THE NAKED MOUNTAINEER

The Naked Mountaineer

MISADVENTURES OF AN ALPINE TRAVELER

STEVE SIEBERSON

Foreword by Lou Whittaker

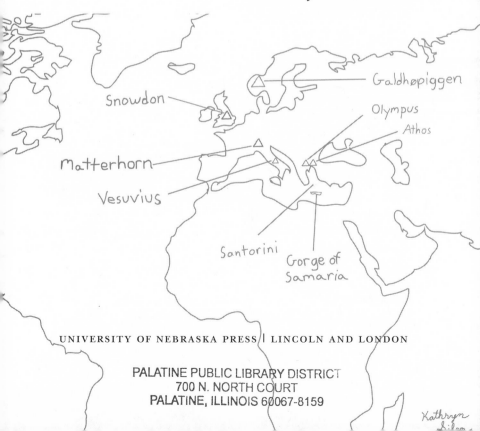

Galdhøpiggen

Snowdon

Olympus

Athos

Matterhorn

Vesuvius

Santorini

Gorge of
Samaria

UNIVERSITY OF NEBRASKA PRESS | LINCOLN AND LONDON

A portion of chapter 12 originally appeared
as "The Last Ascent of Mount St. Helens"
in *Adventure World Magazine* 19:28–35.

Library of Congress Cataloging-
in-Publication Data

Sieberson, Steve.
The naked mountaineer: misadventures of
an Alpine traveler / Steve Sieberson;
foreword by Lou Whittaker.
pages cm
ISBN 978-0-8032-4879-3 (paperback: alk. paper)
ISBN 978-0-8032-8651-1 (epub)
ISBN 978-0-8032-8652-8 (mobi)
ISBN 978-0-8032-8653-5 (pdf)
1. Sieberson, Steve. 2. Mountaineers—United
States—Biography. 3. Mountaineering—
Anecdotes. I. Whittaker, Lou. II. Title.
GV199.92.S535A3 2014
796.522092—dc23
[B]
2014009140

Set in ITC New Baskerville by Lindsey Auten.
Designed by N. Putens.

To Annie, Eric, and Laura
The adventure has just begun

"Now I'm going to give you some very important advice," the British climber said. We had been talking about the next day's summit attempt. We were concerned about the weather, which had been foul for several days. Also, the condition of the route was questionable—the rock was reported to be icy.

"Well, please do," I responded. I gathered that he had a strategy in mind for the climb.

He leaned across the table and looked at me with a sudden intensity. I felt myself glancing down and shifting slightly on the wooden bench. I was anxious to hear what he had to say.

He drew a breath. I waited.

"After you climb the Matterhorn, you must return home and have yourself photographed completely naked."

Contents

Foreword

LOU WHITTAKER

People come at mountains in many different ways. We pay a lot of attention to Himalayan expedition mountaineers and extreme climbers who push the edges of what is possible on vertical rock and ice. Some of these folks are sponsored by outdoor companies, so they are actually paid to climb. Others, like me, have been lucky enough to make a living as professional guides. We get to spend our time climbing and introducing our clients to the sport. And then there are the folks who climb as much as possible without getting paid, often taking odd jobs and living as cheaply as possible. They might be called climbing bums, but really they are productive, talented, good people who live as they please and contribute a lot to mountaineering.

Steve Sieberson is a climber who takes a still different approach. He has had a rewarding career in law and academia, and he hasn't spent as many days in the high country as some of us, but he is a mountaineer through and through. He shares our love of the ranges and our spirit of adventure—it's just that he balances his climbing with other important things in his life.

When Steve contacted me to ask if I would write a foreword for this book, I didn't hesitate for a second. We had never met, but as I saw it, this was a chance for me to support the sport I love so much. When I wrote my own book, *Lou Whittaker: Memoirs of a Mountain Guide*, the foreword was provided by Sir Edmund Hillary, and I was so grateful for his kind gesture. Here is my chance to do the same for someone else.

What I found in *The Naked Mountaineer* was a series of mountain and travel experiences that were exciting and informative but always full of humor. Steve loves his mountains and loves having a good adventure, but he doesn't take himself too seriously. Like any climber who "lives on the edge," Steve has had plenty of surprises and mishaps along the way, but he always manages to pull out of his difficulties and come out smiling. It was easy for me to relate to his situations — we mountaineers always need a great deal of good luck and a guardian angel at our side.

Any expedition, small or large, takes careful planning and some dedicated training to be in condition and skilled enough to be successful. When you leave home and head for other parts of the world, you also need to be prepared to deal with different cultures. This book is filled with fascinating details about the logistics of climbing and the lure of distant lands. My own expedition to the north side of Mount Everest in 1984 is remembered as much for our encounters with the culture of Tibet and its people as for the fact that we were the first Americans to summit by the North Col route. Steve Sieberson's climbs were not record-breaking, but his stories are highly entertaining and, compared with other mountaineering books, highly original.

The Naked Mountaineer captures the essence of what lures us into the mountains and the characters we meet along the way. I have read countless mountain books, but I literally couldn't put this one down. Steve is an explorer and a climber, but more important, he is a great storyteller. Serious climbers will appreciate his insights and his comments on the history of climbing. Independent travelers will be caught up in his enthusiasm for exotic places. Armchair mountaineers and anyone who reads travel literature will treasure these creative and colorful stories.

With so much philosophy and humor in this book, I could have read another dozen chapters. The book concludes with a fascinating account of climbing Mount St. Helens before its eruption in 1980 and after it reopened to climbers in 1987. I lived downwind of the mountain, and after the eruption my house was covered in several inches of ash, my cats were turned ash-gray. Steve's experiences on St. Helens are some of the most interesting I have ever read. It is a fitting "close to home" ending to a series of excursions around the world. I read somewhere that "a man travels the world over and returns home to find what he sought." Welcome home, Steve. I hope you found what you were looking for, and I'm glad you made it back.

Preface

Three decades ago I began a series of trips to what I had identified as some of the world's most interesting mountains. My motivation was no more complicated than a desire to stand on their distant summits, but as it turned out, my journeys were more memorable for what happened along the way than for the actual climbing. You see, there were no big walls, Sherpas, or thin air involved—in most cases it was just me and a pair of boots. However, in getting to the peaks, I bumped into cultures and characters that I wasn't at all prepared for, and as things unfolded, it was these experiences that were most significant. The mountains were always there, and yes, I climbed most of them, but in reality they served as backdrop to the more interesting stories.

As a result, this is not a typical mountaineering book. There are few heroics, and my technical accomplishments will never be written up in the *American Alpine Journal.* The fact is, not everyone with a passion for mountains has the time or inclination to take that interest to the extreme. Most of us don't need to solve the Last Great Problem in the Hindu Kush. We just go on with our lives and escape to the high places now and then for personal satisfaction. Famed expedition leader Chris Bonington titled his autobiography *I Chose to Climb*. Well, I chose to be a lawyer and a professor and to do a lot of other things as well. Climbing was one of them.

With the perspective of time I offer these essays as evidence that mountaineering is a lot like sex. I'm not talking about the obvious metaphor of panting all the way to the summit, experiencing a sweaty moment of ecstasy, and then slinking back to the car. No, what I mean is that climbing and lovemaking share a similar life cycle—the older you get, the less you actually do it, and the more you sit back and reflect on past glories. These are half of my reflections.

Acknowledgments

My thanks go out first to the Creator for filling the world with mountains. On the human plane I want to begin by recognizing the people who contributed to the experiences described in this book. Rather than list them here, I leave it to you to meet them in the chapters that follow. The stories are true, and the people are real. I have used real names in most instances, the exception being where it seemed prudent to do otherwise.

Because these events took place some years back, in most cases I have relied on my own files, photos, and memories, rather than contacting others. Nevertheless, along the way I did speak with Jane and Rupert Pullee, Barbara Ewing, and Gene Yore. I am grateful to them for providing helpful details relevant to the narrative.

Special thanks go to Lou Whittaker, legendary Mount Rainier guide and dean of American mountaineering, for generously agreeing to write the foreword. Also to Don Doll, S.J., for contributing the author photo and to Kathryn Silva Conway for designing the world map. I also want to express my gratitude to Edith Beer at Colorado Mountain College for her encouragement and advice as I sought a home for my manuscript. And many, many thanks to the editors and production staff at the University of Nebraska Press for putting these stories into print—especially Rob Taylor, Courtney Ochsner, Joeth Zucco, and Elizabeth Gratch.

My first mountain instructor was Brian Marts in Estes Park, Colorado, and my earliest climbing companions in Seattle were Lynn Wilcox, Mark Worcester, Kelby Fletcher, Peter Ehrlichman, Ruth Nielsen and Chris Moore—I thank them all for letting me share a rope.

Most of my formal alpine education was through the Mountaineers in Seattle. The club's courses have trained thousands of us for more than a century, and the Mountaineers' field trip leaders have set the standard for climbing organizations throughout the world. Through club outings I met two of my favorite weekend partners, Patricia Gillis and Larry Dolan, along with my confidante, Vera Wellner. In addition to the Mountaineers, let me thank the peerless members of Seattle Mountain Rescue, who accepted me into their ranks for sixteen years.

I am forever indebted to the best friends a climber could ask for—Hans-Christian Jahren, Al Errington, and Luke Reinsma. They have joined me on the peaks and in any number of low places. Their loyalty and good humor are seemingly limitless, and I am alive and happy because of characters like them.

Finally, I trumpet the support and love I have received from my ultra-urban wife, Carmelicia, whose idea of an outdoor adventure is dining *al fresco* on a piazza anywhere in southern Europe.

Prologue

WHERE CLIMBERS ARE MADE

Iowa is the only American state whose landscape is virtually identical from east to west and north to south—nothing but tractors and cornfields as far as the eye can see. In my hometown of Sioux Center we called the land a rolling prairie, but the undulations are subtle, like the ripples on a piece of delaminating GORE-TEX. The monotonous countryside offers nothing to ameliorate the stifling heat of summer or block the Arctic blasts of winter. No lakes, no forests, not even a decent sledding hill, and yet, as a boy I decided that I wanted to live in the mountains, and when I learned that there were people who tied ropes around themselves and climbed for sport, I became convinced that I would be one of them.

I saw my first mountains in the summer of 1959, just before I turned eleven, when my parents took us on what would now be considered a very low-budget road trip to Colorado. Traveling with two other families, we stayed in rundown motels and ate Spam most of the time, but we made it to the Rockies. At first I was intimidated by all the trees and carsick from the winding roads. But then one morning near the town of Evergreen my mother ordered us older children to get outside. "You need some exercise. Go climb the mountain behind the motel, and don't turn back until you make it to the top."

So off we went—my sister Patty, thirteen, cousins Leah, twelve, Leanne, ten, and I. My brother Marvy and the three little kids stayed behind. We Explorers made our way through the trees, up a dirt road. The air was intoxicating, dry and heavy with the scent of pine needles. I had never experienced a warm day without oppressive humidity, and I had never smelled anything like those pines. Laughing and chatting, we hiked on, and we reached the top in twenty minutes. Although we were still in the trees, the slope dropped away in all directions. There were a few boulders to climb on, and from them we could see distant peaks.

"We have conquered the mountain," declared my sister. "Now we get to name it."

Her proclamation instigated a lively discussion, but Patty was ultimately in charge because she was oldest. After considering a variety of options, she decreed that the mountain would be named after all of us—LPL&C, for Leah, Patty, Leanne, and Chucky (my nickname). Mount El-pee-el-cee—and so it was christened. Back at the motel Marvy put up an enormous fuss. He insisted that he had to be included because he would have gone with us if he had known that we would be naming the mountain after ourselves. We Explorers refused, whereupon with great wails and shouts my brother pleaded his case to the mothers. In exasperation they ruled in his favor, and the peak was redesignated Mount El-pee-el-cee-emmm. Later the Explorers did a pinky swear that only the shorter name would be submitted to Rand McNally.

As we drove home several days later, heading east from Denver, I sat on my knees leaning into the rear window of the car. I stared wistfully at the receding peaks and I stayed in that position until Fort Morgan, when the range had shrunk to small, distant bumps, almost like low-lying clouds. Then, without warning, Highway 6 passed over a little rise on the eastern Colorado plain, and the Rockies were gone. A few miles later, when the road rose again, there was nothing on the horizon, and I cried. From that day I resolved to live in the mountains.

Back in Iowa, Grandpa and Grandma Kramer came to lunch. Grandpa was a grumpy old man, a part-time janitor at the Dutch Reformed Church. He mostly sat around with a burning cigar perched on his swollen lower lip, looking sternly through thick eyeglasses and complaining about chewing gum stuck under the pews. I was scared of him. At the kitchen table Grandpa sat next to me. I was wearing shorts. He looked down at my thighs, patted them, and said, "You've got strong legs." I don't know exactly what he meant, but it was the only nice thing he ever said to me, and I never forgot it. Secretly, I took it as affirmation that I should go back to the mountains and climb again.

I decided to prepare for my alpine life as best I could. On lazy afternoons I would lie in the grass staring at clouds, seeing them as distant peaks and tracing imaginary routes to their wispy summits. I became a frequent visitor to the Sioux Center Public Library, rooting around for anything relating to mountains. Besides the *National Geographic*, Mrs. Thompson, the librarian, had two books on mountaineering. They were Maurice Herzog's *Annapurna* and Sir John Hunt's *The Conquest of Everest*. I read them both over and over, and for the first time I started to learn the language of climbing—belays, crampons, crevasses, and the like. I imagined grand expeditions, heady successes, and heartbreaking catastrophes. I feared losing fingers and toes like Herzog, so I spent summer nights sleeping in our canvas pup tent to toughen myself up. That September in a school essay I borrowed the iconic final line of Herzog's book, "There are other Annapurnas in the lives of men." After describing my own climb, I wrote, "There are other El-pee-el-cees in the lives of children." My teacher underlined the sentence and noted, "This makes no sense at all."

It made sense to me. My climbing career had begun on the slopes of El-pee-el-cee, and there were many more mountains just waiting for me. I was no longer an Iowan, and there was no turning back.

THE NAKED MOUNTAINEER

1 *The Naked Mountaineer*

My plan to climb the Matterhorn was hatched when I was eleven, on the heels of my Colorado vacation. In short order I had exhausted the public library's supply of mountain literature, and Mrs. Thompson, the librarian, suggested that I buy a copy of *The Age of Mountaineering* by James Ramsey Ullman. The 1954 book was a comprehensive history of climbing. Mrs. Thompson said she couldn't justify acquiring it for the library because I was likely the only patron who would ever read it. And so I saved up and proudly purchased my first hardcover book, for three dollars. I still have it more than fifty years later.

Ullman's third chapter is titled "A Mountain and a Man," and it recounts how an Englishman named Edward Whymper, along with several Swiss guides, became the first to climb the Matterhorn. Their spectacular success was spoiled by a fatal accident on the descent, and Ullman emphasizes the personal aspects of the incident—a mountain and a man. The book's stark photo of the Matterhorn bears the caption "That Awful Mountain," and I was mesmerized by the image.

Then, in late 1959 Walt Disney released the film *Third Man on the Mountain,* taken from a fictional story written by Ullman. It is the tale of a Swiss boy named Rudi, who is determined to become a mountain guide despite the opposition of his family. After many ups and downs, so to speak, he assists in the first climb of the Matterhorn and becomes a hero. Disney's weekly television show relentlessly promoted the movie, and clips from the film were blended with behind-the-scenes vignettes of the actors being trained in climbing techniques.

For months I pestered my parents to take me to see the film, although I was well aware that our Dutch Reformed church prohibited going to movies. The future lawyer in me argued that we had already crossed the line, because six months earlier we had been to *Around the World in 80 Days* while on vacation in Michigan. Aunt Betty had convinced my mother that it was more of a travelogue than a typical Hollywood film. This, I contended, was precedent—we couldn't consider all movies as evil. Besides, it was Disney, and we watched his show on television. My parents eventually gave in and drove me to the Orpheum in Sioux City. As an impressionable boy already interested in mountain climbing, I was overwhelmed. I felt that the movie had been made especially for me, the conqueror of Mount El-pee-el-cee. This was my story. I was Rudi, and the Matterhorn was my mountain.

Six years later I suggested to my high school class that the theme for our junior-senior banquet (we didn't have a prom, because dancing was forbidden) should be an evening in Switzerland. Surprisingly, they agreed, and "Over the Alps" was born. We painted mountain murals and decorated the gymnasium with fresh-cut evergreen trees that my friends and I had liberated in dead of night from the local cemetery. When the source was later discovered, we had to confess our sins to the Burial Association and then make amends by raking leaves around the tombstones.

The most remarkable feature of the banquet was the fact that we were allowed to screen a movie after the meal. Someone had discovered a nifty loophole in our stringent Calvinism, namely, that the Church did not consider the medium of film to be evil per se. The actual sin (and one that my friends and I had begun to commit regularly) was patronizing a public theater. Apparently the church elders objected to overpriced popcorn and sticky floors, and God knows how the non-Christian people might be carrying on in the back row. Nevertheless, showing a G-rated movie—even a secular one—was acceptable as long as it took place in the school gym. Imagine, then, my satisfaction on that spring evening to find myself at Western Christian High School running the projector for *Third Man on the Mountain*. As I recall, I also did some serious making out with Miss J later that night, but it was not as special as introducing my classmates to the Matterhorn.

Sixteen years later I had taken a two-year position at a bank in Amsterdam, and I could plan a vacation anywhere in Europe. There was never any doubt in my mind that I would go to Switzerland and climb the Matterhorn.

I had naively hoped to find the Zermatt of Walt Disney, a hamlet of simple shepherd huts in green pastures, along with gabled chalets festooned with flower boxes. What I found, instead, were blocks of multi-story apartment houses. The quaint general store had been replaced with a jeans fashion shop, a Christian Dior showroom, and dozens of other boutiques. The cozy inn of the movie had given way to the Ambassador Hotel and restaurants like the Great Swiss Food Disaster Spaghetti Factory. It felt like Disney, but it was the Anaheim version.

Zermatt's main street was teaming with people, most of them in color-coordinated hiking clothes. Their boots and rucksacks were spotless, and a suspiciously large number carried shiny new ice axes. In my army surplus wool pants and thrift shop sweater, and with my well-worn equipment, I was clearly out of place. I was geared for the backcountry in an urbanized playground for the fashionable. With no money to do a makeover, I felt sorry for myself.

My mood changed when I looked up and saw the mountain. The fang of rock soared into a cloudless sky—the Matterhorn in its classic pose, the one on the travel posters and the Alpen muesli box. On the left was the smooth, ever steepening East Face, its rock catching the full warmth of the morning sun, its patches of snow scattering the light. On the right lay the shadowed and sheer North Face, with its massive curtains of ice, utterly cold, uninviting, and sinister. Between the two walls ran the Hornli Ridge, a thin line that leaps upward in graceful sweeps until just below the summit block, where it hooks sharply to the left and gives the mountain its unique and menacing appearance. That was the ridge I was going to climb.

Somewhere in the middle of the tourist trap I located the guides' office, whose modest storefront resembled a small-town insurance agency. It was all but lost among its hip neighbors. The building's principal sign mentioned gondola tickets and information, and it was only on my second pass-by that I saw the word *Bergführerbüro*. A small entry led into a plain room, containing only a table, two chairs, and Herr Kronig. The old man looked up, and I blurted out, "I've come to climb the Matterhorn."

"Well, good," he replied. "Have you climbed before?" I said that I had, and he told me that he would have a guide for me the next morning. It was that simple.

When I returned the following day, Kronig told me that I would be climbing with Hermann Perren. I should meet him at the Hotel Belvedere, a climbers' hostel on the Hornli Ridge. That afternoon my ascent began with a gondola ride that passed over streams and pastures straight out of *Heidi*. Then a second gondola and a third, ending high above Zermatt at Schwarzsee, a guesthouse and restaurant on a promontory at 8,471 feet. From that point a trail ascends another 2,000 feet to the Belvedere.

It was late afternoon, and no one else seemed to be hiking up, except for two young Frenchmen with long baguettes protruding from their bulging backpacks. They passed me, practically on the run and apparently sustaining their pace by cursing at each other constantly. Farther along I began to meet people coming down. Most were day-hikers who grunted "Guten Tag" or "Bonjour." When two men greeted me in English, I stopped to chat. They were Australian, and they had climbed the Matterhorn by themselves that morning, following behind some guided parties. On the way down they were on their own most of the time and had frequently gotten off course. Several times they had wandered onto terrain far beyond their abilities, and the exposure had unnerved them. They kept searching for the correct route, and meanwhile guides and their clients came zipping by. While their ascent took four hours, the Aussies needed seven to get back to the Belvedere. They were exhausted, exasperated, and anxious to get off the bloody mountain. After describing their experience, they admitted, "We shoulduv hoired a goide."

The ridge steepened, and a few of the switchbacks were icy. The exposure below the trail was increasing as well. That evening I learned that only a few days earlier one of the kitchen helpers at the Belvedere had stepped over the edge of the path and had fallen to his death.

The four-story Belvedere, at 10,696 feet, was so weathered that its stucco walls and shuttered windows looked as if they had never been painted. From its terrace, which was simply a level patch of ground with a flea market collection of chairs and tables, I stepped directly into the hotel's great room. It was a large, wood-paneled dining hall furnished with picnic tables, benches, and a Franklin stove. Several mountain posters adorned the walls, and above a sign-in desk was a random display of business cards, advertisements, and newspaper clippings. A judo instructor from the Netherlands had passed through, as well as a car salesman from Lyon. The family of a Southern Baptist minister had posted his obituary, which explained that he had been killed on this mountain. A picture of two smiling teenage boys was tacked nearby, and someone had drawn a cross above the head of each.

The room was nearly filled to capacity. Fifty people sat drinking tea or beer and enthusiastically conversing in a variety of languages. It was almost dinnertime, so the manager quickly signed me in and showed me to a bunk room. As we returned to the mess hall, we passed through the kitchen, and I noticed that there was a table in its back corner. A dozen men sat there eating, and in contrast to the chattering throng in the main room, they were as solemn as the consistory of a Dutch Reformed church. They looked weary and bored, and they spoke in low tones in a strange-sounding German. They were scruffy, with tousled hair, faces weatherworn, and clothes that needed washing. I asked the manager why these people were segregated from the other guests.

"They are the guides," he responded. So these were the legendary men who not only led visitors up this peak, but as citizens of Zermatt, they actually owned the mountain. They looked and behaved as they did because, sitting together as cousins and neighbors, they didn't have to impress anyone. They had no need to regale each other with tales of their exploits, nor did they share the recreational climber's penchant for discussing equipment. They ate quietly because they were at home.

Oddly, there was one man at the guides' table who looked nothing like his companions. His clothes were new and fashionable. His skin was fair, his graying hair long and neatly combed. His silver sideburns flowed out and swept back like the mane of a lion. Although he sat with the locals, he was obviously not one of them. Rather, he resembled a baron out inspecting his lands, the lord of the manor at a yearly meeting with his tenant farmers. The manager saw me staring and explained, "That's the English gentleman who has come here with his personal guide." Now the Matterhorn triptych had been revealed in full: at the center the mountain; on the left the Zermatt guides; and on the right their patron.

Mountain dreams. Climbers and guides. What a strange world for an Iowa boy—and for everyone else at the Hotel Belvedere, when you think of it. There is nothing natural about inserting yourself into a vertical environment, and in the span of human existence, mountaineering is a very recent development. The idea of climbing for sport began in 1760, when a scientist from Geneva visited the French mountain village of Chamonix to further his research on glaciers. Horace-Bénédict de Saussure was struck by the towering presence of Mont Blanc, at 15,782 feet the highest peak in Western Europe. Many visitors before him had been similarly impressed, but Saussure became possessed of an unprecedented idea—that the mountain should be climbed. Remarkably, until that moment the notion of ascending to the top of a rugged peak just for the challenge of it had never occurred to anyone. Throughout human history mountain ranges had been seen as barriers, and individual peaks had been feared as the home of gods or demons. Travelers had negotiated mountain passes but had seen no reason to strive for the summits. Moses had climbed Mount Sinai, but he had done so in response to a divine summons.

After years of thinking and dreaming, Saussure ventured onto the slopes of Mont Blanc, and he persuaded others to join in. Many attempts were rebuffed until 1786, when two men of Chamonix—a physician named Michel Gabriel Paccard and a crystal hunter named Jacques Balmat—reached the lofty summit after two arduous days on snow and ice. Back in the village they were received as conquering heroes, but the real fame would attach to Saussure himself when he ascended the mountain the following year. He was known throughout Europe, and it was he who captured the public's imagination with this new form of adventure. The catch, however, was that if anyone wanted to follow in Saussure's footsteps, they needed to be taught the necessary climbing skills. They needed someone to show the way.

The profession of mountain guiding began when a stranger entered an alpine hamlet and inquired whether anyone there was familiar with a particular valley or peak. A local shepherd or hunter who knew the terrain might step forward and agree to accompany the visitor. Later another foreigner might come for several weeks and hire someone to lead a series of excursions. Over time the villagers became skilled alpinists, and they would actively promote their services. Their neighbors would take travelers into their homes and provide them with meals and supplies. Eventually, in places like Zermatt a mountain tourism industry took shape.

During the seventy-five years after Paccard and Balmat's ascent of Mont Blanc, countless other European peaks felt the tread of hobnailed boots, and the most ardent members of the new climbing fraternity were the English. This might seem strange, because the United Kingdom has no great mountain ranges and most British people spend their lives in misty lowlands. The Industrial Revolution, however, had created a new upper-middle class with leisure time, and these nouveaux riches were eager to travel. Furthermore, recently built railroads offered easier access to remote places, and so the English came to the Continent in droves.

In addition to the Grand Tour of France and Italy, many of the English travelers visited Switzerland, and the more daring ventured onto the peaks. Their explorations culminated in what came to be known as the "Golden Age of Mountaineering," the period from 1854 to 1865, when experience and technical advances in equipment enabled climbers to muscle their way to nearly every mountaintop in the Alps. Of the thirty-nine most significant summits conquered in the final wave, thirty-one were attained by English amateurs and their local guides.

More than a century had passed since the Golden Age, but the Coiffured Englishman had come to carry on a hallowed tradition—retaining a professional guide to lead him up a Swiss mountain. Many of us at the Belvedere that evening were privileged to be doing the same.

Returning to the dining hall, I located a place to sit and found myself across from an American named Prindle. He explained that he was on a business trip to Europe and was attempting the

Matterhorn for the second time. Fifteen years earlier he had actually made it to the summit, but he was so exhausted that he had been robbed of any pleasure and indeed of any positive memories of the climb. Being Prindled is a phenomenon well known among mountaineers, marathoners, and others who engage in drawn-out, physically demanding activities. A Seattle variation is the Mount Rainier "summit special," in which all members of a rope team kneel down in the snow and mark their success with ensemble vomiting. Now, Prindle said, he was more fit and better prepared, so he hoped to enjoy the Matterhorn.

When the sauerkraut, sausage, and potatoes had been consumed, people began to head for their sleeping rooms. That is when the manager introduced me to Hermann Perren—Hemy for short. He was perhaps six foot three, broad shouldered, and well tanned. His surname seemed Italian, but his blue eyes and blond hair were decidedly Teutonic. He told me that he was thirty and had been a guide for nine years. He had already been up the Matterhorn six times that season. His father had also been a guide and his grandfather a shepherd. Hemy had spent a year of high school in Northern California, and he enjoyed climbing with Americans. Although he loved mountaineering, he preferred his winter occupation as a ski instructor. In his tight-fitting jumpsuit he looked as if he had caused more than one vacationing female to melt into her après-ski boots.

We discussed the next day's climb and my mountaineering experience. When I asked him how difficult the standard route was, he told me of a recent article in the *International Herald Tribune* that had disdainfully described the Hornli Ridge as a simple scramble. Hemy bristled as he related how the writer had criticized the Zermatt guides for charging a lot of money for little service. In Hemy's opinion the lack of technical difficulty was only one factor to consider. Route finding was crucial (as the Aussies would attest), the exposure was significant, and falling rocks always posed a risk. He assured me that the Matterhorn was not easy and that I would get my money's worth.

Hemy asked me to get my pack, and our talk turned to equipment. Here I should mention that I had brought along the standard items required by the Mountaineers in Seattle. The club's first rule was "always carry the Ten Essentials." These were emergency items to increase your chance of survival if you were injured, lost, or simply stuck in the wilderness longer than you had planned. The Essentials included things like map, compass, flashlight, fire starter, extra food, and pocketknife. Beyond these basics, all participants on club climbs were required to carry warm clothing, caps, gloves, and rain gear, plus mountaineering equipment such as seat harness, slings, carabiners, crampons, ice axe, and hard hat. Strongly recommended was additional emergency gear—a plastic tube shelter, headlamp, toilet kit, and water purification tablets.

With a sigh that indicated he had had this conversation before, Hemy told me to leave behind everything but my headlamp and crampons. When I resisted, he said, "Look, there will be ten or twelve guides and maybe twenty teams of climbers out there tomorrow. If anything happens, all the guides carry emergency gear. There's stuff in this hut and in the Solvay Refuge, and there is a helicopter in the valley. This isn't wilderness. The entire route can be seen by telescope from Zermatt." Hemy stressed that on this climb I didn't need to be prepared for a night on the mountain, and that speed and agility were critical. When we finished removing what he considered to be the unnecessary gear, my rucksack looked like a deflated balloon.

Having prevailed in the great equipment debate, Hemy suggested that I turn in. He said he would call me at 3:30 a.m., that breakfast would be at 4:00, and that we would start climbing at 4:30.

I was the last person in my room to bunk down for the night, and by that time my roommates were sleeping. Eventually, the Belvedere's humming generator was turned off, and the only sound was the breathing of my fellow climbers. I lay there for a long time, too excited to drift off. My mind just wouldn't let go of the fact that I was finally on the Matterhorn.

Before their historic attempt on the mountain, Edward Whymper and his six companions spent the night in a tent where the Belvedere now stands. The year was 1865, and in all of the Alps only the Matterhorn stood unclimbed.

Articles and books on mountaineering were all the rage in Britain, and several years earlier an English publisher had commissioned Whymper to travel to Switzerland and make a series of alpine sketches. In the course of his assignment he visited Zermatt, where he realized that he could become famous if he were the first person to climb the Matterhorn. During the next three summers he returned and made seven unsuccessful attempts on the mountain. Because the Hornli Ridge looked so severe, all of his efforts began in Breuil (now Cervinia) on the Italian side. Despite, or perhaps because of, his failures, the peak became an obsession, and he earned a reputation as an arrogant man who regarded the Matterhorn as his private territory.

In June 1865 Whymper attempted a new route from Breuil, but he was turned back by falling rock. He briefly left the area, and when he returned, he was shocked to learn that Jean-Antoine Carrel, the leading local guide, had just left with several other men for a new assault on the Italian Ridge. Carrel had been on three of Whymper's previous attempts and had promised to join him again. Whymper was livid. He rushed to Zermatt to form his own party and defeat Carrel from the Swiss side.

Lord Francis Douglas, a noted English climber, agreed to accompany Whymper, as did two Zermatt guides, a father and son both named Peter Taugwalder. By coincidence another group was just about to depart for the Hornli Ridge. It was composed of the Reverend Charles Hudson, the greatest amateur mountaineer of that day; his Chammonix guide, Michel Croz; and an inexperienced nineteen-year-old Englishman named Douglas

Hadow. The two parties agreed to join forces, and, forgoing a gondola ride, they hiked out of Zermatt on the morning of July 13. By early afternoon the team had easily reached their bivouac. They spent the remainder of the day relaxing under the clear sky and mentally preparing for the next morning's summit attempt. At first light on July 14 the seven climbers tied into a single rope and resumed their ascent. All went smoothly until they reached the shoulder of the mountain, where lack of handholds forced them onto the North Face. At that point young Hadow needed help from his companions, but they successfully negotiated the exposed section. They regained the ridge, reached the summit snowfield, and soon arrived at the top. It was 1:40 p.m.

Anxiously searching to see if they were the first, Whymper spotted Carrel's party far below and still ascending from the Italian side. Whymper raised his arms and crowed. He and his party shouted and tossed rocks down the mountain, hoping to catch Carrel's attention. Eventually, the Breuil team received the unwelcome news and turned back. They didn't see much point in being second—Whymper had won the coveted prize.

Whymper's group spent an hour on the summit, enjoying the view and the fine weather. They sang and danced and threw snowballs at each other. Croz tied his shirt to a tent pole and planted it. When the people in Zermatt saw the makeshift flag through their telescopes, they knew that the Matterhorn had been climbed. The partying began.

On the descent Croz led the rope, followed by Hadow, Hudson, Douglas, old Taugwalder, young Taugwalder, and lastly Whymper. Before long Hadow again began to experience difficulty, and on the exposed North Face section it only got worse. At one point Croz set down his ice axe and reached up to place Hadow's feet into footholds. Then, from above, Whymper heard Croz cry out. Hadow had apparently slipped and knocked Croz off his feet, and they fell, pulling Hudson and Douglas with them. The Taugwalders and Whymper braced themselves to arrest the fall of their teammates, but the rope snapped just below the elder Taugwalder. As Whymper himself wrote: "For a few seconds we saw our unfortunate companions sliding downward on their backs, and spreading out their hands, endeavoring to save themselves. They passed from our sight uninjured, disappeared one by one, and fell from precipice to precipice on to the Matterhorngletscher below, a distance of nearly four thousand feet in height. From the moment the rope broke it was impossible to help them. So perished our comrades!"

Some years later the French artist Gustave Doré made a dramatic engraving of the four terrified victims flailing and tumbling down the North Face. I have always been haunted by that image.

Whymper and the Taugwalders were in such shock that they were barely able to continue, and they were forced to bivouac on the mountain before returning to Zermatt the next day. There the tragedy of the Matterhorn took on the color of scandal when it was discovered that the climbers had used their oldest rope on the descent. Some accused the survivors of doing so deliberately. Some even accused old Taugwalder of cutting the rope, but none of the charges were ever proven.

Few events in climbing history have borne the notoriety of the first ascent of the Matterhorn. Whymper personally went on to many other mountaineering achievements around the world, but the Matterhorn disaster and its unanswered questions always dogged him. He had conquered the mountain, but the mountain had also conquered him.

Lying in the dark in the Hotel Belvedere, I saw Doré's engraving, and I imagined myself plunging down the North Face. I was terrified and couldn't sleep. Three thirty came and went, but nobody roused us. The power generator hadn't been turned on, and the building was still dark. I got out of bed, slipped into my clothes, and went downstairs with the aid of my headlamp. In the kitchen I found several guides listening to a radio, while one man was speaking on a telephone. I stepped outside and found Hemy Perren on the terrace looking into a dense fog. He raised his hands and shrugged. "It doesn't look good," he said without emotion. "The weather bureau predicts rain."

"So, no climbing?"

"I suppose we could set out, but even if we weren't turned back by rain, the cloud would stay. We might get to the summit, but we wouldn't see anything. What would be the point?"

Several hours later the gondola heading down from Schwarzsee was filled with shivering refugees from the Belvedere. I stood with Prindle, who was glum. He told me that today was the last day he could spend in Zermatt, so this time he wouldn't get to climb at all.

I spent the next two days sulking and killing time. Every few hours I stopped in to visit Herr Kronig at the Bergführerbüro, always receiving the same bad news about the weather. On the second afternoon I happened to see the silver-haired Englishman standing in front of the famed Hotel Monte Rosa, where Whymper himself had lodged. He was poised with arms crossed, looking expansive and satisfied, as if he were the mayor of Zermatt. I wanted to say something to him, but I was intimidated by his aristocratic bearing. I doubted he would want to talk with a mere colonial like me.

At noon of the third day the Matterhorn finally broke free of the clouds, and I sprinted to the guides' office. As I burst in, Herr Kronig looked up, smiled, and said, "Mr. Sieberson, your guide is Rony Inderbinen, and he is on his way up to the Hotel Belvedere."

Besides me, only six people were riding up to Schwarzsee. A young American couple, both in white jeans, stood at the rear windows of the first gondola. He was pouting, and she was trying to cheer him up. I overheard her saying softly, "You can do it from behind if you really want to. I'll let you do it." I believe she was talking about climbing the Matterhorn from the Italian side.

At the other end of the car stood four climbers speaking German. The tallest one glanced my way; it was Hemy Perren.

We greeted each other, and as we chatted, another member of the group moved toward us. "Steve?" he asked. "Hello. Rony Inderbinen." He was several inches shorter than me, with a wiry physique. His hair was dark, and his face had the blackening tan and deep creases of a southern European who has lived his entire life outdoors. His hands were rough and strong, and he had a perpetual squint from the Alpine sun. In another setting he might have passed for a Greek fisherman or Sicilian farmer. Despite his toughness, there was a sparkle in his eyes, and he smiled easily.

A stiff breeze was blowing at Schwarzsee. Rony and I hiked together, slowing down from time to time to chat. At forty-seven he had been a guide for twenty-six years and had climbed the Matterhorn more than three hundred times. His wife was English; they had three children. They lived on the Zermatt calendar, with Rony working as ski instructor and climbing guide and everyone in the family helping to manage a few guest rooms. Vacation time for them was autumn, when they and everyone else in Zermatt could get away from the mountains.

At the Belvedere, which was all but empty, Rony and I sat in my bunk room for the inevitable equipment discussion. It was an instant replay of my conversation with Hemy Perren three days earlier. When we finished, we agreed that my pack would contain a knit cap, sweater, jacket, gloves, crampons, headlamp, and sunglasses, plus food and drink. At my insistence the helmet would come along too—on my head. The rest of my gear, we agreed, would stay at the Belvedere. Later, without telling Rony, I added back my Ten Essentials. I wanted to be faithful to the Mountaineers in Seattle.

In the dining room Hemy's German clients and another man were drinking beer together in one corner. A French couple—obviously day-hikers—sat near the window with cups of coffee. And there in all his splendor, sideburns flaring out to port, starboard, and then aft in a shimmering wave, stood the Englishman. The star of the show had returned for an encore. He was examining the business cards and obituaries posted above the guest register, and since I had no one else to talk to, I took up my courage and stepped toward him.

"That's an interesting collection," I said.

"Yes, quite so," he replied, turning to look at me.

"You were here on Monday, weren't you?" I asked. There was no doubt, of course, but I couldn't assume that he would remember me from among the masses in the House of Commons, when he had sat in the House of Lords.

"Yes, indeed." He seemed pleased that I recognized him. "It was a pity, the weather."

We introduced ourselves, and at my suggestion we sat down for a beer. When we were served, I remarked about the Belvedere's prices, and he explained that all supplies were ferried up by helicopter, an expensive method but far more efficient than mule trains or human porters. He said it in a way that suggested his own indifference to the cost, and I felt embarrassed at having brought up the subject.

His name was J. LeRoy Harrington-Pumphrey. An engineer, entrepreneur, and sportsman, he came from the West Midlands, where he manufactured safety helmets for race car drivers. He had been a driver himself for a number of years but at age forty-nine had retired from active competition. He was, in his own words, "well known" in British racing circles, and he was still involved in racing associations. He also lectured and wrote on motor sports, and as a celebrity he had done a number of product endorsements.

All in all Harrington-Pumphrey lived the Good Life, attending opening day at Ascot, skiing St. Moritz, and cruising in his Porsche to theater weekends in London. He had become fluent in French, he revealed, in the embrace of a French ballerina. In the same fashion, but with other girlfriends, he had acquired a smattering of German and Italian. "It's quite remarkable what one can learn in bed," he reflected.

As fascinating as his life was, for a while I just couldn't get past the hair. When he mentioned helmets, I thought that perhaps his mane was combed to resemble a full coverage hard hat. His head might have been an advertisement for his company, a way to endorse his own products. In reality it's not often in life that you see a "do" that is absolutely unique. Donald Trump has one, as does extreme skier Glen Plake, with his rainbow-colored Mohawk. I can add Harrington-Pumphrey to the list. I had never seen a man grow his sideburns long enough to comb back like a sideways pompadour, and I have never seen it since. It was a little weird, and it reminded me of a Don Martin cartoon strip in *Mad Magazine*. The prince is standing below a tower and calling, "Rapunzel, Rapunzel, let down your hair." A mass of golden locks is dropped to his feet, and he begins to climb. As he nears the top, he finds Rapunzel standing at the window with her arms raised. The prince realizes that he has just climbed twenty feet of underarm hair.

Harrington-Pumphrey had been in Zermatt for two weeks. His address: the Hotel Monte Rosa, of course. He had done a lot of hiking to get fit. He had also gone on several warm-up climbs with his guide, Erwin Aufdenblatten, in preparation for the Matterhorn.

Our discussion turned to the weather and the condition of the route. Neither of us looked forward to climbing ice-covered rock.

"Now I'm going to give you some very important advice," he said.

"Well, please do," I responded. I gathered that he had a strategy in mind for the climb.

He leaned across the table and looked at me with a sudden intensity. I felt myself glancing down and shifting slightly on the wooden bench. I was anxious to hear what he had to say.

He drew a breath. I waited.

"After you climb the Matterhorn, you must return home and have yourself photographed completely naked."

Well, I thought, why don't you return home and sit on a

running garden hose. What I actually said, after several seconds of awkward silence, was, "Wha . . . what do you mean?"

"I don't wish to shock you," he went on. Too late for that, Lord Hairspray. "You see," he continued, "my suggestion has everything to do with why you are on this mountain."

"It's not by accident that one finds himself here," Harrington-Pumphrey intoned. "It takes a particular type of man, an exceptional man with special qualities, to climb this mountain. Look around you. When the weather interfered on Monday, most of the climbers went home. Who is here now? Who has the commitment, the inner drive, the determination, to come back again and again if need be? Only the few. And the Matterhorn will test these few. Only the best will succeed. We are here, Stephen. We are men set apart from the others."

Having found his rhythm, he rolled on. "In motor racing we say that a man is driving at eight tenths or nine tenths or, when he is at the limit of his potential, ten tenths. I have actually experienced racing at *eleven* tenths, beyond my apparent capacity and yet in control. The man who truly must excel because there is no other way for him . . . that is the man who will learn to perform at eleven tenths. This mountain may call for such commitment from a man. Many people have been unable to meet the demand. Many lives have been lost here. For the man who does succeed, the reward is greater because he has had to give more. And people will recognize that quality in a man. They will be drawn to him like moths to a flame.

"Shall I tell you something? To be the exceptional man, one must believe in himself, in what he is and what he can be. That relates both to the mental and physical aspect of the man. Some years ago, when I was your age, I had a series of photographs taken of myself—naked. My body was trim and beautiful. Now, from time to time, I view the pictures to remind myself of the man that is within me. You should do this yourself, Stephen, with your own photos—an affirmation of who you are."

I didn't know how to respond. I had come to climb a mountain and fulfill a boyhood dream. He, on the other hand, had appeared in this place to announce a new path to self-fulfillment. The hair, the racing cars, the women, and the photos—it all fit together. He had been summoned to this spot by the elemental forces within him; he was answering the call: "Prepare ye the way of Me!" His next lecture would be titled "Mounting the Matterhorn—One Man's Ride to Glory."

I had never met anyone as far over the top as Harrington-Pumphrey. And yet he wasn't saying all those things just to impress me—he actually believed them. As pretentious and bombastic as he sounded, I couldn't help liking him.

I heard footsteps in the hallway, and I was already sitting up when someone opened the door and said, "Guten Morgen." It was 3:45 a.m. As I dressed by flashlight, the hotel's generator started up, and the dangling lightbulb began to glow. Rony stuck his head into the room and told me to take my rucksack down to breakfast so we could leave immediately afterward. The wind had diminished a bit, he said, and the weather was good enough for climbing.

There were six clients in the dining room and five guides in the kitchen. I was still eating when one guide walked in. He and his client roped up in front of me, put on their headlamps, and stepped outside. This is really it, I thought. Those men are climbing the mountain. Next it was Harrington-Pumphrey and his guide. Then Rony appeared, holding a red climbing rope. He looped it once around my waist and started to tie a bowline knot. When I remarked that it wasn't very tight, he said it was good enough. "But if it's this loose, it will ride up on my chest," I persisted. "You're not going to fall," he grumbled.

We shouldered our packs. Rony, still unsmiling, asked, "Do you feel good?" I nodded. "Okay, Steve. Let's go."

I glanced at my watch. It was four forty-five. Rony opened the door, and together we moved out into the night. Stepping off the terrace, we passed the generator shed and hiked up a small knoll. There the wind hit us as it poured from the North Face on our right. I looked up and saw four small lights bobbing above us, moving slowly upward. We walked farther up the ridge and then stepped off to the left and out of the wind. Rony paused and shone his light upward. Putting his hands on the rock in front of him, he turned to me and said, "Here the climbing begins. This is the Matterhorn."

I expected Rony to lead the pitch and then belay me from above as I followed him up. So, as he started to ascend, I just stood and watched, even looking for a spot where I could do a belay from below. To my surprise, after climbing only ten feet, Rony paused and called down, "Okay, climb."

"Shouldn't I wait until you've finished the pitch?"

"No, we climb together."

"You aren't going to belay me?"

"No, it's not necessary. Just climb when I do and stay close."

I wanted to ask how he would catch me if I fell, but I simply started up. We moved in tandem for twenty minutes, and then Rony told me to wait a moment. We had come to a difficult section, and he would climb it first and then belay me. The pitch was no more than twenty-five feet, and although it was slightly steeper and with fewer obvious handholds, it wasn't very difficult. When I reached Rony, I saw that he had established the belay by looping the rope twice around a heavy steel spike driven into the rock. Rony was pleased at how easily I had negotiated the pitch.

Just before six it began to get light, and in the space of ten or fifteen minutes our headlamps became unnecessary. We stopped to take them off, and as I started to place mine into my rucksack, Rony said, "Here, let's just put them under this rock and pick them up on the way down."

"Are you sure?" No climber I knew would *ever* walk away from his headlamp.

"There's no reason to have them anymore. We should keep

our packs as light as possible." I felt my Mountaineers membership card dissolving in my wallet.

We went around an awkward bulge where the rock was not solid—Rony called it Rotten Corner. Here for the first time I could feel the tremendous exposure of our position, but I moved steadily. When the rock became more solid, our tempo increased. I was climbing well, and I kept tight on Rony's heels as we proceeded. Just past a formation called The Jaw we caught up with Harrington-Pumphrey, and he and his guide stepped aside to let us play through. Our route then took us onto the very ridge itself, which in spots was no wider than a single boot. The wind was strong, making balance difficult. At one point Rony gestured to the right and shouted, "The North Face." I didn't stop to savor the view, because I was too intent on maintaining contact with the mountain.

After a tricky slab we arrived at the Solvay Refuge. Tucked into a notch at 13,133 feet, the small, windowless structure was equipped with bunks, blankets, emergency food, and a radio-telephone. A sign in several languages said that the hut was for emergencies only, and those who stayed over would be required to pay a fee upon descending to the Belvedere—if they made it that far. We sat outside for a drink, and it was there that Rony discovered he had forgotten his water bottle. Embarrassed, he accepted my spare, and as we rested he again complimented my climbing. We were making excellent time, he said.

Above the Solvay stood Red Tower, a vertical section that forced us onto the East Face. Once past the obstacle, Rony said we might as well put on our crampons because we would need them shortly. As we strapped them on, I remarked that I had never used crampons on rock. "You'll appreciate them on the ice up there," he said, with a nod toward the ridge above us. "Just climb normally, and don't rely too much on the front points."

In a moment's time the climb was changed. After three hours of the thud of boots on rock, each step we now took caused a metallic clank. My memories of the upper portion of the Matterhorn are rattled with the sound of steel on stone.

We had reached the shoulder of the mountain, where the Hornli Ridge takes its famous bend to the left and where the snow remains even in late summer. Initially, the angle was not terribly steep, and handholds remained plentiful. But then the ridge ran dead into a section of cliffs that leaped upward at a dismaying angle. This was the point at which Whymper and his party had moved out onto the upper North Face, and here Douglas Hadow had required constant assistance. Later, while descending this very rock, Whymper and the Taugwalders had clung to the mountain in horror as their friends, clawing frantically to save themselves, bounced and tumbled out of sight in a shower of stones and ice. I had been climbing well, but the history of this place was unnerving. As Rony traversed onto the face, I wondered what I was getting into.

Then I spotted the rope. Winding through the rock above us, flapping in the wind, a golden brown rope was fixed to the cliff. Reaching its lower end, Rony showed me how to climb with one hand gripping the line, the other searching as usual for handholds. And so, up we went—straight up. The rock was dangerously slippery, and even the rope was icy in places, but we climbed on. Soon the first rope ended in a mass of knots, and a second began. Then another and another, perhaps one hundred yards altogether. I had read about fixed ropes on the Matterhorn. They are disparaged by some who feel that they cheapen the mountain's challenge, but the critics meant nothing to me at that moment—I held on gladly. As I worked my way up, I had profound respect for Whymper's team, who had climbed this section without aid.

The final rope, and then the ridge eased off. Before us was a smooth white slope. Biting into the hard snow with a reassuring crunch, my crampons were finally on familiar terrain. I looked around. The sunlight was dazzling, the sky was deep blue, and we were near our goal. Fifteen minutes later, when the slope began to drop away, Rony turned to offer his hand. "Congratulations, Steve. You climbed well." My only thought was: Yes, I certainly had.

It was 8:50 a.m., and we were standing on the Swiss summit of the Matterhorn, 14,692 feet above sea level. Just ahead and slightly below was the Italian summit, where two other climbers, the first to leave the Belvedere, were sitting in the sun. Below us lay Italy and the miniature houses of Cervinia. Around us in all directions the Alps sparkled like jewels. "There is Mont Blanc, the highest mountain in Europe," Rony said, pointing with a mittened hand. "And there is the Gran Paradiso, in Italy. And there, behind the Weisshorn, is the Bernese Oberland—the Jungfrau, the Monch, the Finsteraarhorn."

We photographed each other with my camera, looked around a bit more, and then descended fifty feet to a sheltered spot in some rocks. There we ate a few snacks, not saying much but quietly enjoying the moment. Rony lit his pipe; I took more pictures. And then it was "We should go, Steve." We had been at the summit for twenty-five minutes.

At the top of the uppermost fixed rope we paused as Harrington-Pumphrey struggled onto the snow. I clapped him on the shoulder and encouraged him. He was tired, suffering from the altitude, and I wondered how many tenths he was running at.

Descending the ropes brought home to me just how steep the shoulder of the mountain really is. The entire section plunges straight down. Lowering myself onto the face, I clutched the line for all I was worth. The abyss tugged at me, and in the wind I thought I heard the screams of Whymper's lost companions.

I was at the bottom end of one rope and traversing a few feet to reach the top of the next, when someone called out from below. I moved farther and had grabbed the second rope when another shout came, and the voice said something in German. Rony immediately yelled that I should stay where I was. A few moments later a young guide appeared from below. He saw me and warned, "Don't hold onto this rope. It's not safe. See here, it's frayed on the rock." The edge he had just negotiated was sharp, and the rope there had indeed begun to unravel. A plastic sheath protecting the rope at that point had evidently broken and fallen off.

I let go of the rope and turned toward the mountain, my hands gripping the icy rock. My left foot could find no hold whatsoever and dangled in the air. Fortunately, the toe of my right boot was secure in a solid, dry step, and I trusted that somewhere above Rony had me on belay. I stood in place as the guide began the painstaking process of tying several knots at the stress point, each time pulling up the entire length of rope. My right leg began to shake, and I knew I had to change my stance. After considering my options, I did a little hop, removing my right boot from the toehold and jamming my left one in. When the left leg tired, I reversed the process.

Eventually, the repair was finished, and after a thoroughly rattled client emerged from below, I was able to grab the offending line and continue down. At the bottom of the final rope I encountered Hemy Perren, whose two clients were moving very slowly below him. He congratulated me and said, "For me it's going to be a long day."

With the fixed ropes behind us, we now began straightforward down-climbing. It was the start of several hours I would like to forget.

It never ceases to amaze me how much misery is involved in getting down from a mountain. To begin with, you are wearier than you care to admit. Despite having paced yourself, you have poured more than half the day's energy into getting to the summit, and you have lost much of your inner drive. Also, down-climbing is more awkward than ascending. Your eyes and fingers lead the way up, but going down, you yield much of the route finding to your leaden feet. You don't know whether to face into the rock and descend with occasional glances over your shoulder or whether to face outward and climb crab style on your heels and the butts of your hands. Gravity seems malevolent—you find yourself making two or three moves too quickly, and suddenly you have started to lose control. The deliberate pace of the ascent is replaced by jerking and jolting, as if you were an actor in an old-time movie. With all of these psychological, anatomical, and physical forces working against you, it is easy to understand why most mountaineering accidents happen on the descent.

Perhaps ten or fifteen minutes below the fixed ropes, Rony said we should take off our crampons. I had begun to appreciate them, and I felt insecure as I re-accustomed myself to the feel of my rubber lug soles. I proceeded cautiously, fearing that a patch of ice was lying in wait on the next move.

Rony promised lunch at the Solvay Refuge, and I assumed that we would be there soon, but the climbing went slowly. Rony insisted that I face out except on the most difficult pitches. I was uncomfortable, unsure of myself. And leading the descent, I was uncertain of the route. Every minute or two Rony had to call out "move right" or "move left." I paused often, and this always garnered a "keep moving." As if to make matters worse, in contrast to my thudding and lurching, Rony himself moved like a cat, silently and in balance. He was in his element, contented. Occasionally, he sang a little song—no words, just pleasant little sounds, like "oh dee dee dah." And, as if to emphasize his nonchalance, that pipe stayed in his mouth.

I lost track of time, but it seemed to be standing still. Visually, our progress was hard to determine. Finally, the Refuge. It was eleven fifteen, two hours since we had left the summit, and only fifteen hundred feet down.

This time we sat inside on a lower bunk, and we ate a lot. Then Rony suggested he photograph me standing in the doorway of the hut. "Someone took a picture of me standing there, and I gave it to my mother," he explained. "She still has it. It's her favorite picture of me."

We moved on, and now the Belvedere lay directly below us. It seemed we would get there in a few minutes, but we had nearly half a mile of vertical remaining. After thirty minutes the hostel seemed no closer. It was maddening, always there in front of me but never any nearer. I was tired, and I knew I was climbing poorly. The knapsack felt like a stone weighing me down, and I began obsessing over the extra gear I was carrying. If only I hadn't brought the Ten Essentials, I would be climbing better. Why did I think I would need fire starter and water purification tablets? I hated the Mountaineers. Moreover, Rony's constant instructions were starting to annoy me, and his little song was like fingernails on a blackboard. "Oh dee dee dah . . . oh dee dee dah."

I slowed down, feeling each step carefully. Now it was Rony who was irritated. "Keep moving, Steve. Don't fight the rock. Move lightly like this." He demonstrated his supple moves. I lumbered on. "Don't fight it."

"Go left," he said for the hundredth time. I moved one step left and started down.

"No, not there," he said gruffly. "Pay attention—there's the route."

I looked up and said, "I'm sorry Rony. I can't always tell where you want me to go. I'm doing my best."

He apologized for getting testy. "You're going all right, Steve. Just have courage. We'll get there."

Now onto the ridge, now back on the East Face, we crept downward. Twelve o'clock. "Oh dee dee dah." Aching shoulders. Rony relit his pipe. Twelve thirty. The Belvedere, is it closer now? Rotten Corner. Retrieve the headlamps. Chew some candy. One o'clock.

Out of nowhere Harrington-Pumphrey came scrambling past, followed closely by his guide. The Englishman was moving smoothly. He later told me that after I had passed him on the way up, he had decided he would do whatever was necessary to catch me on the descent. He wanted to get back to the Belvedere ahead of me. I followed the pair, and for a few minutes Rony did not have to call signals to his dog team. But then we were left behind, and the instructions resumed.

I paused wearily, embarrassed at how stiffly I was moving and mortified that I was so frightened. Rony sat beside me.

"You die on the Matterhorn," he said flatly.

What was this? Was he trying to torment me? The pipe, the song, and now this?

"What did you say?"

"Your day on the Matterhorn, Steve. This is your day."

At last it was over. The final pitch was behind us, and we were strolling up the knoll just above the Belvedere. It was one forty, and the climb down had taken nearly half an hour longer than the ascent. Rony said we should unrope, but I barely heard him. Suddenly the emotions of the past few hours and all those years of dreaming about this place had caught up with me. I had climbed Whymper's mountain, Rudi's mountain, but my confidence going up had been shattered on the descent. I had performed poorly, and I wasn't the mountaineer I had thought I was. I stood numbly as Rony began to untie the rope from my waist. Behind my sunglasses my eyes were filling with tears of frustration.

As we neared the Belvedere, J. LeRoy Harrington-Pumphrey was standing on the terrace, and from a distance I could see that his face was glowing.

When Moses came down from Mount Sinai with the two tablets of the law in his hands, he was not aware that his face was radiant because he had spoken with the Lord. Exodus 34:29.

On the Matterhorn, Harrington-Pumphrey had come face to face with himself, and he was well aware that he was radiant. A small crowd of day-hikers had gathered around him, like moths to his flame. He was describing his climb. When he noticed me approaching, he grandly poured me a glass of mineral water as though it were champagne. He offered a toast, which I accepted, even though I didn't feel like celebrating—I was still distressed at my performance. I had been Prindled.

Harrington-Pumphrey was irrepressible, and he seemed about to burst forth in iambic pentameter. "Stephen," he said expansively, "look back at your mountain. You have succeeded where other men have failed."

I had to admire him—he knew what to do in the winner's circle. And he had won. He had conquered the mountain, and while I had reached the summit half an hour ahead of him, he had bested my time on the descent by a full hour. His total climbing time was eight hours; mine was eight and a half. From that day forward he would tell anyone who would listen that coming down the Matterhorn he had passed a younger, fitter American.

Rony was going to eat dinner and take a nap. Harrington-Pumphrey was also staying around for a while—no doubt his press conference would begin soon. So, after a cup of tea I was ready to set out alone on the trail to Schwarzsee. "It's too bad the supply helicopter isn't here," I said to Harrington-Pumphrey. "I might be tempted to ask for a ride back to Zermatt. I don't think my accomplishment would be any less if I didn't hike that path." He smiled benignly, and we agreed to keep in touch. Then I stepped inside the Belvedere and said good-bye to Rony. I thanked him for taking me up the mountain, and I apologized for my performance on the way down. He shook his head. "You did just fine, Steve. It was your day on the Matterhorn."

I was only a few hundred feet below the Belvedere when the supply helicopter did rise past and land somewhere near the terrace. I really do wish I could take it down, I said to myself. A few minutes later the machine descended, passing tantalizingly close to me. It seemed to hover momentarily, as if to taunt me. I waved and resumed walking.

Two months later I was in London on business, and Harrington-Pumphrey drove down to join me for dinner. He brought with him a large scrapbook he had put together about his Matterhorn experience. There were snapshots of him lounging at the Hotel Monte Rosa, training with his guide, and climbing the mountain. I was relieved to see that he was fully clothed in every picture. There was a certificate signed by his guide, attesting to his achievement—something that Rony had never offered me. There was even a press release from his company, plus articles from two local newspapers with photos of him waving triumphantly from the summit. According to these reports, only 150 people had made it to the top of the Matterhorn that season, and Harrington-Pumphrey had been the only Monte Rosa guest to succeed.

But there was more. My English gentleman told me he had bought the climbing rope that he and Erwin had used, and he had given his personal wristwatch to the guide as a token of his appreciation. To replace it, he had stopped in Zurich on the way home and had purchased a gold Rolex for a sum equal to the price of a sports car.

We rehashed the climb, from breakfast to our final words on the terrace. I mentioned again that I thought the whole thing would have ended nicely with a flight down from the Belvedere. It was only then that I learned what I probably should have suspected all along—that sitting in the helicopter as it brushed past me, silver sideburns billowing magnificently in the breeze, was the splendiferous man himself, leaving his Matterhorn in eleven tenths of style.

2 *Pitching the Horseshoe*

Everybody has heard of Wales, not for its mountains but because Charles, the somewhat dotty heir apparent to the British throne, is the Prince of Wales. He, in turn, is noteworthy for having waited his entire adult life for career advancement, but most of us think of him as the guy who couldn't be content with Diana, ravishing Princess of Wales. Now Charles's second wife, Camilla, could assume the princess part of the title, but she has prudently declined. During Charles's extramarital fling with Camilla, he once told her of his desire to abandon all responsibilities to his subjects and become a cotton plug permanently positioned in her grotto of love. That's doesn't say much for Wales or its people.

The inhabitants of Wales are the "Welsh," which derives from an old Anglo-Saxon word that simply meant "non-Anglo." The English also at one time used *welsh* as a synonym for *renege* because they didn't understand the inhabitants of Wales or their language and thus did not trust them. These condescending intimations have faded away, but *Welsh* is still a serviceable adjective in our language. One tasteful use of the word refers to a comfort food consisting of melted cheese sauce on toast. The English call it "Welsh rarebit" or "Welsh rabbit," which is inordinately peculiar, because there is nothing rare in the ingredients and not even a hint of rabbit.

In the United States the variant *Welch* is ingrained in our culture. When we were children in the 1950s, Buffalo Bob and Howdy Doody urged us to drink Welch's Grape Juice, and the four-pack of small bottles came in a carton that resembled a house. If you drank enough of the stuff, you could assemble the entire village of Doodyville, and your tongue would be purple for weeks. As our interests evolved from puppet shows to the finer things in life, we boys latched onto Raquel Welch. For many of us the 1960s were pretty much defined by the poster for *One Million Years B.C.*, which featured the lusty and busty Miss W in an animal skin bikini, looking for action most primitive. Then Jack Welch became the symbol of American capitalism as chairman of General Electric, but most of us remained fixated on Raquel.

I grew up with these Welch icons, but I have an even deeper connection to Wales through a special bond I share with its prince. I have never aspired to be a tampon, but I was born in the same year as Charles, and I have his name as my middle name. Actually, I am five months older than His Royal Highness, so it is quite likely that Betty and Phil met with their palace retainers and said, "That little Iowa baby is adorable, and he looks intelligent to boot. We have decided to name the next king of England after him." When I eventually discovered that there are mountains in Wales and that Charles's uncle was their earl, I added Snowdon to my bucket list.

Barely the size of Massachusetts, Wales is an easily overlooked land tucked away on the western edge of Britain. Its coastline faces the Irish Sea and the Atlantic Ocean. The western and southern shores of Wales are scenic, but they are also exposed to horrific gales. It is claimed that in a single storm on October 25, 1859, a total of 114 ships were lost in that area. This astounding statistic confirms the conclusion I have reached as a result of my own experience in Snowdonia—namely, that nobody in his right mind would visit Wales to enjoy its weather.

The interior of Wales is largely mountainous and lightly populated. In the south lie the Brecon Beacons. To their north are the Cambrian Mountains, known primarily for unpronounceable peaks such as Pen Pumlumon Fawr, Pen Pumlumon Arwystli, and Pen Pumlumon Llygad-bychan. These peaks do not entice the non-Welsh. Why climb something if you can't talk about it later? "Hey, I had a great hike last week on Pen Pummm, Pummm, oh . . . never mind." For that matter the only reason anyone climbs Mexico's Popocatepetl is because they can call it "Popo."

North of the Cambrians lies Snowdonia, a mountainous region and national park. Both the area and the park refer to Wales's highest mountain, Snowdon. That name is based on two ancient Anglo-Saxon words—*snaw* for snow and *dun* for hill. The fact is, we are very lucky that the English name is in standard use, because the Welsh people call the peak "Yr Wyddfa." Their *dd* is pronounced like a heavy *th*, as in the word *this* (as opposed to the soft *th* at the end of the word *with*), so the mountain comes out something like *Ear With-fa*, which does not exactly roll off the tongue.

In contrast to the Beacons and Cambrians, the summits of northwestern Wales are more than mere rounded humps. A number of Snowdonia's peaks have jagged ridges and cliffs and thus look like actual mountains. I say that advisedly because no less an expert than James Ramsey Ullman has asserted that they "can scarcely be called mountains at all." That is what he wrote in his 1954 bible, *The Age of Mountaineering*. As a boy, I believed every word Ullman wrote. Today I strongly disagree with his dismissal of Snowdonia. It's really a matter of perspective, as I would like to explain.

What does it take to be called a mountain? Ullman was thinking of classic mountaineering challenges such as glaciers and great walls, as well as elevation above sea level. That is why he commented that "the British Isles possess no summits remotely comparable to those of the Alps." True enough. For example, Scotland's 4,409-foot Ben Nevis, the highest point in the United Kingdom, is a full 10,000 feet lower than the major peaks of Switzerland. Furthermore, Ben Nevis is a walk-up, as is virtually every mountain in England's Lake District and every peak in Wales. So, from a comparative perspective Ullman may have been correct. Yet he did add that Britain's high places had proven to be an "unexcelled schoolroom" for climbers. He noted that the cliffs and faces of Snowdonia offer ample opportunity for training in rope work and other aspects of mountain craft.

If the mountains of Wales are a good place to hone your climbing skills, why call them "scarcely" mountains? Is there a good definition that can help us sort this out? You will be disappointed by *Webster's* approach. A mountain, the dictionary says, is "a natural elevation of land rising more or less abruptly to a summit, and attaining an altitude greater than that of a hill." This definition seems to be heading toward something useful until we look up *hill*: "a natural elevation of the earth's surface, smaller than a mountain." Well, if Mr. Webster trips on his own circular reasoning, he could simply refer to Albert Einstein and admit, "It's all relative."

Some definitions focus on the height differential between a mountain's base and summit. To qualify as a mountain, there must be a specific rise. Other characteristics might be prominence, angle, size, and shape—these are the qualities we used to dwell on in the boys' locker room in high school, but they work for mountains as well. Angle, size, shape, and their combinations are nebulous and infinitely varied, but most climbers agree that a true mountain should be prominent. It should stand out by itself, separate from neighboring peaks and visible from different perspectives.

The people of Colorado are justifiably proud of their many Rocky Mountain summits that exceed 14,000 feet in elevation. There are fifty-four of these "Fourteeners"—or is it fifty-five, fifty-six, or fifty-eight? The problem is that several of the 14,000-foot-high points are so close to higher summits—and with so little altitude differential between them and their taller neighbors—that many climbers refuse to count them as separate mountains. One rule of thumb, widely accepted in Colorado, says that a mountain must rise at least 300 feet above the saddle between it and an adjoining higher summit. In the same vein one eminent list of summits in England and Wales (the "Nuttalls") identifies peaks as long as they are 2,000 feet high and have more than 50 feet of prominence, while a separate tally of British "Marilyns" (indeed named after the curvaceous Miss Monroe) requires no minimum elevation but a relative height of 150 meters (492 feet). A more exclusive grouping is that of the world's most prominent mountains—the "ultras." Roughly fifteen hundred peaks on the planet enjoy a prominence of at least 1,500 meters (4,921 feet). Among the greatest of these are the highest mountains on each continent—the famed "Seven Summits"—including Everest, Denali, and Kilimanjaro.

Fifty feet of prominence, 300, 492, or more—try selling that to the folks in the state of Washington, where there is a perpetual debate about the status of Little Tahoma, a sub-peak of 14,411-foot Mount Rainier. When you look south from Seattle on a clear day, freestanding Rainier—an obvious ultra—dominates the horizon to such an extent that locals refer to it simply as "the mountain." In contrast, from the same urban vantage point Little Tahoma appears as no more than a nub on the massive volcano's eastern flank (a climbing friend once tastefully referred to it as "a misplaced nipple on a large tit"). The protuberance juts 818 feet from Rainier's slope, almost twice a Marilyn and three times the Colorado standard, but still a rather small percentage of the great mountain's base-to-summit rise of over 13,000 feet. If Little Tahoma is classified as a separate mountain (and I do not think it should be), the consequences are significant: its 11,138-foot elevation would make it fourth highest among the great peaks of the Pacific Northwest—just behind Rainier and two other ultra-prominent volcanoes, Mount Adams (12,281 feet) and Mount Hood (11,249 feet). It would be ranked higher than two other ultras—Washington's dramatic Mount Baker (10,781 feet) and Oregon's magnificent Mount Jefferson (10,497 feet). Marilyn or not, that's mighty high praise for a nipple.

Returning to the Centennial State, even if Coloradans cannot agree on the exact number of Fourteeners, they are united in their conviction that the Rockies are the grandest of America's mountains. They are quick to explain that outside their state there are only six peaks in the Lower 48 that reach 14,000 feet, while they have more than fifty. They are correct to a certain extent. It is true that the only non-Colorado Fourteeners outside Alaska are Washington's Mount Rainier and five mountains in California. The foremost of California's summits is 14,505-foot Mount Whitney, the highest peak in the forty-eight contiguous states. Colorado's own Mount Elbert comes in second at 14,443 feet, with Rainier third (14,411 feet). The problem for Coloradans is that many of their tallest mountains are not terribly imposing. The Rockies begin to rise just west of mile-high Denver (5,280 feet), which means that in comparison to the foot of the range, the Fourteeners are actually Niners. Furthermore, Elbert itself stands above the town of Leadville, which sits at 10,152 feet in a *valley*. When measured against that base, Mount Elbert is not a Fourteener but a Four-Flusher.

Statistics will never settle the question of what is a mountain, but we can always look to the United States Supreme Court for guidance. In the 1964 case of *Jacobellis v. Ohio* the court had to decide whether an allegedly pornographic French film was protected by the First Amendment to the U.S. Constitution—freedom of speech, freedom of expression, and all that. In searching for a definition of "hard-core" porn, which would not be protected, Justice Potter Stewart helpfully declared: "*I know it when I see it*, and the motion picture involved in this case is not that." Likewise, I believe that most people will be satisfied with: "If it looks like a mountain, I can call it a mountain." It's all a matter of your own point of view.

I once stood with my brother Marv in the countryside near my hometown of Sioux Center, Iowa. He pointed to a cornfield and said, "Someday I'd like to build a house on that hill in the middle of the field."

"What hill?" I asked.

"That one right over there," he replied, still pointing. "The views will be great."

I saw a slight rise a few hundred yards from us. It was no more than ten feet high—nothing remotely resembling a hill. But that didn't matter to my brother. It was his hill and his house plans. Thinking of the Alps, James Ramsey Ullman looked at Wales and saw nothing of consequence. When I went there, I had been living for two years in the Netherlands (the "Low Lands"). In Snowdonia I not only *saw* mountains; I felt their power.

Snodownia is home to fourteen summits higher than three thousand feet. Flexibility on the matter of prominence can expand the list to fifteen or sixteen. One reason they look like real mountains is that the sea is nearby—the range does not rise from a high plateau.

The "Welsh 3000s" are found in three clusters—six in the Carnedd range, five in the Glyders, and three in the Snowdon massif. The three groupings are close enough to each other that every year a number of hardy souls will attempt to climb all fourteen of the 3000s in a single excursion. The "14 Peaks Walk," also called the "3000s Challenge," is a true marathon, with thirty miles of hiking and eighteen thousand feet of up and down. It was first accomplished in 1919. Today most participants hope to complete the trek within a twenty-four-hour period in late June, when the most daylight is available, but of course there has also been competition to set a speed record. The current mark is an impressive four hours and nineteen minutes, set in 1988 by a Scot named Colin Donnelly. Ten years earlier a man of questionable sanity, one John Wagstaff, accomplished the challenge three times in succession in twenty-two hours and forty-nine minutes. Why he stopped at three is anybody's guess, although at the end of the stunt he was overheard to say, "I'm so tired I can't even wag my staff."

The top dog of Snowdonia is its namesake mountain, whose 3,560 feet make it the highest peak in all of England and Wales. (Within Britain overall the mountains of Scotland are loftier, with 283 summits over 3,000 feet and 9 that exceed 4,000 feet.) Snowdon sits at the center of its massif, with ridges radiating outward in all directions. One commentator has likened the extended arms to flying buttresses, those external structures that shore up the roof and walls of a Gothic cathedral. A modern satellite view offers a portrait of something more organic, something that looks very much like a dead starfish decaying above the high-water mark.

Offsetting Snowdon's prominent ridges are the valleys between them. These are deep clefts that add drama to the landscape and emphasize the height of the central summit. They also offer a spelling lesson.

You may recall that when we were children we were taught that the English vowels are "*a, e, i, o, u*, and sometimes *y* and *w*." Nobody in my school could ever figure out the *w* bit, until I, at the age of eleven, read *The Conquest of Everest*, Sir John Hunt's account of the 1953 British expedition that was first to climb the world's highest peak. One of the major topographical features encountered by the climbers was the Western Cwm, a long glacial valley that proved to be the passageway to the mountain's upper slopes. I learned that *cwm* is the standard Welsh word for "valley," and its vowel is the *w*. As a vowel, it is pronounced *oo*, and *cwm* is thus *coom*. I proudly reported this discovery to my fifth-grade teacher, Mrs. Riepma, and she scolded me for disrupting the class yet again with one of my elaborate stories. Fortunately for me, *cwm* appeared in the dictionary on her desk, and I emerged a hero to my classmates.

From the climber's perspective the valley running east of Snowdon's summit is its most significant. Oddly, it is not named on any of my maps. A local man told me that it is sometimes called "Cwm Glaslyn" after a small lake at its head, but he acknowledged that that was not official. For purposes of what follows, I have decided to refer to it (with a tip of the hat to Mount Everest) as the "Eastern Cwm." The great cleft is bounded on the north by Snowdon's northeast ridge, which contains the 3,000-foot summits of Garnedd Ugain (3,494 feet) and Crib Goch (3,027 feet). On its southern side it is flanked by the spiny southeast ridge, whose high point is the near-3,000er, Lliwedd (2,946 feet). These two prominent ridges thus form a lopsided horseshoe, with the summit of Snowdon at the closed western end and the Eastern Cwm occupying the interior. Enhancing the beauty of the scene are three lakes on the valley floor: Glaslyn, tiny Llyn Teyrn, and the largest of them, the mile-long Llyn Llydaw.

The standard ascent of Snowdon follows the well-worn Pyg Track westward up the Eastern Cwm. This trail's name might have something to do with a wallowing pig, or more likely, it comes from the initials for the nearby Pen y Gwryd Hotel. A parallel route is the old Miners' Path, which lies on the valley floor and winds along the shores of the three lakes. At the head of the valley the Miners' Path merges into the Pyg Track, and the single trail then zigzags up to a saddle on Snowdon's northeast ridge. This notch is named Bwlch Glas, and at that point Snowdon sits above to the left, with Garnedd Ugain to the right. Turning left, it is an easy walk along the ridge to the top of Wales.

It is useful to note that the Welsh word for "saddle" or "col" is *bwlch*. The *ch* is pronounced as in the Scottish word *loch*, and thus *bwlch* comes out something like *boolchhh*. In order to get the most out of the experience, you need to pronounce the *ch* with a rolling wave that starts deep down in your gullet. If you do, your *bwlch* will resemble its English cousin, the belch.

More challenging than the Pyg Track is Snowdon's famed

Horseshoe Walk. It starts on the north arm of the horseshoe, heads west along the northeast ridge, then loops around the closed end, over Snowdon, and returns eastward on the south arm, the southeast ridge. This is mountain hiking at its finest, and it includes a bit of scrambling with real exposure. The entire trek is seven and a half miles in length, with a total elevation gain of thirty-eight hundred feet. In 1948 an eighty-year-old man did it in ten hours. In 1961 a younger chap named David Rowlands completed the circuit in one hour and forty-seven minutes. In good weather an experienced mountain hiker can comfortably accomplish the full Horseshoe in four to six hours. I did not. Before I offer my excuses, however, I want to share a bit of local history.

One of Snowdon's valleys is believed to be the site of King Arthur's final battle, but a more recent struggle for survival took place on the mountain's longest ridge. The five-mile-long northwest arm drops gradually from the summit to the town of Llanberis, and since 1896 a narrow-gauge rack-and-pinion railroad train has traversed the route. The Snowdon Mountain Railway snakes upward to a station just sixty-seven feet below the mountain's true summit. The train ride has been a popular attraction for more than a century, but its opening day was a disaster.

The inaugural began with two official trains bearing passengers to the mountaintop. It was April 6, 1896, and on board were dignitaries in frock coats, ladies with parasols and large hats, and perhaps a few of the hoi polloi. After these privileged guests had had a chance to revel in the views, mug for a few summit photos, and tip their glasses of champagne, it was time to return to Llanberis. The first locomotive departed, pulling its two passenger wagons. Unfortunately, not far down the slope the locomotive's rack-and-pinion braking apparatus somehow became disengaged from the center rack rail, and the train began to accelerate, out of control. Realizing the direness of their straits, the intrepid engineer—a Mr. Pickles (actually)—and his equally intrepid fireman (Mr. Onions perhaps?) leaped to safety, leaving the feckless passengers to fend for themselves. At the next curve the abandoned engine detached from the first wagon and took leave of the track altogether. As it tumbled down the mountainside and out of sight, the automatic brakes on the carriages kicked in and stopped them on the track, but not before one passenger had leaped to his death.

As all of this was taking place, a climber in the vicinity, one Mr. Badger, heard what he assumed to be rockfall on the slope above. Looking up, he was more than a little disconcerted to see a steam engine headed in his direction. The story is reminiscent of a recent incident in rural Whatcom County, Washington, where a motorist hit a deer, which sailed through the air and in turn struck a cyclist on an adjacent bicycle path. When interviewed later, the injured man said something like, "Shucks, this is the first time I've been hit by a flying deer."

Meanwhile, back at the summit of Snowdon the engineer of the second train was waiting for the "all clear" signal to depart. Unbeknownst to him, the first locomotive had knocked out the telegraph line, so no message of any sort was received above. Not wishing to inconvenience his important passengers, the engineer departed anyway. Amazingly, at the exact point that the first locomotive lost contact with the rack rail, the second one did as well (possible design defect there). The engine accelerated down the track, and with a frantic toot of its whistle, it proceeded to ram itself into the stationary rear carriage of what was left of the first train. The violent collision had two effects, one good and one bad: First, the rack assembly of the second train reengaged, and the engineer, after peeling his face from the inner surface of the locomotive's windshield and determining that he was still alive, was able to regain the controls and prevent any further movement. Second, the brakes of the first train's carriages were knocked loose, and the two wagons resumed their unpiloted descent.

One can only imagine the thoughts of the first set of passengers at that point. Their train had lost control, its engine had gone flying, and yet they had stopped safely. Then, just as they had completed their prayers of thanksgiving, tidied up their soiled undergarments, and settled back into their seats to wait for rescue, they were smacked from behind by another train and sent careening downhill for the second time. Previously feckless, it now appeared that they were totally fecked. Many of them, we can assume, made solemn vows to limit future transportation to horses and buggies. Miraculously, the two carriages eventually derailed and skidded to a halt, with no further loss of life.

When the Snowdon Mountain Railway opened in 1896, its summit station served as a small climbers' hostel. That building had replaced an earlier cabin. In the 1930s the railway lodge was converted to a restaurant and souvenir stand. Due to its exposure to the elements, the building deteriorated and continued to do so until no less an authority than the Prince of Wales stepped in. Charles has been rather vocal in his criticism of modern architecture, once describing a proposed extension of London's National Gallery as a "monstrous carbuncle." This and other pronouncements have put him at odds with Britain's leading architects, but he has carried on, undaunted.

As to Snowdon's summit lodge, the prince remarked that it was "the highest slum in Wales." To his credit, this comment helped stimulate a campaign that in recent years has led to the razing of the original building and construction of a new visitor center, which opened in 2009. Ironically, the new structure is ultra-modern, a highly stylized concoction of stone, concrete, and glass that resembles a man-made cow pie. If HRH had been expecting something Cotswoldian, he is no doubt deeply disappointed. To him the new station must look positively carbuncular.

My trip to Snowdon began with far less drama than the 1986 railway patrons had experienced. I simply drove to the Pen y Gwryd Hotel and checked in. Located at nine hundred feet in a broad valley, the Pen y Gwryd is surrounded by the Welsh 3000s, and it serves as a handy base for mountain walking. The hotel's name means "head of the Gwryd River," and for those of us who need an assist, *Gwryd* (there's that *w* again) rhymes with *lurid*—full pronunciation: *penny gurid.*

Through the years the hotel has been a port of call for celebrities of all kinds. They have included William Gladstone, David Lloyd George, and Winston Churchill, but also Bertrand Russell and Monty Python's Graham Chapman. Roger Bannister—the first person to achieve the sub-four-minute mile—once passed through, albeit on the run. Even Charles himself stopped in on the way to his 1969 investiture as Prince of Wales. He presented the proprietors with a photo of himself in his "Action Man" bachelor phase, looking all outdoorsy in a bush jacket and leaning with both hands on a chest-high walking staff. This is a younger, more innocent Charles than the one of recent years. He is gazing pensively off into the distance, perhaps imagining himself as a Q-tip inserted into the ear of a Welsh maiden.

The early Snowdon climbers were invariably English and generally from England's educated upper classes. In contrast, the Welsh highlanders were generally poor and unschooled. As a result, visitors and locals did not mix. For the English the Pen y Gwryd was their retreat and their enclave.

Foremost among the many mountaineers to visit the PyG was George Leigh Mallory, who in 1924 was lost as he neared the top of Mount Everest. Several decades later the 1953 British team used the hotel as a base for practice climbs and experimentation with oxygen masks. Their preparations paid off when Edmund Hillary and Tenzing Norgay reached the world's highest point on May 29, 1953, and successfully returned. Word of their ascent reached London in the wee hours of June 2, which was also the day Elizabeth II was to be crowned. With double cause for celebration, everyone in the United Kingdom reacted with a giddiness that was most un-British. At the Pen y Gwryd the proprietors, Mr. and Mrs. Briggs, took a middle-of-the-night call from the

Times, and they immediately summoned their guests to the bar for a series of toasts. Afterward six of the well-fortified patrons dressed and headed out for a night climb of Snowdon. They reached the summit at 4:00 a.m. for more toasting and boasting. For the Briggses the celebrations were just beginning. They decided to expand two small rooms near the hotel's entrance, creating a larger space that they renovated in a log cabin style. There they installed benches and a stove, and the newly dubbed Everest Room became a place for hikers to remove muddy boots and hang wet jackets. Still in use today, its warmth invites you to relax with a pint of ale before heading further into the lodge. In October 1953 the room was officially opened by expedition leader John Hunt and members of his team. That evening the climbers signed their names on the ceiling—the signatures are still visible. In addition, Mr. Briggs assembled a collection of Everest equipment, clothing, and other mementos for a permanent display.

Most revered of the Pen y Gwryd's Everest traditions is the set of silver beer mugs hanging on hooks in the guests-only hotel bar. Mr. Briggs bought them in the late 1940s and set them aside for alpinists who had achieved a first ascent anywhere in the world. Later Briggs established the policy of letting children use them for a drink after their first climb to the top of Snowdon (depending on what the youngsters were offered, this custom might have been designed to keep them quiet during dinner). In 1953 the proprietor had facsimile signatures of the Everest team inscribed on the tankards, and their use was limited to three classes of mountaineers: children, 1953 expedition members (the last died in 2013), and anyone with a recognized first ascent. Everybody else could just look and admire.

During my first few days at the Pen y Gwryd I was trapped indoors by exceedingly foul weather. With each passing day I feared that I might never see the sun in Wales or even set foot on its highest peak.

Late in the afternoon of the third day I was wandering around the building when I stepped into the Everest Room. There sat three young men, soaked to the skin and huddling around the stove. One of them was large and husky; one was medium in build and had very fine facial features; the third was short and wiry. They had apparently just returned from a miserable hike. Completely disheveled and looking slightly deranged, they were talking slowly and deliberately to each other. They bore a strong resemblance to Monty Python's Gumbys, lacking only the handkerchiefs on their heads.

I wanted to learn about the trail conditions, so I sat down and introduced myself. They responded, but I couldn't understand their names. They were speaking some form of English, but I couldn't grasp more than the occasional word. This was intriguing, so I asked where they were from.

In a deep voice the big one said, "Blubbmubbhumm."

"Sorry," I responded. "I didn't get that. Can you say it again?"

Once more he said, "Blubbmubbhumm," so I repeated it back slowly: "Blubb . . . mubb . . . humm."

Looking annoyed, he said, "No, it's Blubbmubbhumm."

At that point I put on my apologetic face and said, "Look, I'm from Canada, and my English isn't very good. Can you write it down here in my notebook?" The big one took my pen and slowly printed out in capital letters "BIRMINGHAM." Then he gave back the book, pointed to the word, and said, "Blubbmubbhumm." At that point the middle-sized fellow and the small one giggled. I was probably the first Canadian they had ever met. (In fact, I am not from Canada, but in my travels I have learned that Americans are not universally loved. In contrast, nobody hates Canadians, and a few Maple Leaf stickers on one's luggage can never hurt. If, however, you do employ this subterfuge, I suggest that you know the names of one or two Canadian cities, be sure to pronounce the word *about* as *uh-boat*, and be prepared to answer the classic north-of-the-border riddle, "Why is American beer like making love in a canoe?")

I asked the three what they had been doing outside, and the big one answered, "Oive bin hoiking and cloimbing with me mytes." I processed those words very carefully and, believing that I had understood, asked how it had been. At this the two smaller ones giggled again, and the big guy just pointed to their wet clothing. He said something that I didn't get.

Ignoring me, the three started talking at once, the big one in his husky voice, the middle-sized one in soft, effeminate tones, and the little one in a nasal and whiny manner. The big one was definitely in charge, and the others seemed to respect his dominance. The small one was a bit of a pest, and the middle one tried to calm him down from time to time. All at once it struck me. They were the Three Bears—Papa, Mama, and Baby. Their stature, intonations, and mannerisms were spot on, and they interacted like a tight-knit, albeit slightly peculiar family. And there I was, Goldilocks intruding on their space.

It was painful for all of us, but I tried to elicit a bit more information from the Bears. I did learn that they were sleeping in a tent behind the hotel, and from this I surmised that one sleeping bag was too warm, one was too cold, and the third was just right. The other thing I gleaned was that they were planning to climb Snowdon the next day. I thought they said that they were going to take the Pyg Track, but it might have been a reference to the Three Little Pigs and the fact that the big, bad storm was trying to blow their tent down.

The next day dawned crisp and clear—a perfect late-autumn morning whose low-angled sun cast everything in ochre. Looking out my window, I knew that this was the day I had been waiting for. Nevertheless, in true Pen y Gwryd tradition I ate breakfast with the other guests at eight fifty and left the hotel at nine thirty. On most climbs nine thirty is a very late start, but the Welsh walks are short enough to permit such institutionalized sloth. As I rose from the breakfast table, Mr. Briggs handed me a white box with my lunch. Then he suggested that I take a thermos of hot tea. I started to resist because a thermos is so heavy, but I didn't want to offend my host. I took the tea and a bottle of water as well.

I drove the mile up to Pen y Pass, a high point (1,168 feet) on the highway where there was a youth hostel and a trailhead parking lot for the combined Pyg Track and Miners' Path. This being late in the season and on the heels of a spell of bad weather, there was only one other car on-site.

Grabbing my knapsack, I fairly flew onto the trail. It started out with a level section, and after less than a quarter mile the Pyg Track branched off to the right, while the Miners' Path continued straight ahead. I turned onto the Pyg Track and started climbing gently toward the west, into the Eastern Cwm. On my right, above me, was the eastern end of Snowdon's northeast ridge descending from Crib Goch. To my left and below was the beginning of the valley. Rounding a slight corner, the scene opened up dramatically. There was Llyn Teyrn, smallest of the cwm's three lakes, several hundred feet below. Farther up was the much larger Llyn Llydaw. Beyond it was Snowdon's dominating pyramid. Directly across this lower section of the valley lay the terminus of the southeast ridge, spilling down from the summit of Lliwedd.

Little more than a mile from the start of the hike, I came to the second junction. This time it was the Pyg Track that continued ahead, while the trail to Crib Goch angled sharply to the right. I took the side path and soon came to a shallow saddle in the ridge with the throat-clearing name of Bwlch y Moch. I believe it means "Mucus Pass" or "Pass the Mucus." After saying its name several times, I felt great.

Now the climbing began as I turned left onto the ridge and started moving upward. There were sections of a faint track here and there, but much of the time I was walking on rocks. Even better, I occasionally had to use my hands—in mountaineering terms, scrambling. It felt good because I hadn't climbed since the Matterhorn thirteen months earlier. The rock was dry and sound, and I moved quickly. Above I could see some steeper sections and above them the eastern point of Crib Goch's summit. From Bwlch y Moch to the top was roughly half a mile. It looked pretty easy, so I didn't pay much attention to where I was going. I just went up.

Without warning I found myself on a high-angle face, and I realized that I had wandered from the ridge onto the mountain's southern wall. The exposure caused my loins to tighten. My heart rate soared. I had strayed into the classic Snowdon trap. Had I slowed down for a little route finding, had I used an ounce of intelligence, I would have seen a way to veer right and avoid this section. But no, I had blithely scrambled in a straight line and was gradually drawn onto the Cliff of Fools. I recalled reading that other unfortunates had made the same mistake and fallen to their deaths at this very spot. Gripping the rock, I envisioned a small obituary in the *Seattle Times* with the headline "Local Man Dies on Walk in Wales."

At that point I did what I do whenever I need to shift into a higher gear—I began to berate myself. Then I quickly realized that my situation was motivation enough, so I focused my attention and delicately began down-climbing. When I could, I traversed to the right, making sure not to lower myself into more treacherous territory. There were just enough small ledges for my toes and nubs for my fingers, and after ten minutes that seemed like two hours, I was off the cliff and back onto the ridge. Panting, I composed myself, shook my fist at the Grim Reaper, and started scrambling again.

The remaining section to the top of Crib Goch was straightforward—this time it really was—and I arrived at the top in ten or fifteen minutes. Actually, it was the eastern prow of the summit ridge, a half-mile-long arête whose apex (six feet higher than the eastern summit) sits at its midpoint. Getting there entailed a very airy traverse on a knife-edge ridge, with sheer drop-offs on both sides. I was reminded of famed Himalayan climber Willi Unsoeld, who described such a situation: "It was pretty much straight down on either side, about 7000 ft. on one side and 5000 ft. on the other. So we leaned just slightly to the 5000 ft. side. There was no use in taking unnecessary risks." I resolved not to fall at all, but I also challenged myself to do the traverse using only my feet, like an ironworker on a steel girder. Bending over for a handhold on a horizontal section wastes a lot of time and energy, and it can have the unintended effect of upsetting your balance. The ridge was stable, and in short order I reached the true summit of Crib Goch at 3,027 feet. It is, incidentally, the wettest spot in the United Kingdom, receiving 176 inches of rain each year. It had been roughly an hour since I had left the car. I paused to drink some water and survey the scene.

The way forward to the mountain's slightly lower western summit was every bit as exposed as the section I had just completed. After that the ridge was wide and rounded—a walk indeed. The next peak, Garnedd Ugain, was nothing more than a broad hump. To its left I saw the Pyg Track emerging from the valley at Bwlch Glas, the col between Garnedd Ugain and Snowdon. Below me I could see the entire Eastern Cwm, its three lakes and the Miners' Path. Opposite, to the left of Snowdon, was the long and impressive southeast ridge, topped by Lliwedd's several summits.

Looking west again, toward Snowdon, I noticed that a band of dark clouds had materialized beyond it and that they were headed in my direction. That was all the motivation I needed to get moving again. In short order I completed my traverse and descended to the saddle called Bwlch Goch. Setting aside that little route deviation on the way up, my experience on Crib Goch had been perfect. The air was crisp, the sun warm. There was no wind. My boots had gripped the rock as if embracing an old friend. Best of all, I had had the mountain to myself. If you climb Crib Goch on a typical summer's day, you are guaranteed to find yourself at many points on the ridge waiting for terrified people ahead of you to complete the next section. I had moved at my own pace. No guide, no other climbers, just me and the mountain.

I paused at the saddle and ate a handful of raisins in

celebration. The technical part of the Horseshoe was behind me. Now it would just be a long hike. I was concerned, however, that the clouds beyond Snowdon were closer, darker, and more threatening. I knew that I could deal with rain, and I could hike in wind. I just didn't want any lightning. There's not much you can do on an open ridge in a lightning storm, other than getting into a squat, lowering your head, and kissing your derrière good-bye. Hoping to beat the weather, I started running up the trail. With roughly three-quarters of the Horseshoe yet to come, I didn't feel that I had much choice. Fortunately, the path was well-worn, and I made rapid progress. There was a short section that required some easy scrambling, but I was soon at the top of Garnedd Ugain, at 3,494 feet the second highest peak in Wales. What I hadn't expected was snow, and it hit me just as I arrived at the stone monument that marked the summit. It came courtesy of a very stiff wind. I paused long enough to take some water and slip on my sweater, jacket, hat, and gloves. Then I started jogging again. In ten minutes I reached the Snowdon saddle, Bwlch Glas, where a huge phallic stone marks the upper end the Pyg Track. At this point the snow was heavier, the wind stronger. I wanted to press ahead, but a voice told me to pause a moment and get my bearings. I might have to retreat down the Pyg Track, and if I had to return this way in poor visibility, I wanted to know how to find the trail. After rehearsing that scenario, I started up Snowdon.

In better conditions this part of the climb would have been a Julie Andrews *Sound of Music* moment. The angle of the path was gentle, and the views would have been great. Instead, in the increasingly awful conditions, I could see little more than the path immediately in front of me. Moreover, the wind caused me to hunch over, and from time to time I lurched and stumbled. I began to wish that I had a hiking staff or ice axe for stability.

I was getting cold, so I stopped and slipped on my rain pants to ward off the wind. At that point I realized that I hadn't eaten anything more than a few raisins, and my body's ability to produce heat was not keeping up with the wind's capacity to chill me. I found a chocolate bar in the lunch box and began to eat it as I continued up the trail.

Time stands still when you cannot see your progress. Now and then I caught a glimpse of the railroad track to my right, but I had nothing else to use as a reference point. I trudged on. After making the summit, I would find a sheltered spot and drink that hot tea. I was glad Mr. Briggs had offered the thermos and that I hadn't turned it down.

When I arrived at a set of stone steps, I realized I was on the final summit cone. A brief moment of clearing confirmed that fact, and I also saw the railroad station just below me. It was boarded up, but I could at least sit on its leeward side to escape the wind and eat my lunch. At the mountain's high point I hugged a stone monument for a few seconds, to avoid being blown off into the Eastern Cwm. I saw nothing but white.

I was carefully picking my way down the summit steps, when at one point I stumbled to the side and onto some rocks. To my great surprise, there was a man sitting there, curled in a ball and hugging his knees. He wasn't moving. He had no jacket or cap and no knapsack. He was plastered with snow. In the howling wind I bent over and shouted, "Are you all right?" There was no response. I yelled again and still got no reaction. Thinking he might be dead, I put my hand on his shoulder and shook him. This time he slowly lifted his head to look at me. I knew that face. It was Mama Bear from the Pen y Gwryd.

"Where are your friends?" I shouted. He didn't seem to understand.

"Your friends, where are they?" Still, he was uncomprehending.

"Where . . . are . . . your . . . mytes?" A look of recognition—he clumsily waved his hand in the direction of the path I had just ascended.

It was obvious that I needed to get him out of there, out of the wind. I shouted, "Listen, I'm going to give you my jacket and hat, but only if you get your ass off the ground and start moving. I'm not going to stand here and freeze my balls while you sit there." I shoved my knit cap onto his head. Then I fought to stand him up and tried to get him into my jacket. It was like dressing a manikin—he was so stiff. Once it was zipped up, I worked my gloves onto his wooden fingers. "Let's go," I commanded, and I grabbed his arm and started guiding him down the steps to the station. He was clumsy, and he nearly pulled me off my feet several times. Fortunately, the station was close at hand, and we made it safely to its sheltered side. There I sat him down against the building.

After fetching the thermos from my pack, I filled its cup and held it to his lips. "Drink this," I ordered, and he took a sip. "Now, put your hands on the cup to warm them." When he didn't react, I pulled up one of his hands and held it against the cup. He then lifted the other one and cradled the cup. "Take another drink," I said, and I lifted his hands and the cup to his mouth. We repeated this procedure until he had consumed the entire cupful. His fingers appeared to soften, and a little color returned to his face.

I refilled the cup, and he drank it eagerly without assistance. Then I handed him my sandwich, which he ate rapidly. After taking a few sips of tea myself, I gave him a little more. I wanted to save the last cup in case we found Papa Bear or Baby Bear.

"Can you walk?" I asked? He nodded. "Okay, then we're getting the hell out of here."

We stepped from behind the station and back into the gale, which was now a certified whiteout. Still holding onto Mama Bear, I led him a few steps up to the path and then we started down, arm in arm. Fortunately, he was less clumsy than before. Also, I could see a few paces ahead, and the path had not yet disappeared under the snow. If I was cold—and I believe that I was—my adrenalin was overriding the discomfort.

As we descended, I tried to look for signs of the other bears, but they were not on the path, and I knew that I had no business wandering around in even a cursory search. My job was to get myself and Mama off that mountain. That was as much as I could hope to do, and it was a nice, definable task that took my mind off the dreadful possibility that two other climbers were lying down nearby and slipping into death.

When we reached Bwlch Glas, we practically bumped into the vertical monument. Visibility at that point was near zero, and the wind was stronger than ever. Grateful that I had paused to reconnoiter the area, I was able to locate the Pyg Track more or less by feel. We started down carefully.

Within seconds the wind and snow eased off. Actually, we started to get below the gale. We were dropping down the leeward side of the mountain as a white plume soared overhead. After ten minutes we were below the bottom edge of the cloud, and the Eastern Cwm presented itself. At that moment I felt a tremendous sense of relief, and for the first time I realized how chilled I was. I stopped and opened my knapsack. Mama Bear and I shared the last cup of tea and ate the rest of the food. We said nothing. When we resumed our hike down, Mama was able to move on his own, so I let him set the pace as I followed a few steps behind.

I wanted to keep dropping, so when we came to a junction in the trail, I told Mama to veer right, onto the Miners' Track. After a bit of zigzagging we arrived at the shore of Glaslyn, the highest of the cwm's three lakes. From the far end of Glaslyn the trail dropped gently down the valley to the much larger lake, Llyn Llydaw.

After skirting Llyn Llydaw, we crossed its narrowest part on a rocky causeway. On the other side we encountered the path coming down from the southeast ridge. Looking up, I saw that the summit of Lliwedd was obscured by the storm cloud. Given our tough times on Snowdon, I did not regret forgoing the second half of the Horseshoe.

The final section of the Miners' Path was more a road than a hiking trail, and we quickly made our way back to the car park.

When we were several hundred yards away, Mama Bear stopped and removed the warm clothing I had given him. Handing the items back to me, he said in his soft voice, "Thanks, Myte, I'm okye now."

Besides my Volvo, the only other vehicle in the parking lot was the same one that had been there several hours earlier. This time I saw that there were two people sitting in its front seat. When Mama Bear walked over to it and opened the back door, I realized that the two silhouettes were none other than Papa and Baby Bear. They didn't bother getting out of the car to greet us or ask how we were. They simply backed up and drove off.

Back at the Pen y Gwryd, Mr. Briggs was waiting at the door. "I've been concerned about you," he said. "That storm came up rather suddenly."

We sat in the warm confines of the Everest Room as I recounted the day's events. Briggs told me that he had helped organize the local mountain rescue group some years earlier, and that its members would be grateful that I had averted a callout. He then instructed me to head to a special shower upstairs, and when I had finished, he would have a reward for me.

The shower (Briggs called it his "Edwardian Bath") was the oddest bathroom device I had ever seen. It was a tall metal cylinder with gauges and dials on the outside and a curving door for ingress. Hoping the temperature adjustments were proper, I stepped inside and turned the faucets. Water began to squirt out from some small holes at the bottom of the chamber around the perimeter. How odd, I thought. I wanted a shower, and I'm getting a footbath. Then I noticed that there were similar holes at various levels on all sides, and water began coming out of the next set of openings above the floor. Then the next level and the next, and eventually I was being sprayed top to bottom with lovely hot water coming at me from every direction.

I lingered in that tank, enjoying the longest shower I had ever taken. When I finally stepped out, I was reeling like Woody Allen as he emerged from the Orgasmatron in *Sleeper*. I dried off and dressed myself, and then I more or less flowed down the stairs like a Slinky toy.

Mr. Briggs was waiting for me in the bar. With an avuncular smile he said, "Your first ascent of Snowdon and your first mountain rescue deserve a token of thanks. Which tankard would you like to use?"

I had climbed the highest peak in Wales and returned in one piece, while the Three Bears were safely on their way back to Blubbmubbhumm. I was well showered, ensconced in a shrine to British mountaineering, and drinking a pint of bitter from the sacred chalice dedicated to Edmund Hillary. This was a fitting end to my second mountain adventure in Europe.

Actually, there was one more thing. Two days later, when I checked out of the Pen y Gwryd, I discovered that, true to his profession, Mr. Briggs had included the celebratory pint on my final bill.

The Unorthodox Climber

MOUNT ATHOS, GREECE, 6,670'

Athens was exactly what you would expect. What happens when a million volatile Greeks are thrown together? Too many cars in too little space. Stone and marble buildings catching the traffic roar, flinging it back, and bracing for more. Add exhaust fumes, oppressive heat, and lack of vegetation, and the air is so thick and foul that every breath is a chore. Apparently, the only way to survive in such a setting is to yell at anyone or anything that crosses your path.

My Greek host, on the other hand, seemed immune to his environment. His name was Klemes Seraphimides, a friend from college and, for a time, my brother-in-law. In the States he had demonstrated an uncanny ability to overcome the stresses of academic life by lighting a cigarette, pouring a glass of wine, and working the *New York Times* crossword puzzle. Now back home in Athens, he remained true to form, the picture of calm.

"How do you do it?" I asked, after a heart-stopping ride from the airport into the city center.

"The wine helps. We should visit my landlord's flat, and then you'll understand."

The landlord was a pudgy older man, mostly bald and deeply tanned. He wore loose-fitting khaki trousers, flip-flop sandals, and a white sleeveless undershirt from which little tufts of gray hair were protruding. After a brief introduction the three of us sat at a heavy wooden table. The other two started smoking. The old man turned to a sideboard and removed a large, ancient-looking carafe. He then set a glass tumbler before each of us. After filling them with wine, he gestured for Klemes and me to take a drink. It was my first Greek wine, and I thought it was delicious.

"Is this retsina?" I asked. I had been warned that Greek wine was laced with extra resin, with the result that it tasted like turpentine. What we were drinking had a stronger flavor than French or California wines, but it was wine nevertheless. Klemes chuckled, then told the landlord what I had asked. The old man smiled and waved his hand back and forth, signaling no.

"Tourists come to Greece expecting to drink retsina," said Klemes, "so we make it for them. It's a cruel joke—Greeks can't stand the stuff. We just drink regular wine." I have recently learned that the same goes for sangria in Spain. Only tourists ask for it, and Spaniards can't imagine ruining a glass of wine by adding fruit juice.

We all had a good laugh and proceeded to work our way through the contents of the jug. At some point I noticed that the landlord tapped the table with his glass before every sip. Looking more closely, I saw that he also raised the glass and sniffed it before each drink. I asked Klemes what the ritual meant. Again, he translated my question, and the old man smiled before launching into a detailed explanation. By the motion of his hands, he was obviously describing each of his wine-drinking movements.

When the landlord paused, Klemes looked at me and translated. "He says that wine is too important just to drink it. You have to experience it with all your senses—with your ears by touching your glass to the table or clinking it with another glass, with your eyes by holding it to the light, with your nose by sniffing it. Finally, in your mouth you feel it on your tongue and taste it with your taste buds. Only when you drink it this way can you truly appreciate it and give it the proper respect."

I immediately picked up my tumbler and reached across the table. The landlord touched his glass to mine. Then I deliberately lifted mine toward the window, peering through the deep red color. I sniffed it carefully and then put the glass to my lips. I felt the liquid roll across my tongue before swallowing it slowly. I looked at the old man, and he nodded approvingly. He then drank from his own glass and set it down. He said something that Klemes translated as "You are doing well on your first visit in Greece," but was more likely "The kid is too skinny, but he's a quick study." Klemes added, "By the way, never drain your glass—here that means you are demanding more, and it comes across as greedy."

"How do you say 'Cheers' in Greek?" I asked.

"Just say 'Yassou'—it means everything is fine." I said it, and we kept on drinking.

The next day we escaped the chaotic city and drove to Meteora, where monastic communities perch precariously on towers of rock. The landscape was inspiring, and I was excited at the prospect of being hauled up to one of the cloisters in a basket, as they do in all the travel films. Klemes dutifully inquired, and we were disappointed to learn that getting into the more isolated communities required special permission arranged far in advance. A guest had to have a legitimate purpose like church business or scholarly research. During our visit only one monastery was open to the public, and access was via a narrow road to a small parking lot just outside the compound walls. Unfortunately, we were denied the chance to see gloomy cells housing shirtless monks on their knees engaged in self-flagellation. The only rooms open to the public were a small chapel and an adjoining shop where the brothers sold postcards and hand-painted icons.

As we left Meteora, Klemes mentioned that a year earlier he had spent a week on the Mount Athos peninsula in northern

Greece, walking from one monastery to another. He had been welcomed into various communities, where he had eaten meals with the monks and lodged in available cells. Knowing of my enthusiasm for climbing, Klemes mentioned that there was a mountain at the end of the peninsula and that it would be an interesting ascent. Now he had my attention.

The Greek region of Macedonia touches on the northern Aegean Sea, and jutting southward from its coast is a fist-shaped landmass called Halkidiki. Three parallel fingers of land extend from the fist, and the easternmost of them is Mount Athos. The mountain at its tip bears the same name.

In pre-Christian times the sea where the peninsula lies was believed to be the site of a great battle between the god Poseidon and a Thracian giant named Athos. As they fought, the giant threw an enormous boulder at Poseidon, but it missed its target and crashed into the water. Poseidon then slew the giant and buried him beneath the land that the rock had created. Apparently, the victory itself was sufficient for Poseidon, because he allowed the peninsula to be named after the vanquished Athos.

Christian settlement of Mount Athos is believed to have come on the heels of a visit by none other than Mary, mother of Jesus. According to legend, years after the ascension of her son, Our Lady was sailing from Palestine to Cyprus when her ship was blown off course roughly a thousand miles northwest to the Athos peninsula. Now that's a serious storm and, I might add, some highly questionable seamanship on the part of the crew. In any event the outcome was felicitous. As a result of being tossed about for weeks on the raging sea, upon making landfall the Blessed Mother was deeply touched by the beauty of the place. Consequently, she prayed to her son and asked him to grant it to her. His voice responded from heaven that indeed Mount Athos would be her garden and "a haven of salvation for those seeking to be saved." The resident pagans were promptly issued thirty-day eviction notices, and the new Christian inhabitants dubbed their home "Garden of the Virgin."

Whether Mary actually set foot there or not, Mount Athos proved to be the ideal location for a haven. It was dedicated exclusively to monastic life, and so it has remained. Its official name is now the Autonomous Monastic State of the Holy Mountain. The peninsula is part of Greece, but the Greek government allows the resident monks and their church officials full authority over the state's affairs.

Today the Holy Mountain is home to twenty monasteries, twelve hermitic communities called "sketes," and an unknown number of solitary hermits. There are roughly two thousand inhabitants, all members of Eastern Orthodox churches. They have chosen to separate from normal society and have dedicated themselves to contemplation and simple, godly living. They do receive donations from the outside, but the monks and hermits must largely support themselves by raising their own food, making wine, and painting icons for sale outside the community.

It is difficult for an outsider to travel to Mount Athos, and not just due to its geographical isolation. There are no hotels and little infrastructure to deal with visitors, so guests must lodge in the monasteries. Needless to say, the monks are committed to their lifestyle, and they do not want to be overrun by casual tourists or, dare we say, the climbing crowd. Therefore, visiting permits are carefully limited. Preference is given to members of an Eastern Orthodox church who wish to carry out a spiritual pilgrimage. Anyone else must apply well in advance and then wait in line. Your prospects are enhanced if you can obtain a recommendation from an Orthodox bishop. Even with the coveted invitation, your stay may be limited to just a few days.

In an era of coeducation and gender equality, it seems remarkable that Mount Athos remains a males-only preserve. There are no communities of monastic women, and females are not only prohibited from living there; they cannot even visit. No women, not ever . . . period. Mary herself would be denied the opportunity to stop in and see how her garden grows. A notorious breach of protocol occurred in the 1930s, when a feminist beauty queen (now that's an interesting combination) named Aliki Diplarakou disguised herself as a man—apparently a fine-featured one—and entered the sanctuary. The monks did not react kindly to this publicity stunt, and the understanding even today is that if the men on duty at the point of entry have any doubts about your gender, you will kindly be invited to drop trouser and display your equipment. In the military this is referred to as a "short-arm inspection."

For any climber endowed with a pocket rocket, the real attraction of the Mount Athos peninsula is the peak at its southern tip. It is an elegant feature with a nicely chiseled summit pyramid, and at 6,670 feet it dominates like the grain elevator in a midwestern farm town. Rising directly from the Aegean Sea, its prominence is equal to its height, and it easily qualifies as an ultra.

Giants, monasteries, and a mountain. The Siren was calling. I told Klemes that I definitely wanted to climb Mount Athos. He said that if I could obtain a letter of recommendation, he would help me with the other logistics.

A year later, in Seattle, I started planning my trip to the Holy Mountain, and my first stop was St. Demetrios Orthodox Church. It was a Saturday in September, when the annual Greek Bazaar was taking place. The church parking lot was filled with smoking barbecues and hundreds of people. Over the course of an hour I ate skewers of grilled meat, drank FIX Hellas beer, and watched a team of costumed dancers moving back and forth, arm in arm. Satisfied that I had consumed enough, I set out to find the priest.

A handwritten sign on the church door said that Father Homer Demopulos would shortly give a lecture, so I took a seat in the sanctuary with two dozen other visitors. A few minutes later the priest strode down the center aisle. Although he was dressed in black, he was clean-shaven, where I had expected a flowing beard. He was smiling, rather than dour, and he was taller than the Greek men I had previously met. He was an imposing and handsome man.

After welcoming us, Father Homer began his lecture by saying, "Worship is not an intellectual exercise, and at St. Demetrios you have the opportunity to worship with all of your senses. When you enter the church, you can touch the holy water near the entrance. Then with your eyes you can feast on the icons and stained-glass windows. When the service begins, you hear the cantor, and you smell the incense. Finally, you will taste the communion bread. We believe it should be an experience for your whole body as well as for your mind and soul."

I was struck by what he said. The Calvinist church of my childhood had been gloomy ("no dancing, no movies"), guilt inducing ("total depravity of man"), and entirely intellectual. Here I was being confronted with a completely different approach to Christianity. It was cheery and inviting inside this sanctuary, and just outside they were dancing and drinking. I was so Dutch, and this was so Greek.

At the end of the presentation I approached Father Homer and asked if I could visit with him. He said yes, of course.

A few days later I called on the priest in his office, and I began by telling him about myself and my interest in Greece. I said that his lecture had been meaningful to me, particularly the part about using your five senses in Orthodox worship. I added that it was similar to what the old man in Athens had said about drinking wine. When I explained it, Father Homer laughed and said, "Well, I've never heard wine drinking described quite that way, but it makes sense, and it sounds rather Greek, doesn't it."

I commented that for some people drinking good wine is so profound that it seems spiritual. It was a casual comment, but he responded seriously. "Of course, any activity—if done with the proper attitude—can be spiritual. Your whole life can praise God, and wine is at the heart of the Christian tradition. Christ turned water into wine, and he instituted the holy supper with wine and bread. However, to be proper about it, just drinking a glass of wine seems to stretch the definition of worship." With a wink he added, "It's a pity, because I do love wine."

I then mentioned my love of mountains and how some climbers feel closest to God when they are in the high places. How about mountaineering as a form of worship?

He smiled. "In the outdoors we do feel a connection with the Creator, but . . . ," he chuckled softly, "I don't want to put myself out of a job. I'm a churchman, and I believe that my calling is to assist people in a very traditional and well-developed form of worship—the indoor kind."

We talked about the lure of Seattle's nearby water and mountains and how it wasn't really surprising that the state of Washington has the nation's lowest rate of church attendance. As we spoke, we had no idea that thirteen years later the flagship store of Recreational Equipment Inc., best known as REI, would be built on the very land where the original St. Demetrios Church once stood. In a bold stroke the one-time house of God was replaced by a quintessentially Seattle alternative—a glass and wood-beamed cathedral dedicated to self-fulfillment and gearhead consumerism.

I told Father Homer about my desire to travel to Mount Athos, and he at once became very animated. "That," he said, "is a very special place." We discussed the details of a visit, and he readily agreed to ask his bishop in San Francisco for a letter of recommendation.

"Now," he added, "there is something I want you to do for me."

"Sure, but what can I do that would help you?"

"It's not so much for me but for some of my parishioners. Up in the North End is a small restaurant called the Lake City Café. It's a little breakfast and lunch place with standard American food, but its owners are two Greek brothers named Nick and Ted. They are third-generation members of St. Demetrios, completely American but proud of their Greek heritage. Well . . . they have a younger brother, Chris, who wanted to become an Orthodox priest, so he went to study at our seminary in Massachusetts. At some point he heard about Mount Athos, and he decided that he would like to spend some time there to deepen his commitment to the faith. So, he joined a monastic community and began a period of prayer and meditation."

"Was he happy with the experience?" I asked.

"In a way, that's the problem. Chris went to Mount Athos seven years ago, and he has never come back. He writes from time to time, so the family knows he's okay. It's just that nobody expected he would stay away this long."

"What would you like me to do?"

"Go to the restaurant and meet Nick and Ted. Tell them you are going to Mount Athos, and see if you can bring anything to Chris for them."

"Are visitors allowed to bring gifts?"

"Actually, anyone can mail things to the monks, and yes, you can bring them gifts if you go there. Maybe Nick or Ted has an idea for something that you could take with you. They can also tell you how to find Chris."

"Of course. I'll call the restaurant and let you know how it goes."

I had seen the Lake City Café, but I had never eaten there. When I phoned, I asked for Ted and then told him that Father Homer had suggested I meet him and his brother. Ted did not sound enthusiastic, but he said it would be okay if I stopped by that afternoon around three, when they had stopped serving lunch.

The café was a freestanding building with large windows on three sides and its own parking lot. It had probably had many identities through the years, with none of the owners caring to risk much expense to make it distinctive. Inside, the furnishings and decor were ordinary and sterile. The clock advertised Coca-Cola, and a photo of the Seattle waterfront bore the logo of Darigold ice cream. The only thing Greek was a calendar on the wall behind the cash register—it showed the Parthenon under a blue sky. Two teenage boys were sweeping the floors. I asked one of them for the owners, and he turned and went into the kitchen.

A moment later two men emerged, both wearing slacks and polo shirts. There was no doubt they were brothers, probably late thirties, although one had a full head of dark hair while the other was balding. The one with hair stuck out his hand. "I'm Nick, and this is Ted." I greeted them both, and we moved into a booth at a window, where I sat opposite them. I began by saying that Father Homer had suggested the visit and that I was going to Mount Athos. Could they tell me how to find Chris, and was there anything I could bring him from home?

Nick began, "Well, it's nice of you to—"

"No it's not," Ted interrupted. "This is just Father Homer trying to make up for what the church has done to us."

Nick winced. "What Ted means—"

"I can say what I mean," Ted said angrily. "The church stole our brother. They lured him to Greece, and now they won't let go of him."

"It's not like that, Ted."

"Yes it is. It's like a cult. He's a prisoner over there."

"No he isn't. He's free to leave any time he wants to."

"But they have control over his mind. He'll never be able to think clearly enough to realize he should come home. He doesn't understand that this is killing our parents and the whole family." Turning to me, Ted added, "Did Father Homer mention that I won't have anything to do with the church because of this?"

"Well, um," I started to answer, squirming uncomfortably. I felt a sudden urge to bolt for the door.

Nick held up his hand and said, "Ted, now let me tell my side of the story. Your opinions are clear enough. I think it's only fair for me to say something to Steve."

Ted waved his hand dismissively. "Okay, I really don't care." He probably would have left at that moment, but he was trapped on the inside of the booth. Instead, he looked down at his hands, scowling.

"Yes, the family is concerned," Nick said, "and we all miss Chris. But he's at Mount Athos by choice, and he has a good life there. You see, I've been there. I saw it for myself. Three years ago I went on behalf of the family and spent two weeks at his monastery. I got to know the men there and how they live. It was the most beautiful place I have ever been." He paused, looking off into the distance. His voice softened. "It was so peaceful there, and I felt so close to God. Actually, I didn't want to come back."

Ted exploded. "Do you hear what you are saying? It's ridiculous. You have a wife and three kids. What kind of bullshit is this?"

"Now, it's not like—"

"Yes it is. What kind of church would do that? Father Homer knows damn well that this is outrageous. Somebody should go over there and deprogram Chris and all the so-called religious men who abandon their families." With that, Ted pushed against Nick and growled, "Now let me out of here." As he stalked away he turned back and muttered, "Stay away from Mount Athos if you know what's good for you."

Without sitting back down, Nick shrugged. "I'm sorry," he said. "I think you'd better go. I guess this wasn't a very good idea."

I was very happy to oblige. As I opened the front door, I looked back and saw that Nick had already disappeared. There were shouts emanating from the kitchen. Later I called Father Homer, and without going into detail, I said that no, I wouldn't be bringing any gifts to Mount Athos. He told me that my letter from the bishop should arrive within a few days.

A month later I was back in Athens, armed with a seal of approval from Anthony, the metropolitan bishop of San Francisco. He commended me in general to his brother bishops and in particular to the officials in Thessaloniki who issued travel passes for Mount Athos. I assumed that Klemes would be able to steer me to the right place.

Klemes was now a single man. After twelve years in Greece his American wife, my sister-in-law, had grown weary of the fact that daily life was a constant battle. Klemes had always been low-key, but his wife couldn't bear the yelling and confrontation that permeates Greek society. She had fled to England, where, except for Question Time in the House of Commons, nobody shouts about anything.

As for Klemes, he didn't seem too troubled by this turn of events. In fact, he had already taken up with a young Greek woman named Zitsa. She was from Crete, but like Klemes she worked in Athens as a representative for English textbook publishers. She and Klemes had known each other professionally and socially for several years, and they were now living together.

Once I had settled into the guest room, I showed Klemes the letter from San Francisco, and that is when he delivered the bad news.

"Look, I called the Mount Athos visitors' office in Thessaloniki a few days ago. There's a problem. There's been a lot of hippies traveling to Mount Athos recently and staying on too long. Dutch, Germans, Brits—you name it. The monks won't kick anybody out, and the hippies seem to be taking advantage of the free food and lodging. A lot of them just sit around and smoke dope, waiting for the next meal. Now the people in Thessaloniki have put a freeze into effect—no visitors unless you are a member of the Orthodox Church. It's bad luck for you. The bishop's letter specifically says you are not orthodox."

Well, I wasn't orthodox, but for a moment I considered becoming so in order to salvage my trip. Of course I knew that wouldn't work, although years later George Costanza did accomplish an express conversion on *Seinfeld* in order to date a Latvian Orthodox woman. Whenever I see that episode, I think of Mount Athos and how I never got there.

"Just great," I said. "Now I've got time to kill. Any ideas?"

"Actually," Klemes responded, "we've been discussing it. We

can't take off work right now, but we think you should consider going to Santorini."

"Why Santorini?"

"It might be the most beautiful place in Greece."

Zitsa showed me a travel guide with pictures of Santorini. After we thumbed through the pages together, she put her hand on my shoulder and said, "Stephen, it's relaxing and very romantic. You should go."

So, instead of climbing Mount Athos, I flew to an island with no mountains at all.

Santorini is one of the most unusual places in the world. Imagine a broadly drawn, backward capital *C* whose outer edge is a curving strip of black sand beaches. From the shoreline the island slopes gradually upward toward its inner rim, which sits atop thousand-foot red-brown cliffs that drop precipitously into a sea of the deepest blue imaginable. A small island sits in the center of the lagoon, and there is a larger one in the gap between the two ends of the *C*.

Thousands of years ago Santorini was a round, cone-shaped island sitting placidly in the southern Aegean. Then one sunny day in 1600 BC the volcanic forces that built it up nearly destroyed it. In one of the greatest eruptions in human history the center of the island simply blew away, creating a hole more than two thousand feet deep and leaving only the outer edge of the previous circle. The sea promptly rushed into the lower half of the chasm, and the island's remnant assumed its current shape.

The eruption of Santorini vaporized its inhabitants. The same event is believed to have caused the disappearance of the entire Minoan civilization on nearby Crete—either because of tsunamis that were generated or as a result of volcanic ash and poisonous gases that spread in all directions from the blast. Historians have also speculated that the dramatic movement of the Mediterranean waters may have had the effect of draining the Red Sea just as Moses and Aaron were standing on its shore scratching their heads and wondering what the heck to do about Pharaoh's approaching army. The most bombastic idea is that Santorini was the lost continent of Atlantis. The story goes that when the Atlanteans abandoned true religion in favor of earthly pleasure, in a snit their gods sank the entire landmass. Whatever history you embrace, that one tiny island was the geological mouse that roared.

Not having seen Santorini for myself, I didn't really know what to expect, and as my plane landed on the island's outer slopes, I was less than enthusiastic. I was stuck on the fact that this was the opposite end of Greece from Mount Athos. I should have been visiting monasteries and climbing an ultra. Despite what Klemes and Zitsa had said, how could this small chunk of volcanic rock be all that interesting? It didn't have white beaches, and it didn't have a real mountain. How could it possibly be worth four days of my time?

My mood didn't change when the taxi deposited me in the town of Fira at the Hotel Apollo. The building was unimpressive on the outside, and it was located on a rough cobblestone lane crowded with parked cars. The hotel's lobby was as uninteresting as its exterior, and my viewless room was austere—the Spartans were Greek, weren't they? On a more positive note I had been assigned to the hotel's shady side, so the room was relatively cool in the punishing heat of midday. I plunked myself onto the bed for a Greek siesta, but I couldn't sleep. Instead, I spent several mind-numbing hours watching Greek soap operas and talk shows on a small black-and-white television. Eventually, I couldn't stand it anymore, and I had grown tired of feeling sorry for myself. I decided to strike out into the village, although I did so with a sigh.

It was still hot, and I walked slowly uphill, staying in the shade where possible. I was hoping I might come across something of interest—perhaps a church or taverna. Then, as I rounded a corner and emerged onto an open terrace, I was unexpectedly confronted with The View. There it was—the crater, the sea, and the arms of the island reaching out on either side. I was impressed, but within seconds I also realized that I had stepped into a swarm of tourists.

The crowd was mostly overweight older folks wearing beach hats and T-shirts that advertised Rome, St. Tropez, and other vacation spots. Everyone was adorned with a colored tag that identified to which cruise line and tour group they belonged. They were chattering in many languages and posing at the edge of the terrace, saying, "Be sure to get our ship in the background!" "Encore une fois!" "Sagen Sie Käse!"

Glancing about, I noticed that the plaza was ringed with souvenir stands. Other tourists were elbowing each other for a chance to shake the Santorini snow globes and twirl the postcard rack. I bolted from the place, only to discover that the entire town of Fira was a series of snack bars, junk shops posing as art galleries, and restaurants whose signs proclaimed "Authentic Grik Food." What were Klemes and Zitsa thinking when they sent me here? Was this Gatlinburg, Tennessee? Would I stumble onto a Ripley's Believe It or Not! museum? What in the world would I do for the next three days in this commercialized hellhole? I retreated to my hotel.

That evening, over a plate of forgettable food on the hotel's small patio—where I was the only patron—I considered returning to Athens the next day and taking the first plane back to the States. But I realized that that would be petulant. I had traveled enough to know that there is always something worth doing, no matter where you find yourself. After mulling over my options and aided by an entire bottle of local wine, I decided that I would do what I had hoped to do on Mount Athos. I would avoid the tourist traps and explore Santorini on foot. This resolution cheered me, and I returned to my room to get organized.

With my mind in climbing mode, I rose early, filled my water bottles, and laced my boots. By prearrangement with the hotelkeeper,

I grabbed a light breakfast and a few sandwiches for my knapsack. Then I headed out into the cool air of dawn, walking north out of Fira toward the northwest extremity of the island. My destination was the village of Oia, which is land's end on the upper half of the island's horseshoe. For most of the five-mile hike I managed to stay on paths near the crater rim, and the views were spectacular. Eventually, I rounded the curve and was able to look back toward Fira. From a distance it shimmered in the morning sun, with nary a tourist in sight.

Oia (pronounced *ee-a*) is a smaller version of Fira. Until World War II it was the island's hub of activity, but in recent times it has been eclipsed by Fira. For the visitor to Oia that's a good thing, because it is quieter and more quaint than its overrun neighbor. Oia's blue-domed churches are the iconic image of Santorini, and its views of the caldera as inspiring as any on the island. I should have lingered and relaxed, but I had a hiking agenda for myself, and so after a quick exploration, I retraced my steps and returned to Fira. I was pleased at having done some walking, but I wanted something a little less tame.

That afternoon I hiked down the zigzag marble walkway from Fira to a boat dock at the bottom of the cliff. For a few dollars I purchased a four-hour tour to Santorini's small neighboring islands. The first stop was Nea Kameni, directly in the center of the water-filled crater. It is the tip of a volcanic cone that has slowly built up since the Big Bang of 1600 BC. Its most recent eruption was in 1939, and I suppose that part of the thrill of a visit is that It Might Happen Today. Not surprisingly, there is not much to do on the uninhabited and undeveloped cinder pile, and most of the tourists on my boat seemed content to emulate one corpulent man, who stepped ashore, picked up a chunk of black pumice, and shouted, "Hey, Mavis, get a picture of me holding this lava rock." I, on the other hand, scampered away and hiked to the high point of the cone. Having ascended the great volcanoes of the Pacific Northwest, I wasn't overly impressed with the experience, but I was grateful to have minimized my time with Mavis and her husband.

The primary object of our tour was the islet of Therasia. A remnant of the original island, it sits along the imaginary circle dominated by Santorini's capital *C.* Like its big sister, it has a wall of daunting cliffs on the crater side, while its outer portion slopes gently away. On a poorly functioning overhead speaker, our boat captain explained in marginal English that Santorini's Greek name is Thera and that *Therasia* means "Thera wannabe" or something like that. He also said that the main village of the island, informally called Therasia Town, sits at the top of the cliff, like Oia and Fira. We could get up to the village on foot or by donkey, or we could spend our two hours onshore at one of the tavernas adjacent to the boat dock.

After spending a few minutes watching some people from Florida haggling over the cost of a donkey ride, I started up the path on foot. I was far faster than the animals and other walkers, and I soon found myself on top of the island in the central square of the tiny village. There were few people in sight, but a couple of taverna proprietors were organizing tables and chairs for the impending visit of the boat people. I had decided to see what I could of the island in the time available, and I quickly left the plaza. Just around the corner I found a second, smaller square, where several old women dressed in black were extracting loaves of bread from a communal stone oven. It smelled wonderful, and I wanted to purchase a loaf, but these people did not look like merchants.

My small map showed a path running downslope and away from the village. After slightly less than a mile, it intersected another path. If I turned left, in a quarter mile I would come to an uphill trail, parallel to the first, that would take me back to the crater rim near Therasia Town. The walkways framed a sloping rectangle of land, and the entire trek would be roughly two miles. This seemed easily doable in the hour and a half I had before the boat departed. I was looking forward to being alone.

The downhill path was actually a dirt road that initially meandered through fields that appeared to be filled with rows of bird nests. On closer inspection they turned out to be grapevines wound in circles along the ground, with the grapes hanging inside. I have since learned that this cultivation technique was devised to protect the fruit from the persistent hot winds that buffet the island. The road straightened, and I found what the map identified as the hamlet of Potamos. It proved to be a collection of rundown houses, few of which looked inhabited. No one was present. I walked a bit farther, found the second road, and turned left.

The second road was level, traversing the gentle slope, and there were cultivated fields on either side. As I approached a small farm on my right, I saw two women in long skirts, sweaters, and headscarves chopping at the dirt with pickaxes. They looked up at me and stared. I waved and began to walk toward them. Perhaps I looked a bit strange to them in my hiking shorts and blue knapsack, because they started laughing in an odd, cackling manner. Both of them were very short and had deeply wrinkled faces—like Mother Theresa in a black babushka. The older of the two was missing her front teeth. Once near them, I had no idea what to do next, so I held up my camera. Through gestures I asked if I could take their picture. They nodded and cackled again.

Just as I was closing the camera cover, I saw a man running toward us from the farmhouse. He was waving a rake and shouting. The rake was not one of those citified ones with the long, flexible tines. No, this was a farm tool with hard teeth bent at wicked right angles. I sensed that this was going to be trouble. Perhaps he thought that I was a threat to his women. Or, because things were fairly primitive out here, maybe he feared that I had captured the women's spirits by recording their images. As he got closer, I could see that he was young, probably a teenager. He must have had some sort of developmental handicap, because he was not saying words—just grunting loudly. In an earlier time he might have been classified as demon possessed, but however we would label him, he was very agitated, and I was certain that he intended to aerate my body with that rake. I made a half-turn and was on the verge of sprinting away when one of the women turned and said something to the boy in a loud and firm voice. He stopped dead in his tracks, clutching the rake in both hands and staring at me. I attempted a pleasant smile. Then I turned back to the women, said "*Efkharisto*—thank you," and promptly left.

Rattled, I figured it was time to get back to civilization. Just past the farm was another intersecting road—apparently the third leg of my hike. Glancing back to be sure I was not being pursued by the boy, I turned left and uphill. This new route quickly deteriorated from a road to a single-track path. I hoped I hadn't turned too soon. There was supposed to be another village—Agrilia—just ahead. I would know in a few minutes.

As the path rose, the smooth slope began to close in on either side, and I realized that I was heading into a small canyon. Very quickly I was flanked by steep walls, and the sunshine gave way to shadow. Above me on each side I began to see houses carved into the rock. They had openings where doors and windows had once been, but now they were nothing but vacant, man-made caves. Agrilia was a ghost town.

Still feeling the effects of my encounter at the farm, I remained apprehensive. I did not want to go back down, but I was concerned that this canyon might prove to be a dead end. I kept moving, and it got darker and spookier. My imagination began to get the better of me. The black eyes of the caves were staring down. Would a wild beast or a Rake Man come leaping from above? According to Lawrence Durrell's definitive book *The Greek Islands*, Santorini is believed to be a haven for vampires. Would Dracula himself accost me to slake his thirst?

My pulse racing, I began to run up the path. I was not going to succumb to the lurking monsters without making them earn their dinner. I ran faster and faster, deeper into the abyss. To avoid stumbling, I kept my eyes on the ground. Then, as I rounded a boulder, I saw something ahead, lying on the path. What! Ten feet from me was the decapitated corpse of a small baby. I don't remember if my scream was audible or imagined, but I felt as if I had been stabbed between the shoulder blades. I was certain that I was going to retch, but instead I found myself looking more closely at the hideous object. Then I heard my intellect say, "There's no blood on that thing." I realized that I had come upon a headless doll. In the distance I thought I heard the old women cackling. Corpse or not, I leaped over it and sprinted forward. The hounds of hell were nipping at my heels.

Moments later I came to the end of the canyon. Mercifully, a path slanted upward on one side, and upward I ran. Several sharp turns, and I was standing back on the open slope in the sunshine, chest heaving, looking down at the gorge and the farmland below it. I had survived Agrilia, and no vampire would pursue me into the light of day. Still on adrenalin, I made quick work of the remaining path and found myself back in Therasia Town. Not wishing to press my luck on this cursed little island, I passed quickly through the village and back down the donkey track to the tour boat. I was more than a little relieved to see Mavis and her husband sitting on deck, filling out postcards. I took a seat near them and quietly contemplated the level of my commitment to solo travel.

Once again in Athens for a final evening with Klemes and Zitsa, I recounted my experiences on Santorini. My hosts responded with much rolling of the eyes and questions such as "Why did you walk everywhere? Why didn't you take taxis? Why didn't you just relax?" I tried to explain that I had tried to turn an island vacation into a climbing adventure, but they just didn't understand. Thinking back many years later, neither do I.

Climbing Backward

Just six months after Santorini, I had a chance to return to Greece for a few days, and my first thought was to climb Mount Olympus. After being denied Mount Athos, I had set my sights on the country's highest peak. I had found enough information to know that the ascent was nontechnical and that I could visit the mountain without dropping my pants for anyone.

I called Klemes for logistical help, and he soon phoned me back to say that the Olympus hostel was still closed for the winter and the upper trails were snow covered. I really should wait to do the climb in summer, and oh, by the way, he had a great alternative. He and Zitsa and I would spend the Orthodox Easter weekend together in Crete.

I protested, "I can climb snow, and I can pack a light tent and do a bivouac."

"Just come with us to Crete," he replied. "You and I can take a hike together into the Gorge of Samaria. Then, if you really want to, you can climb one of Crete's highest mountains."

I hesitated.

"You will see things that not many tourists see, and you will definitely enjoy it. You can go to Olympus another time."

Somewhat reluctantly, I agreed.

Now married, Klemes and Zitsa welcomed me at the airport in Athens, and we drove directly to the port of Piraeus for an overnight car ferry to Crete. Over dinner in the ship's austere dining room they broke the news that Zitsa was pregnant. She looked so tiny that I guessed she had conceived only that morning. As we discussed this new development and the trip ahead, I realized that Mount Olympus could indeed wait. This was exactly where I wanted to be—with my good friends en route to a place I had never thought of visiting.

Crete is Greece's largest island and fifth among all islands in the Mediterranean. Its east-west positioning and elongated shape bear a resemblance—on the map, in any event—to New York's Long Island. Crete, however, is more than twice the size of its American counterpart, and while Long Island is essentially flat, Crete is rugged and mountainous. Its high point, Mount Psiloritis, rises to 8,058 feet. Crete is the southern outpost of Greece, and next stop south is Libya. At the time of our visit the occasional Saharan sandstorms that blew up to the island were locally referred to as "Gadhafi's Revenge."

Crete's south coast is forbidding and lonely, accessed by only a few roads and accented here and there by lonely villages. Most of the island's population lives along its northern shore in four cities—Chania in the far west, then Rethymnon, Heraklion, and Agios Nikolaos. Because of Crete's relative isolation and because it joined Greece only in 1913, the Cretan people consider everyone from the mainland, and especially Athenians, to be foreign. Nevertheless, the island is no longer a remote outpost. It hosts two million visitors a year, primarily Europeans but Americans and Japanese as well. Most tourists come for the famous Minoan ruins at Knossos and Phaestos and to see historic sites in Chania and Rethymnon. Beach resorts are also an attraction, as is watching Cretan men strut about in high black boots and puffy pantaloons.

If you've got a hankering for ancient ruins—and increasingly I do not—then the Perfect Day on Crete will begin at Knossos, just a few miles outside Heraklion, and will end forty miles to the southwest, at Phaestos. My hosts decided that these would be our first stops.

In its heyday Knossos was a massive palace complex, a suitable home for King Minos, whose parents were Zeus and a goddess called Europa. Minos's wife, Pasiphaë, bore him three children, one of whom had the misfortune to be named Androgynous (his or her first day of kindergarten must have been hell). Anyway, one day Minos's half-brother Poseidon, god of the sea, sent Minos a white bull for a special sacrifice. Minos couldn't be bothered, and Poseidon retaliated as only those Olympian gods could by making Pasiphaë lust after the bull. She took the snorting beast for a ride, and that seemed to pacify him. She, however, ended up seriously pregnant and gave birth to something even worse than androgynous—a hybrid creature with a man's body and a bull's head. Not knowing precisely how his species was supposed to behave, the newly minted Minotaur (cruelly named after *Minos + bull*) set about ravaging the countryside. Eventually, he was captured and locked up in a labyrinth beneath the palace. After that, anyone who fell out of the king's favor was sent downstairs to negotiate the maze with something like a one percent chance of getting through without becoming Minotaur's lunch.

The three of us wandered around Knossos for about two hours. We saw the controversial early-twentieth-century restorations—they are very hard to miss—that are intended to show what the original palace looked like, but we never found what the guidebook described as the palace's famous frescoes. The most prominent artifacts we did see were large clay vases called "pithoi." The Minoans used them for storing grain, oil, and other staples. I was not impressed. The jars were brown and rather plain. Any schoolchild with a pottery wheel and large hands could make something more interesting.

Down the road, heading south, are the ruins of Gortyn. Originally a Minoan settlement, it became a Roman redoubt and is principally known today for its wall of large stones into which are carved an ancient code of law. As we approached, Zitsa was reading this description from a guidebook, and because I am a lawyer, she thought I would be interested. Instead, I gently said, "Whoa, that's enough. Really, I don't need to see it." The fact is, I don't read legal books for pleasure or watch lawyer shows on television. I wasn't going to ruin a holiday by looking at an ancient inscription on civil procedure.

Phaestos, a Minoan ruin on Crete's south coast, was our next stop. Its most famous artifact is a six-inch salad plate covered on both sides with symbols set in a spiral pattern. Nobody knows how to interpret the Phaestos Disc, but that has only added to its allure. Archaeology professors have written endless papers, and their students have held ouzo-fueled "interpret the disc" parties, all to no avail. We laymen can only stand back and reverently admire the thing. Actually, we never even had a chance to do that. Turns out the disc is kept at a museum in Heraklion. The main thing we saw at Phaestos itself was an array of those *pithoi*. My irreverent thought was that if we had wanted to see a bunch of big jugs, we should have gone to the beach.

The next day was Good Friday, and we meandered west through the mountains paralleling the south coast. It was slow driving along narrow and poorly maintained roads. It took four hours to cover maybe fifty miles, but the views down to the Libyan Sea were spectacular. Eventually, we arrived at the seaside village of Sfakia. Despite the fact that it can be reached by roads from the north and east, it is truly the Middle of Nowhere. The locals call themselves Sfakiots, and they have a reputation of being proud, independent, and warlike. These consummate isolationists claim never to have been occupied by any of the various invaders who have conquered Crete over the centuries—Venetians, Turks, or even the Germans in World War II. Considering Sfakia's remote location and utter lack of strategic value, I can't imagine why any self-respecting aggressor would bother. For that matter, all of those survivalists tucked away in the woods along southwest Oregon's Rogue River really have little reason to fear being attacked by the Red Army, Al-Qaida, or anyone else.

Our little party of three didn't come to Sfakia to pillage and plunder but, rather, to catch a passenger ferry that would take us farther west along the coast.

Crete's most prominent mountain range is the Lefka Ori, the White Mountains. The massif sits just above the south coast in the island's western reaches, directly south of the city of Chania. Rising to over eight thousand feet, the highest peaks have distinctive light-colored rock, and they sport mantles of snow in the winter, so the name "white" is doubly earned. The uplift forms a nearly impenetrable barrier between north and south Crete. I say "nearly," because although no roads cross the Lefka Ori, the range is split by a deep canyon traversed by a footpath. The ten-mile-long Gorge of Samaria begins in the high plateau of Omalos, drops precipitously through the heart of the mountains, and bursts open like the bell of a trumpet onto the Libyan Sea. Improbably, at its mouth lies an inhabited village, Agia Roumeli, which can be reached only via the gorge itself or by coastal ferry. For our Good Friday visit we took the leisurely approach to Agia Roumeli, by sea.

On our small ship we sat on the open aft deck, sheltered from the wind and warmed by the sun. A few women in black clothing shared the space with us. They appeared to be heading home after some shopping in Sfakia, because they were surrounded by cloth bags overflowing with groceries. The shoreline we were skirting was rough and rocky, punctuated occasionally by small, sheltered beaches, and the hillsides above were a treeless gray-green. A goat or sheep might find something to forage on that barren ground, but there was little sign of human activity. Klemes pointed out a hiking path running horizontally along the slope, perhaps a hundred feet above the water, but it was not in use that afternoon. If I am fortunate enough to return to south Crete someday, I might just fill some water bottles and walk that trail. From the map I estimate the distance between Sfakia and Agia Roumeli to be fifteen miles.

The boat made an intermediate stop at the outpost of Loutros, which was not much more than a dozen whitewashed houses, a small beach, and a boat dock. Agia Roumeli was much grander—perhaps two dozen houses, a beach, and a dock. Actually, it also had several small hotels and restaurants, most of which were closed. We learned that in high season the village carries on a rather brisk trade catering to ferry tourists and hikers emerging from the gorge. Except for the stooped-over shopping ladies, we were the only passengers who disembarked.

We checked into the one hotel that was open and then walked down to the rocky beach. After pausing while Klemes smoked a cigarette, we began to stroll along the waterfront. There we came upon something that startled us. Someone had gathered tree branches and dead brush into a large pile, and above it on a gallows hung a faceless straw man, arms outstretched and dressed in a blue shirt, khaki green pants, and black boots. A small wooden cross dangled on its chest. Was it Christ in army fatigues? One of the now-deposed Greek colonels? Or was it a generic evil spirit about to be exorcised? Good Friday is ripe with symbolism, but this seemed more like Halloween, and we had stumbled onto something rather sinister. We decided to carry our confusion back to the hotel's terrace and reflect over a few drinks in the late-afternoon sun. By the time we finished our dinner, night had arrived, and the few lights in the village did little to dispel the dark.

Lingering while Klemes smoked another cigarette, we were relaxed and feeling good. Then, out of nowhere, we heard a series of loud booms, and we decided to investigate. In front of the hotel we found a small gathering—actually, it was Agia Roumeli's entire population. Several men were holding a stretcher on their shoulders, and on it lay a body draped in cloth. When

Zitsa saw me do a double take, she whispered something to Klemes, and he passed it on to me. "It's called the 'Shrouded Bier.' They are carrying a figure of Christ." In front of the group was a priest holding a smoking censer and waving it toward us. Zitsa crossed herself.

After a few more motions, the priest turned and began moving away, followed by the pallbearers and the rest of the crowd, most of whom were carrying lanterns. An old man in the middle of the group began thumping a drum, slowly and in even strokes. The procession hadn't gone more than thirty feet when it paused in front of the house next door. The drumming stopped, and the priest began shaking the censer toward the house. Three thrusts toward the left, three toward the right, and three toward the center. Then they moved on, and we fell in behind.

Fortunately, Agia Roumeli is a small place, and so the blessing of every house in the village was accomplished in less than an hour. But that wasn't the end of things. Our procession walked to the edge of town and into the entrance of the gorge. A few men moved to the front of the line to light the way with their lanterns. Zitsa, Klemes, and I had difficulty seeing where we were going, and when a man with two lanterns looked back at us, he handed one to me. Before I could remember *efkharisto*, Klemes thanked him.

We walked along a dirt path deeper into the gorge. Canyon walls rose up into the blackness beyond the reach of our feeble lights. A dark stream flowed silently next to us. The only sounds were the drum, shuffling shoes, and a few mumbled prayers. It was so spooky that if I hadn't been in a crowd, I would have turned around, sprinted back to the hotel, and locked myself in my room. We walked on for God only knows how long, but at last I saw a lighted building in the distance. It turned out to be a small, white church whose interior was lit with candles. Once inside, the priest directed the bearers to place the bier on the stone altar. There he blessed it from all sides with the censer. Then he turned to the villagers, said a few words, and abruptly walked out. Some people, including us, followed him back to the village. Others stayed behind to pray silently. Zitsa told me that the effigy would be on display until Easter Sunday.

In the village it was time for the Big Finish. The priest had concluded his own work, and he went home, but the villagers still had something to do. We followed them to the beach, where they surrounded the hanging mannequin. With little ceremony several men knelt around the brush pile, extracted lighters from their pockets, and started the fire. As the blaze grew, the previously silent assemblage began to shout enthusiastically, and the drummer began to pound furiously. Soon the flames reached the hanging man, and he began to sway and dance, as legs, torso, arms, and head flared up. Eventually, pieces of him started falling into the inferno below, and when the final remnants dropped, the crowd screamed in ecstasy. Moments later the drumming stopped and the fire began to die down. The men in charge thanked each other and lit cigarettes. The crowd began to drift away.

Lying in my bed that night, just north of Africa in a tiny village with no roads, I had a hard time processing what I had witnessed. The people of Agia Roumeli were contemporary enough to cater to camera-toting tourists, and yet they were holding on to an unusual combination of ancient traditions. Their Good Friday procession had re-created the burial of Christ, and this was familiar enough to me, but the burning ritual was simply eerie. Like the Yule log or the lighted Christmas tree, the beach fire was a primal element brought forward and incorporated into a Christian holy day, but it was violent rather than joyful. I didn't really understand it; perhaps nobody did.

Saturday found us returning by boat to Sfakia and then driving north through the mountains to Rethymnon, Zitsa's hometown. Known as the intellectual capital of Crete, this small coastal city is a university town, and its old quarter has well-preserved buildings dating from centuries of Venetian and Ottoman occupation. At the family home I was presented to Zitsa's mother, who was clearly pleased about my visit but even more excited about Zitsa's pregnancy. Mother had prepared great amounts of food for the weekend. Later, in the plaza outside the central bus station, I was introduced to Zitsa's father, who had a small kiosk where he smoked cigarettes and sold them along with candy bars and lottery tickets. Neither of the parents spoke any English, but they were happy to converse through their children.

Just before midnight the family, which included a few siblings, cousins, and assorted aunts and uncles, walked together to the city's cathedral and gathered in the square with thousands of others. Despite the hour, many small children were present. These being the Holy Days, a continuous vigil had been held inside the church since the day before. At the stroke of midnight a passel of weary-looking priests emerged, escorting the bishop. The great Bearded One gazed at the expectant crowd, lifted a microphone, and, after a long pause for dramatic effect, proclaimed, "Christos anesti," meaning "Christ is risen!" That announcement precipitated indiscriminate lighting of firecrackers and a mad rush for home. It was time for the first Easter feast, a midnight meal whose hot dish was *avgolemono*, a creamy rice, egg, and chicken soup laced with lemon juice. Zitsa's mother served it with savory breads and sweet cakes.

Having been to midnight mass, more or less, we did not attend services on Sunday morning. Instead, we crammed ourselves into several small cars and headed for the hills. Somewhere south of the city was a hamlet that was the home of Zitsa's late grandmother. After the previous days' experiences I was already an old hand at white-knuckle travel in the Cretan mountains. The village turned out to be not much more than a few houses strung along a curve on a remote dead-end road. All of the buildings seemed poised to plunge down the steep hillside. Just outside one house was a pay phone, the only phone in the village, according to Klemes. He said that if it rang, the nearest person would answer it and then summon the intended recipient.

Our host was Great-Aunt Xenia, a tiny, hunched-over woman with a leathery face and kind eyes. Her home was on the upper side of the road, and in fact it was built into the mountain. The front half had walls and a few windows, but the back section was essentially a cave. On one side was a small, sloping garden, on the other a pen with several goats and sheep. Our meal was held inside at two rough tables positioned end to end. All in all there were thirteen of us sitting for Easter dinner at Xenia's.

Simple as it was, the meal was as good as any holiday dinner I have ever eaten. The salad consisted of tomatoes from Xenia's garden, feta that she had made from the milk of her own goats, and olives and oil from her own tree. The main course was an entire lamb she had raised and butchered herself, and the roasted potatoes were from her garden. She had baked the bread in her stone oven, although I am certain she had purchased the flour and yeast at a shop somewhere down mountain. Not surprisingly, the wine was also homemade, and it was dark and delicious. Dessert was *koulourakia*, sweet pastries that Zitsa's mother had brought up from Rethymnon. Throughout the feast Xenia sat only occasionally, choosing instead to hover about and keep everyone well fed. She looked tired, but she was smiling a lot, revealing poorly cared-for teeth.

As things were winding down, Xenia went to a storage room at the rear of the house and returned holding a dusty bottle. Everyone turned toward her, wondering what this was about. She set the bottle on the table, raised her hand, and began to speak. Klemes turned to me and said that she had specifically asked him to interpret for me. In Klemes's words, this is what she said:

"I am an old woman, and I have lived in this house my entire life. I did not expect that to happen. When I was young, I thought I would move off this mountain and have a comfortable life in Rethymnon. There was a boy in the village, and he asked me to marry him and move away together. I did not accept his proposal because I thought he was not good enough for me. I thought I would get someone better. He moved away, and he became a doctor in Chania. No one else ever asked me. I was not allowed to move away by myself.

"My parents died long ago, and I am old and alone now, but I am grateful that you, my family, have come to my home for Easter. I hope you have enjoyed the food. Now here I have this bottle. It is a special bottle of wine that I made more than sixty years ago, when I was very young. It was going to be the wine that I would serve my husband at our wedding, and I made it from the most beautiful grapes I could find. The bottle has been sitting in my cellar for a long time. When I realized that I would never marry, I decided I would open it only for a very special occasion. Today is very special to me. I have never met an American, and today you have brought one to my own house. This is a great honor to me. And so, with you my family and you my American guest, I will share this wine."

Xenia had tears in her eyes, and the rest of us followed suit. Everyone was dabbing away with a napkin or shirtsleeve. We sat quietly as the old woman reverently opened her special bottle and moved slowly around the table dispensing a few precious drops into every glass. She was like a priest serving his final Communion at his nursing home, savoring the moment and knowing that his eternal reward was imminent. When she came to me, she patted me on the shoulder and poured out a little extra. She served herself the last portion and raised her glass. Everyone joined her and said something I didn't recognize—it must have been in the Cretan dialect. Klemes and I said, "Yassou!" After sixty years the wine had turned heavy and sweet, like a brandy or the Greek liqueur called Metaxa. It was the perfect way to end our meal. No Easter dinner since has ever matched Xenia's feast, and no cordial will ever taste as good as her nuptial wine.

We spent the Monday holiday in Rethymnon, strolling, sitting, and eating. On Tuesday Klemes and I drove west along the coastal highway to Chania and then south into the island's interior. Initially passing through a region of orange groves, the road began to rise gradually up a broad valley. At its head we began to zigzag upward through slopes covered with silver olive trees. Passing through the village of Lakkoi, we entered an alpine zone with stunted pines and barren rocks. Eventually, at nearly four thousand feet, we broke through a cluster of low peaks and paused to look down at the Plain of Omalos, an isolated plateau nearly three miles across and surrounded by rocky foothills that guard the distant White Mountains. This was early May, and Omalos was already coming to life with sprouting fields of wheat and vegetables, but its lonely setting muted the colors.

On the plateau lay a small village also called Omalos. We stopped there, and Klemes made arrangements at a small inn for me to spend the night. The plan was for us to hike the Gorge of Samaria together, and the following day I would climb alone to the highest peak in the White Mountains. Klemes would return to Rethymnon that evening.

At the south edge of the plain, perhaps two miles from the hotel, was a gap in the foothills. There the road ended in a parking lot. This was Xyloskalo, the upper entrance to Samaria National Park and the gorge itself. Ours was the only car on the scene that morning, and the small refreshment stand was closed. I assumed it had been busier the day before, the public holiday, but on the second day of Easter the people of Crete had gone back to work, and we had the national park to ourselves.

Here I should note what is probably obvious—that entering the gorge from Omalos creates a backward climb. You first descend three thousand feet to the floor of the valley and then ascend back to your starting point. Unlike a normal mountain experience, in which you can turn back if the climb is beyond your capabilities, the hike from Xyloskalo presents the risk that you may not know about your limitations until it is too late. Once you have gone down, you have no choice but to climb back up, regardless of your strength. Actually, with a little forethought and the proper conditions, there is an easier way to do it. Many hikers avoid the upward segment by hiking all the way through the canyon to Agia Roumeli and catching the ferry to Sfakia. In high season you can take a prearranged bus tour that transports you from Chania to Xyloskalo, provides a guide for your hike, and picks you up that evening in Sfakia.

Lawrence Durrell characterized the gorge as "one of the most sinister corners of Christendom." During our Good Friday procession up from Agia Roumeli, I had seen his point—we were in near-total darkness following a shrouded corpse into a dead-end canyon—but on that beautiful morning below Xyloskalo, I was of the firm opinion that Durrell didn't know what he was talking about. Where he might have seen us descending into Hades or penetrating Dante's nine circles of Hell, the reality was that we were entering Paradise. The views going down were continuously spectacular, reminiscent of Albert Bierstadt's Yosemite paintings. It was as if we had been dropped at the top of Half Dome or El Capitan and had found the easy way down. Wildflowers of every color were blooming on the slopes. On the day Durrell hiked the gorge, he must have forgotten to take his Prozac.

The sky was clear, the air was warm, and the path was dry, so Klemes and I made good time descending the steep and sometimes zigzagging path. *Xyloskalo* means "wooden staircase," and in earlier days the upper part of the trail had had sections of steps made of logs. They had since been replaced by carefully laid rocks, but the name lived on. In places where exposure would have been daunting to the average hiker, park officials had constructed railings of thin logs at the outer edge of the trail. I doubted that they would hold someone who fell hard against them, but they provided some psychological reassurance to the height-wary.

As we worked our way down, the thought crossed my mind that getting back up when the day was warmer might indeed be a challenge—not for me, but for Klemes. I didn't have the impression that he was in great shape, and he smoked like a diesel truck. Did he underestimate the effort needed to get back up? I recalled my own experience at the age of fourteen when I visited Bryce Canyon National Park with my grandparents. We stood at Sunset Point on the canyon's rim admiring the scene, when I spied the Navajo Loop Path to the bottom. I announced that I wanted to go down, and the old folks agreed that they would relax while I let off some steam. I dashed down the steep switchbacks more than five hundred feet to the canyon floor. After taking a quick look around, I started back, and that's when I discovered that I could not just run up the same trail. It was steep, and I was held back by the force of gravity. Even worse, it was about one hundred degrees on the trail, and the heat soon had me reeling. Halfway up I wanted to sit on a rock and cry, but I just couldn't embarrass myself that way, so I pressed on. Red-faced, dehydrated, and dizzy, I eventually staggered back to the car, where I guzzled a soda and promptly threw it up onto the pavement. My evil older sister, who had stayed behind to suck up to the grandparents, just rolled her eyes in that superior manner of hers. She certainly didn't offer any help. I was sick the rest of the day.

Half an hour into the hike, Klemes and I came to the spring of Neroutsiko, a pleasant pool where we stopped for a short break. We decided not to drink its water, because we had several bottles we had purchased in Rethymnon. Below the spring we entered an endless section of switchbacks through a thin forest of cypress and pines. I envisioned this stretch on the return and in the heat of the day. After passing another spring, this one called Riza Sykias, we were at the bottom of the gorge. In two hours, including several cigarette breaks, we had descended perhaps twenty-five hundred feet from Xyloskalo.

The path now followed a stream called Tarraios, crossing it from time to time. The going was not particularly easy because Tarraios was swollen with spring runoff from the White Mountains. We had to search for places where we could hop from boulder to boulder. Klemes commented that the water flow would have made it difficult and even dangerous to ford our way through the narrowest points of the gorge if we had wanted to hike all the way to Agia Roumeli.

The first sign of civilization was the chapel of Agios Nikolaos, where we sat and took a brief rest. The building was open—in fact it had no door—but it was not very inviting. Its exterior walls were shedding gray stucco as if it were molting, and its slate roof was similarly disheveled. Inside, the small room was divided into nave and sanctuary by an iconostasis, a wooden screen decorated with icons of saints sporting golden halos. Behind an opening in its center was a modest stone altar bearing a candle and a picture of Christ. In the nave were a reading stand for the cantor, a votive candle rack, and pieces of other furniture piled in a heap. Everything was covered with dust. It wasn't eerie, but it seemed sad, like a neglected cemetery.

Just below Agios Nikolaos, the gorge continued to descend but at a gentler pitch. At last we traversed a wooden bridge and arrived at our goal for the day, the ghost town of Samaria. People had lived there until 1962, when the national park was created to protect the endangered agrimi, a Cretan ibex, and the inhabitants were unceremoniously relocated to Agia Roumeli. We found that it doesn't take long for houses to fall into ruin. In fact, only a few buildings still had roofs and windows. One was the park ranger's home, but he was apparently off for his spring holiday. Another was the whitewashed fourteenth-century chapel of Ossia Maria—Saint Mary—whose names blend together to create *Samaria*. We looked inside and saw that its walls were decorated with sayings like "Panos was here" and "Nicholas loves Georgina"—or was that George? A lonely, dust-covered bottle of wine sat on the crumbling altar, a plea for help from the Blessed Virgin or perhaps a dedication to the fading memories of a loved one.

Samaria is an idyllic spot, located in the widest part of the gorge along a rushing stream. In Byzantine times it was a logging camp, and later it became famous for the production of honey. Its isolation made it a perfect place to hide from marauding Venetians and Turks. As the only people in the village that day, we enjoyed it as a refuge from the entire human race.

Lawrence Durrell did not share our sense of well-being in Samaria. His book offers a literary shudder, and he urges you to ward off the spirits by lighting a candle and crossing yourself. Instead, we sat against a wall of Ossia Maria and ate lunch in the sunshine.

As I had expected, the return hike was a chore. Meandering back up the canyon floor along the stream was reasonable enough, but by the time we reached the head of the valley, Klemes was starting to slow down, and twenty-five hundred feet of steep switchbacks still loomed above us. The good news: We hadn't run out of water, and Klemes hadn't run out of cigarettes. The bad: It was getting hot, and, oh yes, we had eaten all of our food in Samaria.

We moved slowly and deliberately, and before long I was hating it. I thought that Klemes was inordinately sluggish and that the ascent would take forever. I wanted to lecture him about the evils of smoking, and I certainly didn't like stopping for him to have a cigarette every fifteen or twenty minutes. Then the water ran out, and I became even more irritated. I was perilously close to unleashing a verbal barrage when I caught myself. Why should I be so angry? I was hiking in the mountains with my best friend. I should be happy to be here. What was going on?

I paused and stepped away from myself. I imagined that I was hovering above a hiker named Steve, looking at a set of gauges on the back of his head. In the gauge that said CONDITION-ING the needle was pointed to high. Nothing to worry about. For BLISTERS I was glad to see the indicator on zero. The TEMPERATURE reading registered somewhat above normal but nowhere near the red line. The problem was that the FLUIDS meter was trending toward low, and BLOOD SUGAR was flashing

"You Need Carbs." Relieved to realize that my mood was caused by my physical state, I decided to focus on breathing slowly and keeping a steady pace. I promised not to react when Klemes declared it was time for another stop for another smoke.

Mind over Matter worked for a while, but my intellect started scolding me for not having carried more water and food. I began to accept that we would have to drink from one of the springs and risk whatever nasties were lurking in the water. I hated that thought, and I moved along obsessing about cool water and the resulting diarrhea.

The next thing I am going to describe will strike you as implausible, but there on that trail in the land of Euripides we had a deus ex machina experience. Plodding along with my eyes focused on the rocky path, I was startled to come upon an orange. An orange!

I bent over and picked it up. It was real, and it was fresh. It hadn't been there when we came down—we surely would have seen it. No, it was recently dropped, but by whom? We hadn't seen anyone all day. Was there someone who had come partway down and turned back before meeting us? If so, why had this person dropped an orange onto the path?

I turned back to Klemes, who had just caught up to me. "Look what I found," I said. "Where on earth could this have come from?"

He took it, felt it, and sniffed it. "Seems okay," he said. "No reason to waste it." He immediately started peeling the fruit.

Crete's oranges are reputedly the best in the world, a product of volcanic soil, sunshine, and the whispers of ancient times. This one was indeed superior to any orange or any other piece of fruit I had ever eaten. We consumed it like the starving men we were.

Amazingly refreshed, we picked up the pace. But then, calories don't last forever, especially on an uphill walk. The effects of the fruit soon wore off, and I started dwelling again on my thirst. Then we stumbled upon the second orange. As before, it was lying in the path, and it was for us. We shared it and moved on.

When we found the third orange a bit farther up the trail, I started glancing around, looking for a fairy or forest sprite and thinking that a supernatural being might be hiding just behind that tree over there . . . or that boulder. I wondered . . . were these magic oranges, like the Turkish Delight in *The Lion, the Witch, and the Wardrobe*, and were we being enticed to our doom? Perhaps the White Witch would soon appear before us with a basket full of fruit and say, "Come hither, my children."

By the time we reached Xyloskalo, we had scooped up a dozen or more Cretan oranges and consumed half of them. We had survived the ascent rather well. Not a single car other than ours was in the parking lot, and no other people were present, so we had nobody—at least nobody human—to thank for these gifts. I don't know what Klemes thought, but I felt a close connection to the ancient Israelites who were sustained in the wilderness by manna that Jehovah deposited outside their tents every morning. I had the strong sense that our fruit had been placed on the path by a divine hand, but if it wasn't, then some poor soul must have arrived ahead of us at the top of the gorge only to discover that he or she was toting an empty sack.

At the Omalos inn, Klemes made arrangements for me with the proprietor, who spoke no English. A simple dinner, a light breakfast, and some bread and cheese for the trail. The old man showed us where my mountain path began and where I could catch the bus to Chania later in the day. Then Klemes left.

That evening I had time to focus on the climb. My goal was Mount Pachnes, which at 8,048 feet is the highest peak in the White Mountains and second highest in Crete. It is a mere ten feet shorter than Mount Psiloritis, located in a different range some fifty miles to the east. By all accounts the White Mountains—once the home of Zeus himself—are far more rugged and dramatic, but their high point is second-best. A guidebook mentioned that chauvinistic climbers from nearby Chania once set out to correct the insult by constructing an eleven-foot rock pile on top of Pachnes. Maps of Crete still show Psiloritis with its three-meter advantage, and none of the photos I could find showed a large cairn on Pachnes, so I assume that the effort was abandoned when the Chaniots discovered that their summit rocks were rather heavy.

Crossing the Omalos plateau that day, I had seen the White Mountains, and presumably the top of Pachnes, and I had observed that the summits still bore large patches of snow. The slopes didn't look steep, but I was concerned. I had no crampons because I had assumed that I could do without. No, what I really wanted was an ice axe, but that was out of the question. So, what now? In the end I thought that a hiking stick or cane would at least offer a third point of contact in case my feet slipped. I decided to ask the proprietor if he could help me.

The old man was sitting in the small dining room with two of his friends. They were smoking, drinking wine, and talking quietly. None of that Athenian fist shaking and shouting—just a low-key conversation to wind down the evening. They nodded at me when I entered. Having gained their attention, I tried with gestures to depict a walking stick. One of the friends, the man wearing a cap, turned to the proprietor and said, "You really should screen your guests more carefully." The proprietor shrugged.

Not having gotten a reaction, I repeated my movements with a bit more flare. The man in the cap asked, "What did you put in his food? Was it those mushrooms from the cow pasture? He seems to be hallucinating."

The proprietor answered, "I think he might have drunk an entire carafe of wine, but he looks harmless enough. If we don't encourage him, maybe he will return to his room."

Frustrated, I took my notebook and pen from my pocket, sat down, and drew a stick figure with a cane in his hand. I showed it to the men and pointed to the cane.

The second guest said, "My five-year-old grandson can draw better than that." The proprietor nodded.

I stood and started prancing around the room to illustrate a person walking in the mountains. In retrospect I must have been quite a sight towering over them, dressed in below-the-knee hiking knickers, long socks, and a white polypropylene undershirt, while they were sedentary and clad entirely in black. After some additional faux hiking, I pointed to my empty right hand, then to the cane in the drawing, then to the proprietor. I repeated this sequence, and the three men leaned in toward each other and engaged in a quiet discussion. At last the proprietor turned to me and said, "Katsouna."

"Katsouna?" I responded. I shrugged, indicating that I had no idea what that word meant. "Katsouna?"

Now the proprietor pointed to the drawing, putting his finger on the cane in the stick man's hand. "Katsouna," he repeated.

"Neh," I responded. "Yes."

He nodded, "Neh, neh." He rose and went to the back room. A moment later he came back, carrying a well-used wooden cane. He handed it to me. I took it and demonstrated walking with it. Then I pointed in the direction of the mountains and said, "Pachnes. *Katsouna.*"

"Neh, neh."

"*Efkharisto* — thank you."

The second guest muttered, "I still think you should lock his door tonight."

I rose before dawn to discover that it was raining steadily. Nevertheless, I dressed and organized myself for the climb, hoping the squall would pass. In the dining room the proprietor was waiting for me with bread, cheese, and coffee, and in an exchange of gestures it was obvious that both of us were concerned about the weather. As I ate, the sky gradually transitioned from black to dark gray, but the rain intensified. Just great, I thought. Wet clothes and slippery rocks—I can't ask for more.

I lingered, drank more coffee, and hoped for an improvement in the conditions. The dark gray became medium gray—a spark of hope—and then dark again. The rain continued unabated. Eventually, the proprietor beckoned me to the window and pointed to a bus idling at the side of the road. He said a single word, "Chania." I looked at him, pointed to the sky, and said, "Okay, Chania." He dashed out into the rain and said something to the driver, presumably that he had a passenger coming.

Within minutes I had grabbed my things, paid the proprietor, and returned his cane. Then I was on the bus—its only passenger—leaving Omalos and my climb in the rearview mirror.

At the central terminal in Chania I was heading for the ticket booth when a man approached me. "Where do you want to go?" he asked.

I am normally leery of these private taxi vultures, but I responded, "Rethymnon." It was a thirty-five-mile trip. He offered to take me there for a price that made me laugh and turn away. But then, without much haggling, we agreed on a fare that was a third of his opening bid. I was delighted, because the back seat of a Mercedes sounded infinitely better than another smelly bus.

And that is how I came to know Nick.

He was handsome and fit, probably in his late thirties. He was eager to talk as he drove, so we soon pulled over, and I moved into the front seat.

Nick had cousins in Chicago. Did I know them? He had spent half a year with them when he was sixteen and had seriously thought about staying on, but in the end the big city wasn't right for him. He was content to live in Chania, where he could enjoy better weather, stronger coffee ("what you Americans drink is like wastewater"), and a more relaxed lifestyle. He thought we had better television in the United States, but that wasn't reason enough for him to emigrate.

When I asked Nick if he was self-employed, he proudly patted the steering wheel and said that he owned his car and ran his own taxi and guide business. He would find clients at the airport or bus station, and he would take them on tours for a few hours, a full day, or even longer. He knew the history of Crete and could take his clients to Knossos and other places. When I asked him how long he had done this, he chuckled and said, "Four years."

"And what did you do before that?" I asked.

Nick laughed again. "You see, Stephen, for ten years I worked the same way that many young men do, as an escort for tourist women."

"An escort? You mean a tourist guide?"

"No, I took care of them in every way."

"You mean, like a gigolo."

He snorted slightly. "We have that word too, but I don't like it. It sounds dirty. I was a boyfriend to my clients."

"Your *clients*—how many did you have? And how could you be a boyfriend to all of them?"

Patiently, as if instructing a child, he explained, "Stephen, many women come to Crete looking for companionship. They are lonely, and they want to find something better, even if it is only for a few weeks."

"Where do they come from?"

"England, Holland, Germany—even America. They all want the same thing."

"What exactly do they want?" I assumed I knew, but I wanted to hear his version.

"First, they want you to treat them like a proper lady. They want you to open the car door for them and hold their chair in a restaurant. Then they want you to tell them how beautiful they are, and they want you to walk proudly with them on the beach or in the town."

"Anything else?"

"Of course, they want you to make love to them all the time."

"Was this your only job?"

"Yes, I had no time for anything else."

"Did you work the whole year?"

"I was very busy in the warm weather and the holidays, but I always took some days to help my father with the olive harvest, and there were times when there was nothing to do."

"But what about the money? Did the women pay you?"

He frowned. "Not at all. I was not for sale, like a prostitute. Not at all. But the ladies, they had money, and they insisted that they would pay for everything—the dinners, the hotels, the drinks. And they did love me, because I loved them, so they would buy me things and give me money as a gift—but never as a payment."

"Well, how did it work? I mean, to have so many clients."

"I had to be very careful to keep a calendar. I would write letters to the ladies and plan their vacations at a time when another client was not here."

"But how did you meet them in the first place?"

"I would go to the airport and to the restaurants and the beach and look for ladies who were alone. Then I would say hello and talk to them. Sometimes they were with another lady, and I would talk to them and tell them that a friend of mine could join us. Sometimes one of my friends would invite me. Really, it was quite easy to see which ladies were here without a man, and all of those ladies were interested in being with me."

"All of them? No exceptions?"

"All of them. . . . Look, Stephen, Crete has something for everyone. You came for the mountains. Some people come for the history. The single ladies come to meet a nice Greek boy. My girlfriends, they came for me."

Sometimes a woman would be reluctant to jump into bed with the first good-looking Greek man she met. In that case, according to Nick, it was important to start with a low-key pitch, such as inviting her to take a walk on the beach or go on a scenic drive.

The subtle approach was nicely illustrated in the 1989 film *Shirley Valentine*, in which Pauline Collins portrays an Englishwoman who takes a vacation in Greece to escape her dreary existence. There she meets Costas, a local man, who invites her for an excursion on his brother's boat. When she hesitates, he appears to be hurt, but then he masterfully pleads his case: "You afraid that I want make fuck with you. Of course I want make fuck with you—you are beautiful woman—a man would be crazy not to want to make fuck with you. But I don't ask you to fuck. I ask you to come on brother's boat—different thing. Boat is boat. Fuck is fuck. . . . I give you word of honor. I don't try to make fuck with you."

Before long, of course, the boat ride becomes that different thing.

I asked Nick, "Did you see the same women year after year?"

"Of course. Once they met me, they would come back every year for their vacation, just to see me. And they would write letters and send me gifts the whole year. We were really in love."

On my flight from Amsterdam the previous week I had sat with a weary-looking Dutch woman named Carien. A lawyer in The Hague, she was a partner at one of the country's premier law firms. She was successful, but her practice was highly demanding. I asked why she was going to Greece, and she explained that her Greek boyfriend lived near Corinth. He would be picking her up at the airport, and they would spend the next two weeks together. He never visited her in Holland because he was busy year-round as a tour guide. He always accommodated her vacation schedule, however, and took time off when she was able to come to Greece. They both looked forward to the as yet unspecified day when she would move to Greece or he would join her permanently in The Hague.

An American woman once told me about her best friend in San Francisco, a legal secretary in her fifties who had never married. Ten years earlier she had saved her money and taken a package tour to Greece. On Corfu she met a handsome young island man, and the next year she maxed out her credit card so she could return to see him. After the second visit she knew she had found her destiny. Back home she moved into a smaller, less expensive apartment, and she lived as cheaply as possible fifty weeks of the year. But during the annual visit to her boyfriend, she spent lavishly and lived like the queen he assured her she was.

As we neared Rethymnon, Nick explained that during his career as an escort he had saved his gift money until he could afford a small house. Then, when a wealthy client from Connecticut had bought him a new car, he promptly retired from the hosting business, married a local girl, and started his taxi service. Soon he was the father of two children.

Nick was not ashamed of his years entertaining women, but he now disapproved of the practice. It was all behind him. He and his wife had an unwritten agreement never to discuss the subject, and he would never let his son do what he had done.

As he dropped me off, Nick asked if there was anything else he could do for me. He could arrange anything I wanted, really. Here, take my card. I have enjoyed spending this time with you. Call me when you come back to Chania. Anything you want. Really.

The next day Klemes brought me to the airport at Chania for the first leg of my trip home. The facility did not have Jetways to connect an airplane to the terminal building. Instead, passengers rode a shuttle bus onto the tarmac and then boarded via a movable stairway. On my shuttle I noticed that most of the other riders were women, and many of them were crying. I looked out the window and saw that above the terminal was an open-air observation deck. Many dark-haired men were standing there, blowing kisses and waving good-bye.

5   *No Gods but Me*

I was finally on my way to a Greek mountain, on a bus tracing the coast northwest from Athens. It soon became apparent that each and every one of the other passengers (and every seat was occupied) intended to smoke without letup for the entire trip. After five minutes I felt violated, and two hours later at our first stop, I staggered out, presented myself to a butcher shop, and begged to be wrapped and hung in the window with the other cured meats.

A second coach took me inland on a lesser highway, still bearing northwest. This was a local run, stopping every five minutes in small villages and anywhere else a person might be waiting. We passed through gray-green hills and broad valleys that may have been scenic, but the ambient smoke on board made it difficult to see much. I can't be entirely sure how long the trip took, but it seemed like weeks. In desperation, on several occasions I stepped into the small water closet in the rear, even if I had no business to do. The cabin smelled like any toilet on any bus—a miniature hog confinement. Nevertheless, the scent of aging urine offered a welcome respite from the cigarettes.

Although I was heading to Mount Olympus, the highest peak in Greece, my initial destination was Trikala. I had come to meet the family of my pizza maker.

Spiro Aliagas came to the United States from Greece as a young man seeking his fortune. He settled in Seattle, and he worked hard, opened a restaurant, saved his money, and never married. He might well have emulated many other bachelor immigrants by returning to his homeland in his sixties with buckets of cash, marrying a girl a third his age, fathering two children, and then dying, leaving behind a wealthy young widow and a couple of spoiled brats. We will never know if Spiro intended to follow that script, because he died of cancer at the age of fifty-six, still in Seattle. The reason I mention him is that in addition to feeding my pizza habit, he played a role in my visit to Mount Olympus.

Spiro's Olympia Restaurant was a tiny place at the top of Queen Anne Hill, and it held no more than a dozen booths and tables. Its kitchen was open to the sitting area, where patrons could watch Spiro barking orders at his cowering assistants. Although he was diminutive and balding, he was loud and seemingly angry all the time. I understood that he was just being Greek (his obituary noted his "soft heart"), but watching him at close range was a little unnerving. Oddly, he was always friendly to his patrons. Unlike *Seinfeld*'s Soup Nazi ("No soup for you!"), Spiro loved to work the room, smiling and having a brief chat at each table. Then he would return to the kitchen to resume browbeating his staff into making the best double cheese and capocollo the world has ever known.

One evening Spiro was doing his rounds, and I pointed to a framed picture of Meteora on the wall above my booth. I mentioned that I had been there a few years earlier. His face lit up, and he sat down to talk. He asked if I had passed through Trikala, a town near the monasteries. I told him I had, and sensing where this might be heading, I said that it was a very nice place. He beamed with joy. He then told me he was from that area and had several family members in Trikala. Well, from that day, whenever I set foot in the restaurant, Spiro would call out from the kitchen and see to it that my order was taken promptly. And every time I stopped in, he asked me if I had any plans to visit his home town. When I finally reported that I was returning to Greece to climb Mount Olympus, Spiro insisted that I stop in Trikala along the way, and he wrote a note to introduce me to his cousin Stavros.

Stepping off the bus in Trikala's main square, I immediately spotted the Taverna Diana, just as Spiro had said. I knew only one word—*Stavros*—and I said it to an older man who was sitting in the shade smoking a cigarette. Startled, he stood up, put his thumb on his chest, and said, "Stavros." I handed him Spiro's note, pointed to myself, and said, "Steve."

At that very instant I realized that I had no idea what I was getting into. I couldn't read Greek, and I hadn't thought to ask Klemes or Zitsa to translate the note for me as I passed through Athens. I had a momentary flash of anxiety, fearing that the words were something like:

> Stavros: The man bearing this note is named Steve. He is a lawyer from Seattle, and he is probably carrying a lot of money that he stole from his clients. He is traveling alone and may be ripe for a little excitement. Unfortunately, I don't know which way he goes when he is away from home, so you might bring out young Nick in his leather pants and busty Elena in a low-cut dress—then see how he reacts. I suggest cousin Vassos for the role of the outraged father and Uncle Ianis to play the magistrate. When all the fines have been paid, save 25 percent for me. With great affection, Spiro.

When he finished the note, Stavros smiled and reached out to shake my hand, which he did vigorously. "Steve, Steve," he said, and then let loose a string of excited utterances that either meant "You are welcome here" or "You are a pigeon ready to be plucked." In any event he sat me down at his table and called to a waitress, who promptly brought out a glass of chilled coffee topped with some kind of creamy foam. After issuing additional instructions that sent the young woman scurrying away, Stavros turned to me and offered a cigarette. For a fleeting moment I wondered whether I should accept it to avoid insulting him. Then I realized just how dumb that would be—I would look far worse trying to smoke the damn thing than declining his offer.

Stavros and I nodded repeatedly at each other, occasionally saying things that the other didn't understand. After ten or fifteen minutes a good-looking young man (not in leather pants) rushed onto the terrace and introduced himself as Dimitris. Fortunately, he spoke English.

As luck would have it, I was not rolled for my wallet. That evening I was the guest of honor at an outdoor dinner with a large group of relatives eager to tell me how proud they were of Spiro and of the fraternal ties between Greece and the United States. A great deal of red wine and lamb were consumed, many cigarettes were smoked, and there was much shouting. I spent the night at the village's best hotel, the Achillion, and the next day Dimitris drove me through the monastery region. Actually, it was a tour of his family haunts, and he stopped frequently to introduce me to his relatives. All of them—farmers, villagers, elders, and young people—were thrilled that I was a friend of Spiro. Ouzo was readily offered and accepted at each stop. That evening the Trikala contingent and I had another five-hour feast, and I was beginning to get the impression that there was some kind of competition to offer the highest praise of Spiro. Perhaps the intent was that I would report these compliments and Spiro would conclude that Cousin Panos or Aunt Adelpha deserved a bigger inheritance. At the end of the meal I was laden with gifts for my family and for Spiro. I carried them back to Athens a few days later and gave most of them to Klemes and Zitsa.

It took several more bus rides to get me north to the coastal village of Litochoro, the gateway to Mount Olympus. There I checked into the Hotel Aphrodite, which is named after the goddess of love and sensuality. Her Roman name is Venus, and according to the ancient stories, she was born in a family squabble that would make excellent reality TV.

It seems that proto-god Uranus was unhappy with most of his offspring, so he imprisoned them deep in the earth. Their mother, Gaia, retaliated by convincing her youngest son, Kronos, to attack his father with a sickle. The lad complied, and in the struggle he sliced off the old man's genitalia, leaving him with nothing but the last two syllables of his name. Kronos then tossed the naughty bits into the Aegean, and where they landed, a mass of foam arose like the head on a warm beer. From the bubbles there emerged a stunning young woman, Aphrodite herself. (Here I would like to remind my mountaineering friends that there are more enjoyable ways to reproduce the species.) The goddess climbed onto a giant clam and floated to shore, a scene nicely captured in Botticelli's *Birth of Venus*, also known as *Aphrodite on the Half-Shell*. For his part Uranus retreated to the cosmos, and he lives on as our seventh planet. His name is also the root for *urinate*, and this fact combined with the loss of his *cojones* should qualify him as the patron saint of all climbers about to embark on their first rappel.

At the Aphrodite I placed a call to the Mount Olympus hostel, whose manager explained how I could get there the following day. I was coming at the very end of his season and would be one of his final guests that year. I would have a bunk room to myself.

The ancient Greeks may not have known the exact height of Mount Olympus, but they made a good choice for the home of their gods. In a country filled with mountains, the Olympus massif towers above all others, and its many summits constitute a rugged and inspiring setting for the deities. Homer's *Iliad* describes Zeus pontificating from "the many-ridged Olympus," and the *Odyssey* depicts the mountain as "the reputed seat eternal of the gods." The *Odyssey* goes on to sing of a place that "never storms disturb, rains drench or snow invades, but calm the expanse and cloudless shines with purest day." Well, almost. In fact, like any mountain,

Olympus experiences its share of harsh weather, and it catches enough snow in winter to play host to a modern ski resort.

The apex of Olympus is a cluster of six named summits that exceed 9,000 feet. Highest of them at 9,570 feet is Mytikas, and just next to it is 9,544-foot Stefani, whose chair-like shape gives it a second name, "the throne of Zeus." These peaks and two others, Skala and Skolio, form a semicircle around a deep basin called Kazania, the "Cauldron." Thousand-foot vertical cliffs rise from Kazania to the mountaintops, and they offer highly technical climbing routes. Most visitors avoid the steeps and simply hike to the summits on well-developed trails. Only Mytikas and Stefani require exposed scrambling on their easiest routes.

The origins of the name *Olympus* have been lost in time, although Robert Hixson Julyan has suggested that it may derive from nothing more colorful than an ancient Caucasian word for *mountain*. Nevertheless, due to the enduring influence of Greek culture, the name *Olympus* will forever be associated with divinity, and its adjective connotes something grand or superhuman, as in "an Olympian feat." In this context it is appropriate that the highest known mountain in our solar system is an eighty-eight thousand–foot volcano on Mars that astronomers have named "Olympus Mons."

In doing my research on Olympus, I was somewhat disappointed to learn that there are no ancient ruins on the mountain. Christian and even pre-Christian artifacts have been found on several of the sub-peaks, but evidently no one ever attempted to honor the early gods with a grand temple like the Parthenon or even a small shrine. Okay, it would have been a bit rough hauling marble pillars to nine thousand feet, but as architects are quick to say, "That's just labor." Perhaps the Greeks were too busy fighting each other or wrestling in Crisco, or perhaps the gods were too intimidating for mortals to come knocking on their door. In any event Olympus is not a playground for archaeologists. It is only a mountain, albeit a rather famous one and an ultra to boot.

Olympus remained unclimbed until 1913, when two Swiss adventurers and a Greek guide reached the summit of Mytikas. This was nearly fifty years after Edward Whymper's ascent of the Matterhorn. Because a climb of Mytikas requires no technical equipment, one might wonder whether Olympus had been overlooked during mountaineering's Golden Age or whether earlier climbers simply hadn't bothered to publicize their successful ascents. Neither one, actually. Beginning in 1856 and to the end of the century, a number of attempts were reported, but Zeus had apparently rebuffed them all. Nothing like a few thunderbolts to send you scurrying back to base camp.

At noon the next day a taxi drove me from Litochoro up a rough, winding forest road some ten or twelve miles to the Mount Olympus trailhead at Prionia, elevation thirty-six hundred feet. A sign in the car park identified the path as "E4." As I was paying the driver, I noticed an old man steering a group of six donkeys onto the trail. They were carrying loads carefully balanced on their sides. I asked the driver about it, and he said that the donkeys haul supplies to the hostel and return with garbage. They were trained to go by themselves, and indeed the old man just stood there and watched them leave.

It turned out that the donkeys didn't appreciate anyone coming up behind them because as I tried to pass, they attempted to nudge me off the path and into the trees. Hanging back wasn't an attractive option, however, because they were moving much more slowly than I was willing to go, and they were emitting copious whiffs of sweet and sour flatulence. I bided my time, trying not to breathe too deeply and pondering this most unusual mountaineering challenge. At last I saw a steep switchback ahead, and I plunged into the forest to cut off the turn as the beasts ambled on. After a minute of uphill scrambling I emerged onto the trail above the packtrain, which was just rounding the corner. I looked back at the donkeys, offered them a raspberry, and resumed my hike.

The Spilios Agapitos hut—also called Refuge A—sits at the upper reaches of the forest, at sixty-nine hundred feet. The trail from Prionia to the hut is three miles—three miles and thirty-three hundred feet of gain means a steady slog uphill. With the donkeys behind me, I moved quickly and enjoyed the exercise. It was late October, the air was cool and fresh, and the angle of the sun signaled that we were well into autumn. The forest was predominantly black pine, but clusters of beech trees added color to the scene. Their leaves had turned yellow and brown—winter was not far off. It felt great to be on a real mountain trail.

In two hours I arrived at the hostel, where I was greeted by its manager, Kostas Zolotas. He was a handsome man in his forties, somewhat tall for a Greek, but unlike his urban countrymen, he seemed relaxed and happy. "Welcome, Steve," he said. "It looks like the weather is holding for your climb tomorrow. You are fortunate. Some years we would be closed by now." He went on to say that a British couple and a Boy Scout troop from Thessaloniki had been on the mountain that day, and he expected them back in the next hour or so. They would stay the night and hike down in the morning. I was the only guest who was on the way up.

After I had put my things into a bunk room, Kostas asked me about my mountain experience, and he seemed pleased to learn that I had done some technical climbing. Then he asked how long it had taken me to hike up from Prionia. When I told him two hours, he smiled and said, "Well then, you will have no trouble tomorrow making the grand tour."

Kostas pointed to a topographic map on the wall and continued, "Look, from here you will walk up the E4 trail to Skala. Then you can go to the right along the ridge and scramble to the top of Mytikas—although I don't recommend that to most of my guests, and most people don't try it. It is rated Class 3, and the exposure is too much for people who don't climb. After Mytikas you can return to Skala and go the other way along the ridge—like this—to Skolio and then to Agios Antonios. From there you complete the circle and take a different trail back to here. After Mytikas it's just walking, and it will be easy for you. All the trails are marked E4, and you can see where you are, so you can't get lost. If you take time to relax on the summits, you can do the tour in six hours. No need to go any faster. You have all day. I wish I could go with you, but I can't leave the hut. My wife is already down at our house in Litochoro, and the summer workers are gone. It's just me up here right now."

I sat down and started reading a book on local plant life. Before long the British couple arrived, and Kostas welcomed them back. They went to their room to change clothes, and Kostas came over to me. "Steve," he began, "I have an idea. It's two hours until dinner. Why don't you hike up the trail and get onto the ridge above the tree line. You will get to see Mytikas and Stefani from this side."

I followed his suggestion and had a pleasant stroll up a well-worn path through scrub pines. I hadn't gone far when I met a group of fifteen coming down—obviously the Scouts and their leaders. We exchanged greetings. A bit farther, when I broke free of the trees six hundred feet above the hut, the Olympus panorama revealed itself. There was the deep, forested valley leading up from Prionia and in the distance, the Aegean Sea. Above me the towers of Mytikas and Stefani jutted into the sky. They were the high points on a ragged, irregular skyline, and the whole summit bloc was intimidating. Still, with a few more hours of daylight I might have gone for it right then. I wondered whether I should have come up that morning and made the climb that afternoon. I hoped Kostas was right that the weather would hold one more day.

Dinner was not a Greek feast. Boiled potatoes, fried meat, and a few vegetables—I surmised that Kostas's absent wife was the real chef. After a day of hiking, however, it was good enough. I shared a table with Colin and Meryl, who had come from London on a walking holiday. That day they had climbed Skala, and from its summit they made the decision to skip Mytikas. Too daunting, they said. Instead, they completed the half-circle of Skala, Skolio, and Agios Antonios, an experience that they said compared favorably to the Snowdon Horseshoe. Actually, it was far easier than the Horseshoe. It was mostly walking on a well-beaten path along broad ridges. Easy terrain and fantastic views. Bit of a lark.

The hut was alive that evening with the energy of a dozen Boy Scouts, aged twelve and thirteen. They bounced around from sofa to sofa and table to table, teasing each other and chattering loudly. I visited with one of their leaders, a man named Nick. He was a schoolteacher and scoutmaster, and climbing Olympus was a fall tradition for his troop. He had done the scramble up Mytikas in the past, but he would never do it with a gaggle of boys. He had a cousin in Chicago and wondered whether I knew him. I didn't. As we finished our brief chat, I noticed that the other two scout leaders were talking together on a nearby sofa. Looking more closely, I had a great shock. One of the men was my brother, whom I hadn't seen in ten years.

The man had blond hair and blue eyes—decidedly un-Greek—and he wore wire rim glasses. His facial features were unmistakable. My brother. What was he doing there with a group of Boy Scouts from Thessaloniki? Why was he in Europe? I just couldn't understand what was happening.

Quietly, I sat and absorbed the situation. There, fifteen feet from me, was the brother whom I was effectively estranged from. For ten years he had kept his distance from the family, not show-ing up for holidays, skipping other special occasions. I felt very bad about it because being seven years older, I somehow felt responsible for his alienation. You see, I should have spent more time with him when he was little. I should have taught him to play ball. No, I was always too busy with my friends. The only time I paid attention to him was when I volunteered to babysit him in order to stay home from church. I never should have sold him my Voigtlander camera when he was in high school—word came through the family grapevine that he thought I had ripped him off. I should have just given it to him. Whatever the reason, I always felt that I had botched the job of big brother and that my shortcomings had caused him to withdraw.

My brother! How bad I felt for him and how sorry I was for having failed him. But what was he doing there? Had he, without my knowing it, left the United States and moved to Greece? Had he tried to escape to a place where he would never have to see his family again? Or maybe it was more miraculous than that. Maybe God had simply plucked him from his home and transported him to Mount Olympus on the very night I was at the hut. No, this was crazy. None of it made sense, but there he sat. I had to go to him, offer my apologies, and tell him that I was still his brother, that I would buy the camera back, and that I loved him.

I stood and walked over to the men. They looked up. To my brother I said, "Hey, it's me. What in the world are you doing here?"

My brother looked confused. He said something in Greek, and then the other man said, "Sorry, Panos doesn't speak any English. What do you want to tell him?" They must have thought I was out of my mind, because I just stood there and stared, my mouth hanging open.

When I recovered, I stammered, "Please tell him that he looks like my brother in America. That's all." Panos heard the translation. He nodded, and I hastily retreated to my bunk room. I was embarrassed, and I wanted to disappear. The Greek man bore an uncanny resemblance to my brother, but really, what was I thinking? Uncharacteristically, my emotions had gotten the better of my common sense.

Twenty-five years later the encounter at Spilios Agapitos still weighs on my mind. Most likely it is because I still haven't had that conversation with my brother.

It is a luxury to start a climb at eight o'clock in the morning, and most of my day on Mount Olympus was that pleasant. As I left the hut, the sun had risen over the Aegean, and the sky was cloudless. The late-autumn air was crisp, but there was no wind. If ever a day was made for mountain hiking, this was it.

Retracing my steps from the previous evening, I quickly reached timberline. At that point the thought struck me that I had the entire day to climb. No need to hurry, and so I settled into a relaxed pace, somewhat slower than my normal speed. It had taken four trips to Greece to get here, and I could enjoy every minute of it.

Above timberline the trail reached the spine of a ridge, a prominent feature that would lead directly up to the peak called Skala. A signpost reminded me that I was on the E4 trail, and its arrow pointed up. Because the right side of the ridge dropped steeply into the Prionia valley, the path stayed just to the left of the ridgeline and proceeded upward in lazy zigzags. Coming so early in the day, the monotony of the terrain and the sections of loose scree didn't bother me; I was fresh and happy. The summit would come soon enough. At any point I could pause and look back at the forest and the Aegean.

At ten o'clock I arrived at the top of Skala—the name means "step"—which is not much more than a bump on the summit ridge, but at 9,402 feet its height is only 168 feet lower than Mytikas. In other words, the 2,500 feet I had just climbed from the hut constituted most of the elevation I would gain that day. From the peak of Skala, with the ascent path behind you, the view ahead is straight down into the Kazania valley, the Cauldron. To your right is the ridge leading to Mytikas, a very rugged-looking summit. To your left the E4 trail follows a ridge that rises gently to Skolio—nothing but an easy stroll. No wonder most people head left. At 9,550 feet Skolio is only 20 feet shy of Mytikas, and who's counting? Take the easy route and claim your summit. I set out for Mytikas.

The next hour was glorious and annoying, just like the rest of Greece. The glorious part was the climb itself. Excellent rock with good handholds and enough exposure to keep you well focused. The annoying part was that some geniuses with cans of paint had marked every move with yellow squares containing red arrows. "Walk this way." "Now move to the right around this boulder." "Now go up, you imbecile." This was the mountaineering version of Paint by Numbers. It reminded me of art class in eighth grade, where my magnum opus was a set of black metal bookends, each displaying a colorful heron that I had painted by the numbers. Even at the age of thirteen I knew what a cheesy non-accomplishment it was. My parents, of course, said that they were proud of me, and fifty years later they still had those silly bookends. Well, I did climb Mytikas, but as I reached the summit I felt cheated because of the ubiquitous route markers.

Then I just relaxed. I lingered for an hour, perhaps the longest time I had ever spent on top of a mountain. The sun was warm, and I indolently ate my lunch and drank in the views. Seeing the northern Aegean in the distance, I knew that just beyond the horizon was Mount Athos, and I was disappointed that I hadn't been able to get there—it was still off-limits to the unclean. On further reflection, however, I knew that climbing Olympus was a worthy substitute. After all, it was the highest point in Greece and an ultra as well. It was a beautiful summit, and there wasn't another soul in sight.

Scrambling down from Mytikas, I discovered that additional red arrows had been painted on the tops of rocks, so the descending climber would know where to go. Grumble, grumble. Actually, as I had learned on the Matterhorn, route finding on the descent is much trickier than on the way up—it is easy to get off route and into trouble. I knew that I would save a lot of time and potential grief by following the marks, and it would have been silly to ignore them. So, I proceeded along the dotted line and moved swiftly. Nevertheless, my official opinion is that the summit of Olympus has been defaced by the paint warriors.

With the actual climbing accomplished, I decided to follow Kostas's suggestion and walk the Olympus horseshoe. I passed over Skala, rejoining the E4 trail, and followed the undulating ridge to Skolio. If Skala is a bump on the ridge, then Skolio is simply a bigger bump. Its name means "curved" or "bent," and when viewed from the proper angle, it sweeps in a gentle curve to a prominent summit. Interestingly, its name can be found in English as a spinal deformity, *scoliosis*. In addition to being the high point of choice for most Olympus climbers, Skolio offers impressive views back to the west faces of Mytikas and Stefani. Their vertical walls rise out of the Cauldron and have provided a playground for serious rock climbers since the 1930s.

The E4 continues south from Skolio along a wide, curving ridge, dropping and ascending again to Agios Antonios—Saint Anthony—the final peak of the horseshoe. Its broad, rounded summit reaches 9,236 feet. The trek from Skolio is more than a mile in length, but for me it was heaven. It was early afternoon, and the slight breeze was just cool enough to offset the warmth of the sun. Perfect hiking weather, and the views in every direction were stunning.

There are many saints called Anthony, but the first and most famous of them was an Egyptian known as Anthony of the Desert. He was the father of ascetic monasticism, and he lived alone on a remote mountaintop. Despite the harsh environment, he survived to the ripe old age of 105—an inspiration to all of us to Stay High and Live Long. Oddly, there is a nasty rash called "Saint Anthony's Fire," and the man's memory is invoked for curing skin diseases. Climbers, keep that in mind the next time you suffer from sunburn or blisters. In any event, whether as a healer or man of the heights, Anthony was a worthy namesake for the sub-peak of Olympus, and he should join Saint Bernard of Menthon as a patron saint for mountaineers.

Given the Greek propensity to build chapels and shrines, and given the stature of Saint Anthony, I should not have been surprised to find his mountain littered with memorials, but I was. As I approached the summit, I noticed a cluster of protrusions on the otherwise smooth slope, almost like stalagmites or giant anthills. On closer inspection they proved to be piles of rocks.

There were hundreds of them, but why? I inspected one that was four feet high, and embedded in the stones was a picture of an old man and woman. The next pile held the portrait of a young child, another displayed a soldier in uniform, and on it went. Then I looked at the tallest of them, a ten-foot tower. It held the stylized icon of a saint, presumably Anthony himself.

I had never seen a place like this, and I certainly wasn't expecting it here. Mountaineers do build cairns, but only to mark a climbing route or the true summit of a peak. This was quite different, and I found it to be a little creepy. I had seen gravestones that display a photo of the deceased person, but why take the trouble to climb a mountain and create a memorial? Was Anthony so powerful as to make the effort worthwhile?

I sat there a while, contemplating the scene, and my initial disquietude gradually faded. It wasn't eerie any longer; it felt serene. Coming to Mount Olympus, I had hoped to see ancient shrines to Zeus and his comrades. Instead, I found a place for memories of ordinary people. After arriving at that peaceful thought, I decided to build my own cairn.

In retrospect I'm not sure why I wanted to erect a memorial. Normally, I am of the "leave no trace" school. But that day and that mountain were different. I had plenty of time on my hands, and I had a room reserved at the hut that evening. Better to spend more time outdoors in the sun than sitting in the hostel reading *Wildflowers of Greece*. Also, it's not as if I was going to deface the mountain—my monument would be one of hundreds.

After some reflection I decided that the cairn would be dedicated to my children, who I missed very much. "This shouldn't take long," I said to myself. "There is scree everywhere, so all I have to do is stack it up." I picked a spot nicely spaced from several other monuments, created a level base, and set the first stones. No problem. The next layer went up rather quickly as well. Three layers, four, and then I discovered that the new rocks wanted to slide off. It was difficult to make one layer level enough to hold the next. I tried to place the stones very carefully, but at one point an entire section came tumbling down. Restraining the urge to utter profanities, I began to replace the stones that had fallen. Somewhere in the process I discovered that the flat rocks had sharp edges, and I scraped my knuckles. When an actual cut opened up, the flow of red was accompanied by expletives that I uttered in Dutch, hoping that Saint Anthony would not understand.

When I reached what I hoped would be the midpoint of my cairn—it was only two feet high at that moment—I decided to prepare the contents of the memorial. From my wallet I took photos of my three children and wrote their names on the backs. In my notebook I wrote about what great kids they were and how much I loved them. I put the photos and note into a sealable plastic bag and set it into the center of the cairn. Then I started building again. With a few more scrapes and rockfalls along the way, I eventually stood back, looked upon my handiwork, and said, "Behold, it is a bit sloppy, but good enough."

My next task was to identify the precise location of the monument, so perhaps someday one of my children or grandchildren would be able to find it and see what I had done. First, I took a photo of it. Next I looked around and took a compass reading on the great monument to Saint Anthony. Finally, I carefully paced off the distance to the larger cairn. Sitting near the saint, I wrote in my notebook something like "From the n. side of St. Anth. cairn sight nnw. Go 45 paces—1 yd. ea.—nnw. Can't miss. 4 ft. high." To confirm my directions, I followed them, only to discover that I had either miscounted the paces, or they weren't one yard each, or I had misread the compass. The cairn I arrived at looked like mine, but it showed a picture of an old woman. Okay, I thought, I'll just look for one that has no photo on display. It turned out that in the general vicinity were at least a dozen identical monuments that had no photo. I went back to Saint Anthony and tried again. No luck. At that point my only options were to (1) start tearing down monuments to find which one contained my sandwich bag or (2) let it be.

Note to my children: Somewhere on top of Mount Olympus in Greece is a pile of rocks containing your photos and a message from your father. You will never find it.

That evening Kostas and I shared another of his simple dinners and had an enjoyable visit. I would be heading down in the morning to return home. He would spend the next few days closing the hostel for the winter. He would then join his wife and children in Litochoro. He did not anticipate any further guests, although as long as he was there, he would take people in.

Kostas was very curious about the Pacific Northwest and our Cascade volcanoes. He had done a lot of winter climbing locally on seasonal snow slopes, but he had no experience on glaciers, so Mount Rainier and Mount Hood were of great interest to him. We agreed that if he ever had a chance to come to Seattle, we would climb together.

Mainly we talked about Olympus—his home and his passion. He had climbed it for the first time as a boy and had decided then and there to spend his life on the mountain. As a young man, he had trained in technical climbing, and in 1957 he and a friend had made the first ascent of the west face of Mytikas, a fifteen hundred-foot vertical line from the Cauldron directly to the summit. It had taken fourteen hours. That feat had cemented his reputation as one of Greece's leading mountaineers, and when the Hellenic Mountaineering Federation later offered him the job as manager of Spilios Agapitos, he decided to make it his summer home. Several years later an attractive German woman visited the hut on a hiking trip, and he convinced her to stay permanently—as his wife. I was tempted to ask him whether prior to his marriage he might have offered personalized tours like the taxi driver in Crete. I didn't.

Kostas was an innkeeper and mountain guide. He had climbed Olympus countless times, and he knew every inch of it. He handled the flow of human traffic up and down the peak. He presided over visitors from around the world. At that point in history he *was* Olympus. In a way I envied him and his life. On the other hand, I don't think I would have been satisfied staying so long in one place. I was too restless, too American, for that.

Sitting there in the hut, I realized that Mount Olympus was the capstone of my visits to Greece and in fact the culmination of my interest in the country. I was quite certain that I would not return for a long time—I was ready for new adventures in other places. I told Kostas how much I loved his country and the history that was present everywhere. "So," I said, "tell me what you think. Are there any gods dwelling on Olympus?"

His answer was simple and befitting someone who lived at the highest point in the birthplace of Western civilization: "No gods but me."

*

Although I had made my last trip to Greece, I wasn't quite finished with Mount Olympus. On my flight back to Seattle I realized that I had never heard of anybody who had climbed both the Greek mountain and its namesake in Washington. Seattle climbers on a trip to Europe will focus on the Alps, while European mountaineers traveling to the Pacific Northwest will naturally be drawn to a more prominent peak like Rainier or Hood. Having the opportunity to climb both peaks named Olympus would require a rare planetary alignment, and it had happened to me. I had made enough trips to Greece to get past the other attractions and visit its loftiest mountain. I lived in Seattle, where the Olympic range dominates the horizon across Puget Sound. I simply had to complete the pair.

Washington's Mount Olympus is the most remote major peak in the state. It sits smack in the middle of Olympic National Park, a true wilderness with roads only around its perimeter. At 7,965 feet it is the highest peak in the range, and yet it is virtually invisible. From most vantage points, including Seattle, it is hidden behind intervening ridges and lower summits. If you want to see it without climbing one of those other mountains, you have to drive to Hurricane Ridge, at 5,200 feet, on the north edge of the park. A winding road takes you to a visitor center for one of the most spectacular alpine views in the United States. A display board on the terrace identifies the myriad of summits before you, and that one little bump in the middle of them is Olympus.

My Olympus team, members of Seattle's Mountaineers, met at the Hoh Rain Forest Visitor Center, on the west side of the national park, on Saturday of the Memorial Day weekend in late May. A few of us had camped near the town of Forks the night before, after eating the loggers' dinner in a crumbling restaurant. Actually, the entire town seemed to be falling apart. If Michelin gave stars for dilapidation, Forks would earn three. It may be due to the incessant showers. Seattle, of course, has the reputation as Rain City, but it receives only thirty-seven inches per year—actually less than New York and Atlanta. The bad rap comes from the fact that in Seattle the precipitation comes in tiny amounts, nearly every day of the year. A favorite local T-shirt says "Seattle Rain Festival—July 1 through June 30." Well, compared to Forks, Seattle is a piker. On the west side of the Olympic range and not far from the Pacific Ocean, Forks receives over one hundred inches of rain annually. The town's recent fame as setting for the *Twilight* novels hasn't helped its appearance. It is still a sad little place.

Our plan was to hike in sixteen miles to base camp on Saturday, climb Olympus on Sunday, and hike out on the Monday holiday. A saner approach would have been to take five days, but I was the climb leader, and my time was limited. There were nine of us on the team, five of whom—three men and two women—were enrolled in the Mountaineers' basic climbing course. They would get credit if they summited. Two of the others, Maury and Wes, were more experienced and were assigned as rope leaders. The final member was Doreen, Maury's girlfriend. I was acquainted with Maury, but Doreen was new to me. Dorie and Maury, as she called them, were both in their forties, she unmarried, he divorced, both looking for something on this climb.

There are three types of significant other who attach themselves to mountaineers. Category 1 says, "Just go off and leave me for another weekend. I'll stay home, pay the bills, and struggle with the children." A popular variation of this one is "Go and do your thing. I'll find someone else to sleep with." Category 2 says, "I'll go along just to be with you, but I'm scared of heights, and I'll hate every minute of it, you bastard." Finally, category 3 says, "I'll go with you because I want to share this part of your life. If I participate in your hobby, you will find me even more attractive, and you will know I'm a keeper." (A fourth category, the spouse who happily encourages and supports your climbing career while not feeling the need to participate, is not known to exist in real life.)

Dorie was a category 3. She never stopped talking to Maury, apparently to remind him of her presence. My first taste of her routine took place at Maury's car in the ranger station parking lot. The rest of us were ready to go, so I walked over and saw Dorie looking into the back seat. Then I heard her say, "Shall I take the gray sweater or the blue one? Gray or blue, gray or blue . . . look, I'm taking the gray one!" Maury just nodded. Then Dorie turned toward her backpack and said (apparently to Maury), "Shall I pack it on top or in the side pocket? Top or side, top or side . . . look, I'm packing it on top!" Maury nodded again.

The climbing guide describes the Hoh River Trail from the visitor center as the "shortest, easiest, and the most direct" approach to Mount Olympus. It adds, "Total round trip distance is about forty-four miles." It was indeed the most direct route, but for someone carrying fifty pounds of overnight gear and snow-climbing equipment, it proved to be neither short nor easy. Compounding the effort was the fact that it was early in the season. The trail was wet and muddy in many places, and downed trees forced us to slither over or under them.

The Hoh Rain Forest was fascinating, with moss hanging from

every limb of the towering western red cedars and Sitka spruce, but the thrill was soon gone as our pack straps began to dig into our shoulders. At the Happy Four Shelter, actually five miles up the trail, we took a lunch break. Dorie, who had provided us with nonstop narration for the past two hours, looked around and said to Maury, "Shall I sit on this rock or this log? Rock or log, rock or log . . . look, I'm sitting on the log!" Maury nodded. Then, reaching into her pack, Dorie extracted a food bag, dug out a few things, and said, "Shall I eat the apple or the granola bar?" The rest of us ate quickly, anxious to be on our way. One of the other climbers approached me and asked softly, "Do you mind if we get out ahead? We can't listen to her anymore."

Eleven miles later we arrived at our campsite, Glacier Meadows. We had climbed from six hundred feet at the ranger station to forty-two hundred feet. As we organized for the night, Dorie treated us to more of her one-woman debates—where to pitch the tent, where to set up the stove, and what to cook first. With a mixture of curiosity and dread, several of us quietly speculated whether she would discuss where to relieve herself. Oh, look, I'm squatting here!

At four thirty the next morning we left camp and stepped onto the Blue Glacier. There we set up three rope teams of three climbers each. I led the first, Wes the second. I asked Maury to head up the third rope, which meant that Dorie would be second or third behind him, as far back from me as possible. Most of us were still tired from the approach hike and a little cranky at that early hour. Fortunately, Dorie was feeling great! She chattered merrily as if on a special visit to a preschool.

That early in the season the snowpack was deep and firm, and we made good progress on the glacier. At a hump called the Snow Dome we ran into a bergschrund, a deep crevasse separating the glacier from the rocky outcropping that is the mountain's summit. We were forced to retrace our steps and approach from a different side.

The seventy-five-foot summit block itself was a chore. It was coated in ice, and my lead would have been difficult. Fortunately for me, another group was already on the summit, and they kindly offered a top rope. With no shame I accepted it and then anchored myself atop the vertical cliff and began to belay up my teammates, one at a time. As Dorie made her way up, I could hear her deliberating about which handholds to use. Eventually, everybody joined me on the rather crowded fin of rock that is the true summit—all, that is, except our teammate Jason. Watching the others struggle on the icy rock, he got completely spooked and could not be persuaded to come up. He had hiked more than sixteen miles to our camp and then another six on the glacier, and he had had enough. Even without him it took me four hours, standing in the same spot in a brisk wind, to get everyone up and back down onto the glacier.

I was exhausted, and so was everybody else. Even Dorie was silent as we slogged back to camp. At Glacier Meadows people flung down their packs and started crawling into their tents, but at that moment my reputation as the Ogre of Olympus was born. I called a team meeting and said, "Look, our climb took eleven hours, and I'm as tired as the rest of you, but I do not want to hike out sixteen miles tomorrow. So let's take an hour or two, relax, and make dinner. Then we're going to strike camp and head down the trail. Every mile we can manage this evening is one we don't have to do tomorrow." What I didn't say was that I was feeling guilty about leaving my family at home. I wanted to get back to Seattle ahead of schedule the next day and salvage a few hours of the weekend. Climber's guilt accompanied me every time I went to the mountains.

I thought they were going to run me through with their ice axes. A wave of grumbling built into a crescendo, with someone eventually shouting, "Are you nuts? Are you trying to kill us?" I calmly argued the merits of my position and then put it to a vote. A majority agreed on my plan, but several voting in favor said they didn't like it a bit.

Down the trail we went, stumbling more than walking. We managed perhaps five miles, to the point where we entered the flats of the Hoh River. When it finally got too dark to keep going, I called a halt, and we stopped for the night. None of us bothered to pitch a tent—we just threw our bags onto the ground. The last thing I heard before passing out in the rain forest was: "Shall I lay my bag over here or over there? Here or there, here or there . . . look, I'm putting it here!"

On Monday we reached the visitor center at noon. Carrying heavy packs, we had covered forty-four miles and seventy-four hundred feet of gain in fifty-two hours. After a group picture one of the women pulled me aside and said, "Well, Steve, I'm glad we made it, but I'll never climb with you again."

On the way home Wes, Maury, Doreen, and I stopped for lunch in the town of Sequim. Dorie had a difficult time choosing between the chicken and the fish, but before she could do her full litany, I suggested she order a piece of each. Just as our food arrived, she excused herself and headed for the restroom. Wes was well into his plate of spaghetti marinara when Dorie returned. She sat down and in a loud and cheery voice said, "Well, that's interesting—I just got my period!" Maury nodded, but Wes paused, took a long look at his plate, and then slowly pushed it away. "Please," Dorie said, "don't stop. I'll catch up. Now, what shall I try first?"

⑥ *Crawling for Sushi*

To many people Mount Fuji is the most beautiful peak on earth, and they are right. Its perfect symmetry and unbroken lines are sublime. Its snowcap is delicate and ethereal, radiating a pure light as if directed by the gods. Okay, maybe that's a bit much, but Fuji is truly stunning. Along with the Matterhorn the Japanese volcano is one the most recognizable of all the world's mountains, but where the Swiss peak is a jagged and intimidating fang, Fuji is serene and inviting. Only a daredevil or skilled climber will attempt the Matterhorn, but countless pilgrims and romantics are drawn to the slopes of Mount Fuji. The two are continents apart but joined in popular imagination; they are different but complementary, like yin and yang. If mountains have gender, then in classic terms these two peaks embody masculine versus feminine—the Matterhorn is rough and raw, while Fuji is smooth and refined. They are Humphrey Bogart and Grace Kelly, Ozzie Osborne and Sade.

At 12,388 feet Fuji is the highest peak in Japan and its geographical glory. Located at the midpoint of the country's main island, Honshu, the mountain lies sixty miles west of Tokyo. When the air is clear enough, Fuji is easily seen from hillsides in the capital, and lawsuits to protect these coveted vistas are a regular occurrence. Outside the city a highly prized view is from the *shinkansen*, the famed bullet train that speeds along Honshu's south coast between Tokyo and Nagoya. As the train nears the towns of Fuji and Shin-Fuji, passengers gasp and rummage for their cameras as the mountain appears, unobstructed and a mere twenty miles away. Visual perspective is lost, and it seems you could just extend your hand and touch it. At two hundred miles per hour, however, opening the window is frowned upon.

In Japanese the peak is referred to either as Fuji-yama (*yama* is simply "mountain") or Fuji-san, with *san* being the designation for "honorable." The meaning of *Fuji* is less clear. Some scholars have speculated that it connotes immortality, abundance, greatness, or (my personal favorite) "beauty of the long slope hanging in the sky," but those definitions were most likely assigned long after the name had attached. According to Robert Hixson Julyan, the most plausible interpretation is that *fuji* was an aboriginal Ainu word associated with fire and the mountain's volcanic activity. Thus, he proposes "mountain of the goddess of fire." I think all of these are good ideas and would be even better if combined into one grand definition. Fuji will henceforth be officially known as "the most honorable and immortal volcano goddess whose long, sensuous slopes sweep upward and whose beautiful, snowy summit hangs in the sky like a mound of soft-serve vanilla ice cream."

One of the curiosities of Mount Fuji's reputation is that many people assume it is snowcapped year-round, because that is what you see in all the photos. The reality is that the snow melts off every summer, leaving behind a reddish-brown cinder cone. In such a state Fuji is not particularly photogenic, but that is precisely the point at which it can be climbed most easily.

And the climbers do come, in staggeringly high numbers. In a typical summer more than 200,000 people will ascend Fuji-san. They are able to do so via a series of zigzagging paths that wind upward through the pumice and rocks. The ascent entails nearly five thousand feet of elevation gain and can take from five to ten hours, depending on your conditioning. The person who greets the sunrise from the summit is said to receive many blessings from the gods, and thus most climbers (as many as 20,000 on a single Sunday) choose to hike through the night for a predawn arrival at the top. Some will stop along the trail and sleep for a few hours at one of the resting huts (they are generally described as crowded, overpriced, and filthy), and nearly everyone pauses at some point to purchase a cup of tea and some food. It must be quite a sight to see thousands of flashlights bobbing along in the dark. On the other hand, to a true mountaineer the idea of sharing the trail with a horde of panting hikers sounds positively dreadful.

If you achieve the summit, the dawn is uniformly described as awe-inspiring. When the first flash of sun appears on the horizon, the respectful pilgrims will raise their arms and shout, "Banzai!" which is said to mean "Ten thousand years." For some, no doubt, the climb may seem to have taken that long. Incidentally, recent etymological research has established that the unabridged meaning of the cry is "May my Toyota's transmission last another ten thousand miles."

Everyone who has struggled to the top has earned the beauty of the sunrise, and it leaves a lasting impression. In fact, the daybreak view from Mount Fuji likely inspired the red sun on the country's national flag, and the Japanese name for the nation—Nippon—means "the land of the rising sun."

The first ascent of Mount Fuji is believed to have occurred in AD 663, long before any European had even conceived of climbing the Alps. According to legend, Fuji's pioneer was a Buddhist monk named Enno Gyoja. He was the first to make the climb, and in his honor today we eat gyoza as an appetizer at Japanese restaurants. Interestingly—and this too is highly speculative—Brother Gyoja is also credited with the discovery of acute mountain sickness. To his considerable surprise and consternation, after reaching the top of his sacred mountain, he initiated the oft-repeated ritual of peering into Fuji's summit crater, leaning heavily on a protruding boulder, and tossing up his lunch.

Although the Seattle Convention and Visitors Bureau seems to have decreed that every picture of the city must have Mount Rainier in the background, the Japanese have been at it much longer. In Japanese landscape art, even in pictures going back hundreds of years, it seems quite standard to have an image of Mount Fuji plunked into the scene. The mountain serves as both a reference point and a common design motif, so much so that a Japanese painting seems incomplete without it. The best example of this style is the famed *Thirty-Six Views of Mount Fuji*, a series of woodblock prints created between 1826 and 1833 by Katsushika Hokusai. These exquisite and highly stylized pictures show scenes of Japanese life, including farmers, fishermen, and woodworkers plying their trades, but always with the mountain hovering over them. Most iconic of Hokusai's images is *The Great Wave off Kanagawa*, which shows a giant sea swell rising up and threatening to destroy three small boats. Sitting calmly in the distance, neatly framed within the wave's curl, is Mount Fuji. When copies of this one picture reached Western Europe, the image set off a flurry of interest in Japanese art, and Hokusai's style exerted an influence on both art nouveau and impressionism.

I first saw Hokusai's work in the Sioux Center, Iowa, public library when I was a boy. I was always hanging out there reading the *National Geographic* and anything remotely related to mountains. One day the librarian, Mrs. Thompson, took me to a section with books on art and pulled a tall, slender volume from the shelf. "You may want to look at these pictures," she said. "They have mountains in them." It was the collection of Hokusai's Mount Fuji prints. As I studied them, I was fascinated but also frightened. My fears arose from the fact that these pictures were so utterly foreign. The people and buildings were nothing like my Iowa farm country. But it was more than that. There was something about the *style* of the pictures that was strange. I didn't know words like *abstract* or *impressionistic*, so I could only think that the images were somehow not quite right. Things were out of proportion, and the perspective was slightly weird.

There in the library I started to feel sinful because in my ultra-religious Dutch immigrant community the only truly acceptable form of painting was representational. Modern art, like rock-and-roll music, was of the Devil. But Hokusai wasn't modern—these prints were more than a hundred years old. Perhaps my problem was that I knew so little about Japan. My only exposure to the country was at Sunday school one time when a missionary talked to us about his obviously daunting divine call to convert the ninety million or so godless Japanese into no-fun-on-Sunday Dutch Calvinists. Maybe Hokusai's art was disturbing because he was a heathen.

I began to wonder whether Mrs. Thompson was trying to lead me astray. She wasn't Dutch, after all, or at least her husband wasn't. We were taught to be wary of anything different from ourselves and anything that was too innovative. In the end I decided to take a risk. I would study the pictures for their content, but I would do all I could to avoid any spiritual taint from Hokusai's suspect artistic style. I would concentrate my thoughts on the mountain, and after all, God had created the world and all of its mountains in precisely six days.

Vowing that I would never tell anyone about how I had flirted with temptation, I carried on, looking at every image of Mount Fuji again and again. I started to believe that I knew this mountain. I was able to imagine myself in the Japanese countryside, sitting in an open-air teahouse and staring at the peak from a distance. Then I saw myself on the snowy slopes, yodeling and hiking to the top with a Sherpa. I had had a momentary bout of religious anxiety, but I convinced myself that I would emerge from the library with my faith intact. One thing was absolutely certain—someday I would climb Mount Fuji. I just wouldn't do it on a Sunday.

More than twenty-five years passed before I had my first opportunity to travel to Japan. I was invited to accompany a group
from the Port of Seattle to a conference at its sister port in
Kobe. Somehow I convinced my law firm that participation in
the meetings would be good for business development. Actually, I wanted to go just to climb Mount Fuji. I would attempt
the ascent after the conference, even though it was November,
well past the official climbing season. Our delegation traveled
first to Taiwan, then to Kyoto, and finally to Kobe, and I dutifully tagged along. As we moved from place to place, it was a
bit embarrassing that I had two large suitcases while everyone
else had one. My second bag contained my winter climbing
gear—boots, crampons, knapsack, emergency items, and lots
of clothing. My only regret was that my ice axe was too long for
the suitcase, so I had decided I would buy a new one in Tokyo
just before the climb.

At the conference we were forced to sit through endless formal
welcomes and speeches about container terminal management
and our "mutually beneficial relationship," all of which were
transmitted through headsets and the disembodied voice of
an interpreter—someone with a robotic accent and who had
apparently never had a conversation with a native speaker of
English. There was, however, a bright side. To compensate us
for enduring hell-in-a-chair, they served us a lot of food.

There were too many people at the meetings to allow for a
sit-down lunch or dinner, so each meal was held in a large hotel
ballroom with small tables scattered around the perimeter and
lots of standing room. In the center were two long rows of buffet
tables. One, the hot food lineup, had stations where chefs were
cooking sukiyaki, tempura, udon, and other dishes. The other
row was a twenty-foot spread of sushi and sashimi presented on
elaborate platters, with servers constantly flowing in and out to
replenish the supplies.

A hotel hostess did me the courtesy of explaining that sushi
is a piece of raw fish served on rice that has been pressed into

a flattened ball, while sashimi is just the fish. She said it was acceptable, however, for a foreigner like me to use the word *sushi* for all of these dishes. She suggested that I take a bit of wasabi paste, mix it with some soy sauce, dip a piece of sushi into the mixture, and then eat it. With these basic instructions and a pair of chop sticks firmly in hand, I tried my first sushi. The little placard said it was raw tuna—well, why not? With no further guidance I immediately learned several valuable lessons: First, the green stuff is not lime Jell-O but industrial strength horseradish that will cause you to wheeze and double over in agony. Second, you must eat the whole sushi in one bite, or it will fall apart and cascade down your necktie. Third, if you use your fingers instead of chopsticks, the room will go silent and two hundred people will stare at you in wonder and revulsion.

Okay, after a few colorful failures I had the hang of it, and I was off and running. I discovered raw squid, salmon, and shrimp—actually the entire array of ocean creatures—and everything was delicious. Why had I lived my whole life thinking fish had to be cooked?

During three days in Kobe I ate a lot of sushi, and I found that between meals I was developing intense cravings for it. I didn't know what was happening to me, but I responded by eating even more sushi at the next occasion. On the third day, just before lunch, I decided to ask a senior member of our delegation about it. He was an old Japan hand, undoubtedly familiar with exotic Asian diseases. He told me that I probably wasn't used to the salt in the soy sauce and that my body was demanding salt, not fish. I thanked him and headed for the sushi table.

After trying three or four of everything, I concluded that my favorites were the various kinds of sushi described as "maki" or "naki." They consisted of a ball of rice formed around some type of fish or vegetable, with the entire item wrapped in a paper-thin strip of seaweed called "nori." The *nakis* were fresh, easy to eat, and loaded with flavor. I learned that some of the standards are:

- *kappa-naki* — a roll with spears of cucumber
- *ikura-naki* — sushi containing salmon roe
- *tekka-naki* — a piece with raw tuna.

Although the featured ingredient of *naki* is usually vegetable or raw seafood, I did hear rumors of a "Mount Fuji naki" containing certain morsels of bovine anatomy. In the western United States these delicacies are known as Rocky Mountain oysters. In Mexico they are *huevos del toro*, and in Canada they are simply "lunch."

Sushi chefs are known for the rigors of their training. For this we are grateful, because we trust that the raw fish we ingest will by and large be trimmed of the parts containing mercury, tetrodotoxins, and tapeworms. Entrance to the renowned Edo Institute for Sushi Preparation is highly selective, and its graduates must pass a series of demanding exams. The institute's graduation rates are low, and its pressure cooker atmosphere has earned it the nickname "The School of Hard Nakis."

On the final evening, after dinner, one of Seattle's port officials (I'll call him Harry) and I were talking to Mr. Suzuki, an urbane Japanese businessman who spoke excellent English. At one point he asked if Harry and I would like to accompany him to his private club for a few drinks. Harry accepted immediately, and Suzuki went to call for his driver. Harry then turned to me and said, "This is a great honor, Steve. These clubs are highly exclusive and ridiculously expensive. You must be invited to join, and membership is very limited. On top of the monthly fees you probably pay fifty dollars for a drink. I have known Suzuki for years, and this is the first time he has invited me. He obviously likes you a lot, or he wouldn't have asked you to join us."

Harry continued, "Now when we get there, don't say much. You are young, and Suzuki will expect you to be deferential. Just sit politely and observe what is going on."

Suzuki's limousine took us to another part of the city, where we entered a nondescript door in a row of older buildings. Inside, a host welcomed us and escorted us up a long staircase. At the top was an elegant parlor with groupings of furniture, lots of drapery, and soft lighting. The dark paneled walls were lined with old paintings, and the overall look was more European than Japanese. Parties of men and women sat quietly, and cigarette smoke filled the air. Suzuki selected a vacant spot with two settees positioned at right angles, along with an overstuffed chair. He directed Harry and me to the loveseats, while he took the chair, directly in front of us. No sooner had we sat down than four young women glided in and sat, two with Harry and two with me. They were beautiful, elegantly dressed, and smiling. Suzuki leaned forward and, with obvious pride, said, "These girls all speak very good English." Then he ordered four glasses of white wine for the hostesses, three glasses of single malt scotch for the men, and Cuban cigars for Harry and me.

I nodded to the woman on my right and then to the one on my left and said, "Good evening." They immediately responded, "Good evening, Sieber-san, and welcome to Kobe." I had no idea how they knew two-thirds of my name, but the other two knew Harry's, and they were beginning an animated conversation. The woman on my left said that her name was Aika, and it meant "lovebird." The other was Harumi, which means "spring beauty." I felt a slight swoon coming on, and I was about to start babbling like a mad fool. Recalling Harry's admonition, however, I forced myself to say very little.

My hostesses had other ideas. Calmly, they worked to draw me out. They asked about my tastes in music, art, food, and travel. Whatever I answered, they were truly impressed. When I mentioned that in a few days I would climb Mount Fuji, they gasped and looked at me in awe. Harumi said that she had never "been" with a man who would dare to go up Fuji-san in the winter. I realize now that I was completely taken in by these modern geishas, who had me believing that I was the most significant man on the planet. Meanwhile, Suzuki sat back in his chair, smoking a cigarette and smiling paternally.

After several drinks and copious amounts of fawning by the hostesses, Suzuki leaned forward and said, "Perhaps the girls would like to take a little rest now." All four of them nodded respectfully. Aika and Harumi looked longingly at me, lightly stroked my arms, and said, "Thank you, Sieber-san. It has been wonderful to visit with you. We hope to see you again." And just like that, they rose and gracefully left the room.

Now Suzuki leaned forward with a twinkle in his eyes. "Harry, Stephen, did you enjoy the girls?"

"Oh yes," Harry replied. "They were the most beautiful girls I have ever seen." I chimed in with a few words to the same effect, and I thanked our host.

"Now," he continued, "you are my honored guests here in Kobe, and I want your visit to be a happy one. Would you like to have one of these girls for the night?"

I was stunned, and I felt a ribbon of drool running down onto my chin. I didn't know what to say, but Harry stepped right in.

"Thank you, Suzuki-san," he said with a slight chuckle, "but I must give a speech in the morning, and it is time for us to return to our hotel." I noticed that he had said "us" and "our" hotel.

Harry continued, "Steve and I have had a wonderful time, and you have been an excellent host. We cannot ask you to do anything more for us tonight."

As we left, I looked over my shoulder several times, hoping for one last glimpse of the women who admired me so much.

The Kobe conference came to an end with a final sushi party and thirty or forty farewell speeches. The next morning, wishing I could linger for one more injection of raw seafood, I boarded the bullet train to Tokyo. Once we were under way, it was quite fun to contemplate how fast we were moving, but in truth it didn't feel much different from any other train ride. The air in the wagon was stuffy, and someone near me had eaten garlic for breakfast.

Near the town of Shimizu, I got my first good look at Mount

Fuji. It was a clear morning, and the peak was exactly as advertised—breathtakingly beautiful. The mountain's early-winter snowcap extended nearly halfway to its base. With an index finger I traced its lines on my window, thinking of Hokusai and my suitcase full of climbing gear.

Thanks to an elaborate set of written directions, my white-gloved taxi driver got me to the home of my friend Jim, an American working in Tokyo. It was Sunday, and Jim had volunteered to take the next day off to drive me to Mount Fuji. After I settled in, I told him that I needed to find an outdoor shop to buy an ice axe. He just shook his head as if I had said something in Swahili, but I impressed on him how important it was. There ensued a long, silent period in which Jim was flipping through the phone book to find a mountaineering equipment outlet. Finally, he said that there was nothing remotely close by and he had no intention of traveling two hours to the other side of Tokyo to help me find something I should have brought from home.

I contemplated my fate for a while, realizing that I would have to do something creative or else cancel my climb. It would have been unthinkable to attempt a winter ascent of Mount Fuji without an ice axe. Eventually, I asked Jim if there was a hardware store in the neighborhood. "Yes," he said. "From the corner where you turned onto this street, turn right one block, then left at the next intersection. There's a hardware store." He was deep into his *New York Times,* and he did not volunteer to go with me.

As I set out on my vital errand, I tried to think of what I might find. Perhaps a large adze like the early Swiss mountaineers had used, or perhaps a short-handled rake. I would figure something out.

The shop turned out to be smaller than I had hoped. Given the fact that Tokyo is primarily concrete, it is not surprising that the shop had no gardening tools beyond some small hand spades. I looked at every item in the store, trying to visualize how I might use it in place of an ice axe. A clerk offered to help me, but we had an impenetrable language barrier, and my pantomime of climbing a mountain just made him retreat in fear. I considered buying a pair of long screwdrivers and holding them in my hands like ice picks that I could stab into the slope if I slipped. The problem was that I wanted something for balance as I walked uphill. As an alternative, I could buy a wooden rod for a walking staff, as Fuji trekkers do in summer, but that would not be of any help if I started sliding and needed to catch myself. Maybe a stick in one hand and a screwdriver in the other?

Eventually, I settled on a practical, if unusual, solution. I purchased a hammer with a straight claw, plus a wooden dowel that was about an inch in diameter and three feet long. My third item was a roll of silver duct tape. My plan was to tape the hammer's handle to one end of the stick. I would climb with my hand on the head of the hammer, using the device as a walking cane in the same fashion I would use an ice axe. If I started slipping downhill, I would pull the shaft under me and drive the claw into the snow for a more or less standard self-arrest. I sincerely hoped I would not need to test this out because I was not sure that the tape would hold under pressure. If it failed, I would have to stop myself with the hammer alone, assuming I hadn't lost it when the apparatus came apart. As a last resort, I would have my ten fingers to dig into the snow. In fact many mountaineers have resorted to this method after having their axes ripped from their grasp. It is not recommended.

Back at Jim's I sat on the floor and assembled my new Japanese climbing tool. Jim watched, incredulous, as I wound the tape. I assured him that this was in the best tradition of climbing, that mountaineers often have to jury-rig equipment when something is broken or lost—you know, clothing as a rope, bent wire for crampons, all that. To his credit he didn't believe a word of it.

To my surprise, the next morning Jim was able to navigate through the endless tangle of roads in Tokyo, into the countryside, and finally up the flanks of Mount Fuji. After much zigzagging and increasingly expansive views, we reached our destination at road's end, the Kawaguchiko Fifth Station at 7,562 feet. The trip of fifty miles had taken more than three hours.

There are four main trails up Fuji, each of which has ten stations from base to summit. The stations may range from provisioned huts to nothing more than a bench and a monument. The Kawaguchiko Station is the preferred starting point, and it is by far the most developed. It has an enormous parking lot, restaurants, multistory hostels, and souvenir shops. It is essentially a tacky tourist trap. When Jim and I arrived there, the parking lot was empty, and everything was closed except one snack bar that also sold official walking sticks. Pilgrims and souvenir collectors will buy one of the five-foot staffs, lean on it for support as they climb, and have it stamped at each of the stations along the way to the summit. Many of the sticks had small bells attached with silk cords. When I saw those bells, I was even happier that I was not climbing in August. My winter ascent might be difficult, but at least I would not be stuck with thousands of people kicking up dust and rattling incessantly.

At the snack bar I asked for sushi but had to settle for a bowl of ramen. The cashier gave Jim directions to Sato Goya, the hut where I would spend the night—Jim had called ahead and made a reservation for me. He had also checked the bus schedule and showed me where to begin the first stage of my trip back to Tokyo. The bus would take me to a train station at Fujiyoshida, then a train would take me to a second train, that train to a subway, the subway to his neighborhood, and a taxi to his house. He wrote it all down in English and Japanese—my Tokyo lifeline. It sounded so complicated that I assumed the next day's climb would be the easy part.

On one edge of the parking lot stood a billboard with a trail map and warnings in several languages that the official climbing season was July and August only. At other times of the year the icy slopes and strong winds promised certain death to anyone who set foot on the mountain. Intriguingly, the English portion mentioned that the wind would often come in a series of seven gusts, like ocean waves, with each one stronger than its predecessor. After reading all of the caveats, Jim turned to me and asked, "Are you sure you want to go through with this?" I responded that the sign was undoubtedly there to scare away the people who had no business on any mountain, and that I was confident of my experience on snow and ice.

A hundred yards up a short trail, and surrounded by trees, was Sato Goya. Jim explained that this simply meant "Sato's hut" and that the proprietor was a Mr. Sato. The building was a single-story affair with dark-brown siding typical of a mountain cabin. It had large windows and a small portico that was supported by two gnarled logs and framed with several signs in Japanese characters. We entered and placed our shoes into a large rack just inside the front door.

Sato's hut had a great room with a freestanding wood-burning stove in the center. The knotty pine walls were festooned with randomly placed calendars, postcards, and photos. On the plank floor sat benches, chairs, and a few low tables that were either handmade or of garage sale quality. Straw mats and cushions lay strewn about. Around the perimeter were shoji screen doors opening to what I assumed were sleeping rooms. Overall, Sato Goya was cluttered and rustic, and with a tea kettle bubbling away on top of the warm stove, the room felt cozy.

As Jim and I stood there looking around, a man emerged from what I assumed was the kitchen. He was short and trim, his face dark and weathered. It was impossible to determine his age. He looked every bit the mountain dweller, and it was obvious that this was Mr. Sato. He bowed slightly, without smiling.

Jim returned the bow, looked at me as if to say, "Don't just stand there." I gave a slight, unpracticed bend of my own in Sato's direction. There ensued a somewhat tense conversation in Japanese between Jim and Sato. Based on the men's body language, I believe it went like this:

Jim began with: "This is Steve Sieberson. He will stay here tonight and climb tomorrow."

Sato responded, "Does your friend have shit for brains?"

"Yes, honorable Sato."

"Is he completely incapable of reading one of the seven languages on the sign in the parking lot?"

"Apparently so, Sato-san."

"Who is he anyway?"

"An American lawyer, Sato-san."

"Has he ever climbed a mountain?"

"So he says, Sato-san."

"Does he have proper equipment?"

Jim then asked me to show Sato my equipment. I opened my knapsack and took out my crampons. Then I showed them my gloves and goggles. Finally, I pulled out my homemade ice axe.

Sato looked horrified. "What does he expect to do with that hammer taped to that dowel?"

Jim shrugged. "Search me, Sato-san. He says his axe was too long for his suitcase."

"Is he out of his fucking mind?"

"Yes, Sato-san."

"He might as well make one out of Legos."

"Yes, Sato-san."

"Will you come back next spring to claim the body?"

"Yes, Sato-san."

A most awkward silence ensued, and eventually Jim drew a deep breath and said, "Well, Sato thinks you are crazy, but he will put you up for the night. You should start before dawn. Now I have to get back to Tokyo." With that, he shook my hand and said, "Good luck." Then he bowed to Sato, quickly put on his shoes, and left.

I stood there stiffly as Sato stared at me. I couldn't tell if it was a look of curiosity, pity, or scorn, but I smiled and said my only word of Japanese. "*Arigato*, Sato-san—Thank you." I wasn't sure I had anything to thank him for, but at least I was breaking the silence.

Sato gave a very slight nod and gestured for me to follow him. He led me to a screen, which he slid open to reveal a small room with rectangular tatami mats and several stacks of futon pillows. Having slept on a futon the night before at Jim's, I knew that this was my bedroom. Again I said thanks, and I set down my pack. Sato then beckoned for me to return to the main room, where he showed me the hot water, a tin of tea, and a teapot. I filled the pot, put it on a low table near the central stove, and sat on one of the cushions. Sato nodded and disappeared into the kitchen.

With an afternoon ahead of me and nothing to do, I drank several cups of tea as slowly as I could. I heard Sato's radio in the kitchen playing exotic-sounding music. Looking around, I noticed a stack of old magazines on a corner shelf. I shuffled through them and found that none were in English. The ones in Japanese were focused either on outdoor sports or naked geishas, while the rest were newsmagazines in French or German. I passed on the girlies—perhaps I would spirit one into my room later. For the longest time I tried to glean something from the European journals, but I was just killing time.

After several hours of this excitement, the front door opened. Sato emerged from the kitchen as someone stepped into the room. The newcomer was an athletic-looking Japanese woman, perhaps in her late twenties. She was wearing an ivory-colored knit cap, but her long black hair extended beneath it. Her clothing was of the outdoor type, and she carried a knapsack. The visitor and Sato engaged in a brief conversation as I looked on. At several points I noticed Sato nodding in my direction. Eventually, he directed her to a sleeping room, where she deposited her pack. She returned and walked to where I was sitting. Then she said, "Hello?"

Surprised at hearing an English word, I stood and returned the greeting. Somewhat carefully she said, "You are American, yes?"

"Yes, my name is Steve. I am visiting from America." I extended my hand, and she shook it.

"I am Tumiko. I am from Japan."

Tumiko told me that she had come to the Fifth Station by train and bus and would return to Tokyo the next day. She was not planning to climb Mount Fuji but simply wanted to spend a quiet day at the Fifth Station, perhaps hiking up the trail to where the snow began. Sato had told her of my own intentions—and of my impending doom. She said that the hutkeeper wanted her to tell me that it was very dangerous to climb at this time of year. In response I asked her to tell Sato that I was an experienced mountaineer and that I would be very careful. I would turn back if conditions became too risky. She nodded, somewhat gravely.

At one point I asked Tumiko to look at Jim's written instructions on how to get back to Tokyo, and she said that she would wait until midafternoon for me to return to Sato Goya after my climb. Then she would escort me into Tokyo to the point of my final taxi ride to Jim's house. I thanked her profusely. Later I asked if she would like to get up early the next morning and hike with me as far as the trail went. She agreed that that would be a nice thing to do. At no point did I offer to show her my faux ice axe, which would likely have prompted her to end our relationship.

The two of us drifted in and out of conversation for an hour or more. There were pauses, during which she read a book and I looked at the magazines. At around six Sato invited us to sit on some cushions at a low table, and he served us dinner. It was basic, but good enough—miso soup, vegetables, a bit of beef, and lots of steamed rice. I did not dare to ask for sushi. Eventually, I asked Tumiko to tell Sato that I had enjoyed the meal, that I was going to bed, and that she and I would leave at first light. She conveyed this message to him and translated his response: "He will make us a breakfast."

In my small sleeping room I sat on the floor to sort my gear. When I went out to the kitchen to fill my water bottles, Sato just nodded at me. A few minutes later I was repacking my knapsack, when there was a soft knock. "Come in," I said, thinking Tumiko might want to tell me something. The screen slid open, and there stood Sato. He was holding an ice axe. With two hands he extended it to me, almost as if it were a ceremonial dagger for hara-kiri. He might have been thinking, "I will help this lost soul on his journey to the next life." When I took it, however, he made a motion indicating that I should use it for climbing, and then he pointed up toward the mountain. I made a deep bow and said, "*Arigato*, Sato-san. Thank you." He bowed in return, said something I did not understand, and backed out of the room.

I rose in the dark, dressed, and went into the main room. A fire crackled in the stove, and the kettle was steaming. Tumiko was sitting at the low table, drinking tea. I joined her, and Sato came out with rice and vegetables. Tumiko and I talked quietly about the day ahead; it was clear that she was still worried about me.

Outside it was very cold—certainly below freezing. Leaving the hut at six fifteen, we hiked in predawn twilight through a thinning forest. We soon arrived at timberline, and above that lay a barren landscape with a few shrubs. The path was well-worn and as wide as a road. The early-morning air was very crisp, but there was no wind and the sky was cloudless.

We passed the Sixth Station, a collection of ramshackle buildings that makes the Fifth Station look like a luxury resort. The closed and boarded-up huts resembled abandoned gas stations. The trail now became a series of switchbacks, and I thought of Hokusai and his picture *Climbing on Mount Fuji*. It shows men in conical hats and white togas struggling up a steep and rocky trail, using long staffs for support. Patches of snow appear here and there. There is a ladder at a steep section, and steps are carved into the red rock just above that. In contrast, our trail was smooth and well trampled.

After a few easy switchbacks we arrived at the lower edge of the snowfield, where the path disappeared. It was seven o'clock. We were six hundred feet above Sato Goya and four thousand vertical feet from the summit. It was time for me to strap on my crampons and take the ice axe in hand. It was also the place for Tumiko to turn back. Figuring that I would need at least three hours to make it to the summit and two to return, I told Tumiko that I would be back at Sato Goya at one. She said she would wait for me. She wished me good luck, we shook hands, and I stepped onto the snow.

Because the past few days had been sunny, the snow was firm and stable. My crampons bit nicely into the surface, and the angle of the slope allowed me to walk straight uphill. In short, these were ideal climbing conditions. Setting out at a good pace, I felt great. Things got even better when the sun rose from behind the mountain's eastern slope to my left. The direct rays offered a welcome bit of warmth.

As I climbed I began to calculate the timing of this ascent. If conditions stayed as they were, I felt that I could make between fifteen hundred and two thousand feet of elevation gain per hour. Optimally, I could arrive at the summit in as little as two hours.

I was soon bypassing the Seventh Station, which sat well off to my left. That meant that I was at nine thousand feet. I felt a breeze coming from above, and it cooled me enough to make me re-zip my jacket. For a time there were ribs of black rock to my left and right, meaning that I was in a broad gully. Still, the snowfield was relatively smooth, and I was doing well.

Between the Seventh and Eighth Stations the breeze turned into a steady wind coming directly down on me. That forced me to exert more effort to continue my pace, and eventually I had to slow down. Somewhere around the ten thousand-foot level I found myself panting and leaning on my ice axe from time to time. I realized that I needed food and water, so I sat in the snow for a few minutes to refuel. There I took in the panorama below me. Most prominent were Lake Kawaguchi and its surrounding resort towns. Rolling hills ran out to the distant Akaishi Mountains. The foothills were mostly forested, but here and there were checkerboard squares that indicated logging clear-cuts. Farms and golden fields completed the scene. I had a fabulous bird's-eye view of central Honshu.

Feeling better, I began moving again and made good progress into the strengthening wind.

As I approached the eleven thousand-foot level, with the Eighth Station to my left, the slope steepened. At the same time I noticed that the wind was no longer steady but was starting to come in bursts from above. It would hit me hard for five or ten seconds, then let up. After a brief lull it would return a little stronger and then pause again. Remembering the billboard at the Fifth Station, I started counting, and I realized that the gusts were indeed coming in series of seven. After the seventh one, it was peaceful for half a minute, and then the pattern would begin again.

As these cycles came and went, there was an overall increase in intensity, and the wind now roared like a jet engine. I found it necessary to pause during the stronger gusts and lean forward on my axe. When the wind abated, I could resume walking. As conditions continued to deteriorate, one especially strong blast nearly knocked me backward. I didn't want to be blown down the slope, for fear I couldn't stop a slide. So, I began to climb between the gusts, leaning during the first three or four in a series and lying down during the final few, chest on the shaft of the ice axe, face in the snow, and toe points dug in below me. In this up-and-down fashion I proceeded slowly but kept going. It must have looked like someone in a calisthenics class, alternating between jumping jacks, toe touches, and push-ups.

Looking back so many years later, I wonder what kept me moving upward. I don't like loud noises, and this was the loudest thing I had ever heard. I was getting cold. From time to time I wasn't confident I could hang on. I was still hundreds of feet from the summit, and it was getting desperate. Oddly, I never thought of turning back. I was more angry than scared; I fought the wind and screamed at it. I lunged madly up the hill when I could. When I stabbed the axe into the slope, I imagined that I was plunging it into the heart of the wind demon. At times I found myself lurching, but I kept moving.

The only thing I knew was noise and wind and cold, and a tilted field of ice. The feeling came over me that I was no longer that person who was clawing his way up a frozen slope. Instead, I was a hawk circling in the sky and watching a scene far below. What was going to happen to that speck of a man down there? After an especially violent episode I lost the energy to jump to my feet. I started crawling on my belly, face down, but I was near the end of my ambitions. I became oddly distracted by random thoughts. A Christmas tree with bubbling candles . . . high school algebra class . . . the back seat of my '58 Chevy and . . . Wait a minute! Why were these things flashing before me? Surely I wasn't about to die. Wasn't this just a fun climb? How did I get myself into this mess?

Then a more powerful thought took hold: "Sushi, I really need some sushi." The tiny scrap of intellect that was still functioning tried to tell me that it was just a salt craving, but I became convinced that sushi would save my life and that a buffet table was waiting for me at the summit. Desperate for raw fish, I crawled on. After what seemed like ages, I found myself in a spot where the wind was not quite as strong. Still prone, I lifted my head and was confronted with a staircase leading up to an open gate. On either side of the steps sat two fierce-looking lions. I let out a little shout of surprise. Actually, it was an all-out scream arising from the certainty that I had perished and was lying in front of the Pearly Gates. I looked down and clung to the ice axe, gasping for breath.

A few moments later, with a little more oxygen feeding my brain, I lifted my gaze again. This time I realized that the lions were made of marble. Behind them was a rough set of steps leading to a Japanese torii, a symbolic Shinto gate. Behind the gate was the profile of a building. This was the Tenth Station, the summit of Mount Fuji.

I garnered the energy to wriggle up the steps. They were snow free, probably because of the constant wind. Passing through a torii represents movement from the profane to the sacred, and for me it meant leaving the maelstrom for the leeward side of the summit hut. I found a calm spot and began to eat and drink. The food warmed me, and I started to think rationally again.

My watch told me it was ten o'clock. It had taken almost four hours to get there from Sato's hut, a gain of forty-seven hundred feet. That wasn't a blistering pace, but it seemed reasonable in light of the fact that the last thousand feet had been such tough going. I knew that I didn't want to linger in that spot, but I had one more thing to accomplish. Given the strong winds, hiking around Fuji's crater to the true summit on the far side was out of the question, but I did want to see the crater. So, I put my camera into a pocket, cinched everything up, and stepped out from behind the building. The blast of wind was unkind, and I was brought to my knees. I found that I couldn't walk, and I couldn't even crawl on all fours. So, I once again resorted to slithering on my belly like a salamander. Because of exposed rocks, I had to meander a bit through the summit snows, but I eventually reached the crater rim.

Mount Fuji's crater is over seven hundred feet deep and sixteen hundred feet across. The rim around it is punctuated with eight high points, the "peaks of Fuji," which are sometimes described as the petals of the mountain's inverted lotus flower. I wanted to get to the rim to take a photo. Still slithering, I made it to the edge, but I couldn't even sit up in the gale. Then I saw a wooden post about twenty yards away, positioned at the very lip of the crater. I crawled to it, wrapped my legs around it, and sat up. The pillar was covered with notes and coins that pilgrims had inserted into slots in the weathered wood. They were no doubt prayers and offerings, and I felt bad about using this monument for something as trivial as a photo. Nevertheless, I extracted the camera from my pocket, leaned around the post, and snapped a single summit picture.

I still had to get down, so I worked my way around the summit station and began preparing for the descent. Sitting there, sheltered from the wind, I thought how nice it would be if the hut were open. I could be inside drinking hot tea and eating sushi. But no, I had to step back into the fierce wind and biting cold. Also, except for a few attendants at the weather station on the far side of the crater rim, I was the only person on Japan's highest mountain that day. I needed to get organized and get down with no help.

As I ate another granola bar, I tightened my crampon straps and got my clothing and knapsack in order. I crept through the torii and scooted down the steps on my rump. Passing between the lions, I regained my feet and started down. Again on the snow, I tried plunge-stepping. This is the technique of taking long straight-legged strides onto one heel, then the next. While doing so, you hold the head of the ice axe in your hand, with your arm extended outward so you don't accidentally stab yourself if you lose your balance. On soft snow, plunge-stepping allows for rapid progress. On Mount Fuji it didn't work. The snow was still firm, so I had keep my legs flexible and place my feet slowly and carefully.

I hadn't gotten more than a few yards onto the slope when I was hit with the full force of the wind, now at my back. I had hoped that I could keep moving, but out of caution I lay down as I had done on the ascent. Then I picked myself up, took a few steps, and fell onto the snow again. I did this through several seven-wave cycles, and I became highly annoyed. Jumping up and down was tiring, and it was going to cost me a lot of time. My impatience is likely the reason that when the third series of gusts had spent itself, I came up with one of the brighter ideas I have ever had: I would ignore the wind and just keep moving. At most it might give me a little boost. And that is how I, a grown man with a heavy knapsack, became airborne.

To be sure, during the first waves of the next series I was able to continue my way down the slope. The wind pounded at my back, but I maintained my balance. At gusts four and five I had to struggle to avoid falling forward, but I stayed on my feet and kept moving. It was number six that finally got me. I thought I was in the momentary lull, and so I took a series of rapid, giant steps. In the middle of one of them the wind took me by surprise and hit me with such force that I felt myself rising up. I was in the air, and I was soaring.

I had flown before. When I was four, I had a vivid dream of floating at treetop level and drifting slowly down Main Street. People stepped out of their houses and shops and looked up in admiration. When I awoke, I quickly dressed and ran outside. I lifted my arms just as I had in the dream, but for some reason I didn't leave the ground. Perplexed, I looked back at the house, then ran up the front steps and climbed onto the porch railing. I launched myself upward and outward, and in a second I was back on the lawn with a severely sprained ankle. I was not only hurt—I was confused. Later, as I lay on the sofa in pain, I started to believe that the dream had been one of Satan's evil tricks.

Later, as a judicial law clerk in Seattle, I discovered that one of the elevators in the federal courthouse began its descent so rapidly that if I jumped at the precise moment it started dropping, I was able to float for a second or two, like one of those astronauts practicing weightlessness in a reduced gravity aircraft. I did this from time to time for amusement, until one day I inadvertently jumped when a woman was in the car with me. Hovering next to her in that confined space, I scared the crap out of her. Later I wrote a cheesy poem whose final line was "One could do worse than be a jumper of elevators."

For a while I took up skydiving. It was flying for real, but on my twenty-ninth jump the wind shifted unexpectedly, and I found myself landing on the median strip of a heavily traveled divided highway. I immediately sold my parachute and bought my first mountaineering backpack. I would go high, but I would try to keep my feet on the ground.

I'm not really sure how long I drifted down the icy flanks of Mount Fuji. It was probably no more than a second or two, but everything moved in slow motion, and I remember having several very clear thoughts in my head:

1. Do not fall on the ice axe, but keep a firm grip on it in case you need it when you come back down.
2. Do not land on your head.
3. When your feet touch down, do not try to stop all at once. If you do, you will be permanently compressed into a lump of torso like Mr. Potato Head.

As I flew, I made windmill motions with my arms, like a long jumper over the landing pit at a track meet. This helped me keep my feet in front of me. When my crampons finally hit the surface, they stayed firmly in place (that's what they are supposed to do) and the rest of me kept moving. The result was that I lurched forward and flopped onto my chest, head downhill, arms out to the side. As an inverted, top-heavy cross, I started sliding down the slope, and I instinctively kept my chin up to avoid spending the rest of my life without it. Fortunately, the snow was smooth—there were no outcropping rocks or chunks of ice.

There are times when your training kicks in and you react automatically. It will take me far longer to describe what I did than it actually took to accomplish. While sliding, I rolled onto my back, still moving downhill headfirst. Then I pulled the ice axe on top of me across my chest, gripping it with both hands. With it securely under control, I rolled to my right and jammed the pick into the snow. My legs swung out to the side and then down the slope. I kept my knees bent with my feet in the air—I did not want my crampons to snag. With my weight fully on the shaft of the axe and its pick in the snow, I skidded to a stop.

I lay there, taking an inventory of my body. I could move my head, fingers, and toes; I felt air moving in and out of my lungs; and there were no fluids leaking out of any old or new openings. I hardly deserved it, but I was able to get up and start moving again.

The sport of Unaided Mountain Flying has not yet been officially recognized, and it has no organizing committee or corporate sponsors. After my experience I am certain that UMF has only one rule: Don't Try It.

With much more caution I resumed down-climbing when the wind permitted. The snow retained its excellent consistency, and I made good progress when I wasn't doing push-ups. Gradually, I got below the roaring freight train, back to where it was just windy. When I thought it was safe, I stopped dropping and kept walking. Far below me I saw the end of the snowfield near the Sixth Station, and never had dirt looked so good. A bit farther down I could see the trail. Someone was standing there, at the edge of the snow. It was Tumiko. She was facing uphill and waving.

I shouted and waved back, and then I quickly navigated the last few hundred feet. As I stepped onto the path, still in my crampons, Tumiko came to me, and in a most un-Japanese show of emotion, she reached out her arms and gave me a very big hug. It was twelve thirty, around five and a half hours after we had parted company. Tumiko told me that she had arrived at the trail's end fifteen minutes earlier. She had been terribly worried, because down in Sato's hut the radio had reported unusually intense winds at the top of the mountain. She had come to wait for me, and she was greatly relieved to see me descending the snowfield.

Twenty minutes later we were back at Sato Goya. As we entered, Sato came out from the kitchen. With two hands outstretched I returned his ice axe with a rather emotional "*Arigato*, Sato-san." He accepted it, stepped back, and for the first time in two days, smiled.

With Tumiko's help I told Sato about the climb and the fierce winds. I left out the flying episode. I told him I could not have done it without his ice axe and that I would always remember his generosity. When he had heard the story, he went to the kitchen and made me some food. I was aching for sushi but gratefully accepted rice and vegetables.

Tumiko was true to her word, and she shepherded me back to Tokyo, to a taxi that took me to Jim's house. Jim was so relieved to see me that after my shower he insisted on taking me out to celebrate. I begged him for sushi, and he readily agreed. "Actually, all that mass-produced banquet food you've been eating is second-rate," he said. "You need to see a real sushi chef at work to appreciate the artistry of it."

We sat at the counter in a tiny bar, facing an array of fish chilling on ice. Jim ordered one round after the next, and the chef expertly prepared servings of sushi and sashimi. Off to one side there was a tank with live shrimp crawling around. I asked Jim about it, and rather than explain anything, he ordered a pair for me. The chef plucked two wiggling shrimp out of the water with a long set of tongs and set them on the counter. Working quickly, he took the first one and held its body on the marble as he deftly cut off its head. Then he sliced the underside of the shell, spread it apart, and cleaned it, all but the tail. He set the fresh gray meat diagonally onto a small square plate.

Meanwhile, as the first shrimp was being butchered alive, the second one had seen what lay ahead and had tried to scurry away. The chef reached along the counter, retrieved it, and proceeded to behead and strip it in the same manner as the first. This one he draped across the first, so the plate had an X of fresh raw shrimp on it. The chef triumphantly set the plate in front of me.

"Pick one up with your chopsticks and admire it," Jim instructed.

I raised it for all to see, as the chef looked on proudly. Then, to my great surprise, the shrimp *moved*. It twitched in a series of pathetic jerking motions. What was left of this recently dispatched sea creature was still in its death throes, its little nerves continuing to send signals as I held it aloft. Horrified, I set it down.

On my ten-day Asian odyssey I had endured a hundred speeches on seaport operations, stuffed myself with thirty or forty pounds of sushi, and, most significantly, survived a somewhat perilous winter ascent of Mount Fuji. But there in that small Tokyo restaurant I finally hit the wall. I was not going to eat that raw shrimp any more than I would swallow a live eel. I would never crawl for sushi again. It was time to go home, sit on my couch, and eat a hamburger, well-done.

7 *Knickers in a Twist*

In 1821 a thirty-five-year-old Englishman named James Holman worked his way to the top of Mount Vesuvius at nighttime with only a walking stick and his feet to find the way. The meager moonlight was scarcely enough to illuminate the terrain, but for Holman that was not an obstacle—he was totally blind. He was accompanied by an Irish surgeon and a Neapolitan guide, but he refused their assistance as he walked. In fact, he insisted on completing the ascent even when the others wished to turn back. He later wrote that he accepted their participation in the climb "rather . . . for amusement and information than guidance and protection." Holman had even turned down the offer of a mule ride on the lower slopes because, he said, "I see things better with my feet."

Vesuvius was in the middle of an active eruption cycle, and Holman's party was greeted at the belching crater with overpowering sulfuric fumes and unstable ground so hot that standing in one spot for more than a few seconds was impossible. The men quickly retreated to a hermit's cabin four miles downslope. Understanding that Holman was the first blind man to climb the mountain, the trio celebrated with copious amounts of locally made wine.

Holman went on to become what biographer Jason Roberts has called "history's greatest traveler." He made his way alone across Russia and later accomplished a circumnavigation of the globe, but his efforts on Vesuvius nicely illustrated his drive and tenacity. In *A Sense of the World*, Roberts describes Holman's insistence on marching to the beat of his own drum: "Such reasserted freedom wasn't just a sop to his dignity. It was, in his opinion, the only thing keeping him alive."

Holman's journey to Vesuvius had begun in England. Mine took place 165 years later, and I set out from the Netherlands. I had spent a week in Rotterdam teaching comparative law, and coincidentally, I had been introduced to the Dutch version of mountaineering.

The Netherlands is a small coastal nation whose name translates as "flatter than a pancake and below sea level." The high point of the country has a dizzying elevation of 1,059 feet. Known as the Vaalserberg, it sits in the southern province of Limburg (meaning "a lumpy pancake, slightly above sea level"). The actual spot would be completely unnoticeable were it not marked by a monument alongside a flat road, where the borders of Germany, Belgium, and the Netherlands intersect. Lacking any natural features worth ascending, the Dutch have embraced gymnasium climbing for their vertical thrills. During my visit to Rotterdam a group of students inducted me as an honorary member into an exclusive society known as Hermes, and after several rounds of drinks they took me outside and proudly pointed out a new climbing wall on the side of the fraternity house. Fueled by a mixture of Heineken and *jenever*, I managed to ascend it, albeit clumsily, in a business suit and dress shoes.

The next day, my last in Holland, I paid a brief visit to the quaint village of Loenen aan de Vecht, where I had lived for two years while working in Amsterdam. I strolled along Loenen's cobblestone lanes, occasionally knocking on a door and saying hello to a former neighbor. At the local bakery I chatted briefly with Mrs. Koning, and as I left, she insisted that I take a package of *speculaas* cookies that her husband had baked that morning. These sweet biscuits are fragrant with clove, ginger, and cinnamon—a wonderful treat. I had grown up with them in my Iowa farm town, where we called them windmill cookies because of their shape. I accepted them gladly, but back at my hotel I grumbled about stuffing one more thing into a suitcase that was already bulging with boots and climbing clothes. I thought I might just leave them behind, but in the end I packed them, and they became The Cookies That Saved My Life.

My lectures accomplished, I flew to Rome and caught a train to Naples. Somewhere on that train it occurred to me that this was my first time in Italy, and I had just bypassed all the sights of the Eternal City in order to add a four thousand–foot volcano to my climbing résumé. I made a mental note to grow up someday.

I arrived in Naples on a Friday evening, and at the station I stopped at a currency exchange to cash some traveler's checks. This may sound strange to some of you, but there was a time when ATMs did not exist and many establishments did not accept credit cards. Thus, it was necessary to carry cash (that is, real money) and traveler's checks. Banks and currency exchanges were a regular feature of European travel. The man in the *cambio* cage at the train station took one look at my Visa traveler's checks and waved me off. "No good," he said, using two-fifths of his English vocabulary. "Only American Express." Here I would like to mention that in the past I had always carried American Express checks, but my banker back in Seattle had told me that the new Visa checks were cheaper and just as widely accepted. Apparently, she had never tried to present them at the train station in Naples.

I waved the checks and said, "What? Where do I cash these?"

The teller waved back and said "No good. Banca. Banca."

This I took to mean "bank," and I pointed toward the station entrance. "Banca? Where is banca?"

He gestured as if dusting lint from his sleeve. "No banca. Chiusi. Chiusi."

I didn't understand this at all, so I said, "Muchas gracias," and walked away. I looked around and saw a tourist information office, which fortunately was still open. There a very nice young woman explained that all of the banks were closed by now—"chiusi"—and that this was the start of a three-day holiday weekend, the Weekend of No Money. Did I have any cash at all? Yes, a few Dutch guilders. The woman suggested that I at least exchange my guilders and then try to use my credit card, although she feared that many restaurants would be closed for the holiday. She also kindly offered that if my hotel, which was just across from the station, did not accept plastic, she would find me one that did. A few minutes later, with my precious lire laid out on the counter, the woman and I calculated what it would cost me for public transportation to Vesuvius and Pompeii. Add a few entrance fees, and I had just enough cash to see the sights. There would be no money left over for incidentals like food.

The desk clerk at my hotel said yes, he could accept my credit card in payment for the room (oh joy!). Because of the holiday weekend, however, the hotel's restaurant and breakfast room were closed (oh *merde!*). But I would be pleased to know that because I would not be receiving any breakfast, there would be a small discount on my room rate. I said that I really needed a hotel with food, so I lumbered back across the station square with my bags to the tourist office. In the fifteen minutes since I had last been there, it had closed. Once again to the hotel, where the clerk accepted me back with a rather insincere welcome.

Before I unpacked my bags, I made my first foray into the neighborhood in search of a credit card meal. I was unsuccessful. I returned to my room, where I discovered among my things the nearly discarded package of *speculaas* cookies. After lustily eating several, I realized that these might be my lifeline for the next three days. I counted them carefully and calculated that for each of my remaining meals in Naples, I could eat four cookies.

Wash them down with some questionable tap water, and it was time to party.

Naples was a certified dump. It has a most beautiful bay, but the city was little more than crumbling buildings and piles of garbage being ignored by the people who were paid to collect it. If the Neapolitans had not invented pizza and three-flavored ice cream, their home would dwell in much-deserved obscurity—the Sioux City of Europe.

Saturday didn't dawn so much as ooze into place. The sky was gray, and it was raining brown drops of something or other. Not a day to climb Vesuvius, obviously, so I took a leisurely breakfast in my room—four cookies and a glass of water. I tried watching television, but the two channels didn't offer anything but women in too much makeup thrusting their large breasts toward the camera and shouting for us to buy something. I decided to visit Pompeii.

I am certain that on a sunny day, when it is not too hot, Pompeii would be worth a long, leisurely stroll. I am certain that I would hear the echoes of ancient chariots on stone pavement and people excitedly conjugating together in a public square. I am certain I would conclude that Pompeii is the most spectacular ancient ruin anywhere in Europe. The problem was, it was raining heavily. In my hiking boots and foul weather gear I navigated around great puddles, but the marble streets were so slippery that I couldn't relax for a moment. I wondered how the Romans had survived such conditions in togas and those silly high-strap sandals. I had to keep my guidebook in my pocket, so I didn't know what I was looking at, and frankly everything looked the same. Eventually, I tired of the whole business and found shelter under the awning of a closed-up souvenir stand just outside the complex.

Standing there, shivering, I ate my *speculaas* lunch. I also tried to engage in conversation with a thoroughly drenched Austrian couple who huddled next to me. As it turned out, they spoke only German and a little Italian, while I could offer only English, Dutch, and some elementary Spanish. We exchanged a variety of words and phrases, searching for cognates. Every so often we would connect on a thought, but we soon tired of the effort and went our separate ways. I returned to my hotel.

Dinner that night was the same as breakfast and lunch, and I was already tired of those cookies. They were bearable only because one of the television stations was playing some kind of quiz show in which an incorrect answer forced the contestant to remove an article of clothing—a sort of *Strip Jeopardy*. The hostesses were skimpily clad from the start, and they seemed to enjoy assisting with the disrobing. Eventually, one unfortunate man was down to his undershorts, but just as the Full Monty was about to occur, some dancers surrounded him and escorted him from the set. I take it that he did not win a vacation in the Seychelles.

Sunday morning was gray on gray, but it was not raining. I had to go to Vesuvius. I nearly skipped breakfast out of boredom, but the twelve cookies the day before had not provided much nourishment, and I was ravenous. I ate my allotment unenthusiastically, as if taking Pepto-Bismol.

Access to Vesuvius is through the coastal village of Ercolano, a six-mile train ride south of Naples. From there a local bus takes you uphill onto the mountain. Except for an old woman in black who disembarked at a church, I was the only passenger that morning. After much climbing and winding, the driver pulled into a parking lot, pointed into the swirling mist, and said, "Vesuvio." He had no sooner left than the skies unloaded a torrent of rain. I scrambled to a boarded-up snack bar and found a somewhat protected spot beneath its overhanging roof. The rain was coming down so hard, it bounced off the ground in little geysers. I wasn't going anywhere until it let up.

At one point a car drove up and a woman in the passenger seat rolled her window down just enough to shout something in strangely accented Italian. I just shrugged. Then she asked in very carefully pronounced English, "Is this where the Vesuvius trail begins?" I recognized her accent and responded in Dutch. She was startled, and she thanked me in Dutch. I thought she might want to invite me to sit in the car and wait out the rain, but she didn't. As I hugged the kiosk to stay dry, the Dutch people waited, engine idling. I suspected they were eating sandwiches and drinking hot, steaming cups of coffee. Eventually, they gave up and drove off.

Finally, the rain stopped. Since it had momentarily washed out some of the mist, I easily spotted the trailhead and a picture sign that illustrated the mountain. Despite the fact that I was risking exposure to further showers, I decided to start hiking.

This is probably the point at which I should discuss the logistics of the climb that lay ahead. I knew that the summit of Vesuvius is forty-two hundred feet in elevation. Assuming a start near sea level, I had anticipated a vigorous workout. What I didn't learn until I got off that bus and looked at my altimeter was that the trailhead lies at thirty-three hundred feet. In due course I discovered that the path hits the crater rim approximately six hundred feet above the starting point, with the mountain's true summit on the opposite side of the crater, some three hundred feet higher. Today all of this information is available on the Internet, but none of my resources at the time offered these statistics. Had I known that my total elevation gain would be no more than six or nine hundred feet, I would not have bothered coming to Naples.

As the fog moved back in, I set out from the parking lot. The path was wide and relatively smooth, and it was crisscrossed with rivulets of rainwater. Despite the limited visibility, the track was easy to follow. The trail's cinder surface crunched underfoot, and on either side was a jumble of brown and black rocks. After a few initial zigzags the route proceeded upward in a fairly straight line. Ten minutes into the hike I paused to remove my jacket, and I glanced at the nearby slope. How nice, I thought. Look at those patches of white flowers growing in this meager soil.

Nature is truly impressive. Then I stepped off the path to take a closer look and discovered that the white objects were plastic bottles and food wrappers.

A few hundred yards up the trail I came upon a small, open hut. An old man inside pointed to a sign in several languages, directing me to buy an entrance ticket and pay a guide fee. I asked him, "Are you the guide?"

He shook his head and pointed upward. "Guide is Pietro. He is at top."

Not more than ten minutes later I came to a T intersection that marked the crater rim trail—I proceeded to the right. There was a great black void to my left—the crater itself—but in the mist I sensed it more than saw it. In short order I stumbled upon a building, the summit snack bar. I stepped inside and was assaulted by the smell of coffee and food. Knowing that I couldn't buy anything was almost too much to bear.

I asked the attendant for Pietro, and he pointed to a person at a nearby table, a middle-aged man lustily eating a sensational-looking plate of pasta. I approached him and said his name. He looked up and said, "Yes. I am Pietro. You wait a few minutes. I will come." So, I stepped outside onto a wooden deck with a railing on the far side. I assumed that it offered a view into the crater, but at that moment the only thing out there was fog. A gray-haired woman in walking clothes leaned against the building, staying out of the wind and presumably waiting for her guide as well. As discretely as possible, I stood near the wall and took the four lunch cookies from my knapsack. I knew it was silly, but I was embarrassed to be seen eating them. I felt like the two men from *Alive* who, upon meeting the first outsider after their grueling hike across the Andes, were ashamed to be nibbling on the flesh of their rugby teammates.

A few minutes later Pietro emerged, slipping on a jacket. I noticed that he was wearing ordinary street shoes. He stepped up to the railing, turned back toward us, and gestured for both of us to come closer. "English?" he asked. The woman and I both said yes, and Pietro launched into a three-minute talk about Vesuvius and its great eruption in AD 79. He said that it had erupted many times since then, most recently in 1944. Then he excused himself and went back into the restaurant.

I turned to the woman and said, "I imagine he is putting on his hiking boots to take us on the guided walk. By the way, I'm Steve." She introduced herself as Jane, and I realized she was British. We waited. And waited. It was cold standing there in the mist, and I wanted to get moving. After ten minutes I turned to Jane and said, "I'll go see what's keeping him."

Inside the building I was startled to see Pietro sitting at the table eating his pasta. "Pietro," I said, "aren't you coming back?"

"No. Tour is finished."

"But aren't we going to hike around the crater?"

"No, very dangerous."

"But aren't you our guide?"

"Yes, I gave you lecture. Tour is finished."

"But I want to hike around the crater."

"Bad idea. You see nothing today, and it is very dangerous. Bad idea."

"But I want to go to the summit."

"This is summit. You stay here. Bad idea to go farther."

He was wrong, of course, about the summit. The mountain's high point was across the crater, but that was of little consequence to him. I returned to the terrace and explained the situation to Jane. She was disappointed, but looking at the brighter side, she said, "At least we didn't pay much for the guide fee."

"Yes," I responded, "but I came here for a serious hike. Look, I've got a knapsack with all of my emergency gear, and I'm wearing my boots, jacket, and hiking pants."

She immediately blushed and said, "Oh dear. *We* wouldn't say that."

"Say what?" I asked.

"Well, you know . . . pants. It means undergarments."

"Oh, I'm sorry. I meant my knickers."

She drew in a deep breath. "Oh my. That's even worse. That's what we call *women's* undergarments."

"Well, what do you call these things?"

"Plus fours, or simply trousers. You Americans have a most peculiar way of expressing yourselves."

I was about to say that I was Canadian, when the mist off the deck parted briefly and the deep crater came into view. I quickly set down my backpack to retrieve my camera, but by the time I had it in my hands the cloud had re-formed itself.

"Well," I said, "this looks hopeless. I think I'll be heading back down."

"Before you go," she said a bit hesitantly, "may I ask you something?"

"Of course," I responded, hoping to regain a bit of my dignity after the Knickers Incident.

"Steve isn't your real name, is it?"

"What do you mean?"

"You're that singer John Denver, aren't you?"

You should understand that years earlier Mr. Denver had shamelessly copied my hairstyle and wire-rimmed glasses, and this sort of mistaken identity had happened before. Nobody today would confuse me with the man born as Henry John Deutschendorf Jr., particularly since he is dead.

"Actually, Steve is my real name. John Denver is just a stage name that was created to suggest an association with the state of Colorado."

"But I rather enjoy your music. So typically American, I think."

"In a way I'm a John Denver fan too," I responded. I was tempted to tell her that she filled up my senses like a night in the forest, but she didn't. Instead, I said thanks and good-bye, gave her my best rock star smile, and walked away humming a few bars of "Rocky Mountain High."

That evening I should have celebrated the Conquest of Vesuvius with wine and good food. Instead, it was all I could do to avoid gagging on those damnable pieces of *speculaas*. I desperately wanted to get to Rome, where I could surely find an expensive restaurant that would accept my credit card. Unfortunately, I had a reservation on the next evening's train, and I doubted that on the Monday holiday I would find anyone who could help me change my ticket. I spent the next day walking in light rain along the Naples waterfront, scrutinizing piles of garbage, and trying to avoid pickpockets. I ate my lunch cookies while leaning against a statue as I tried to make out Capri across the bay. After I boarded the evening train, I consumed my dinner allotment with a side dish of self-pity.

Not surprisingly, I arrived in Rome just after my hotel's kitchen had closed for the evening. And no, the desk clerk had no idea where there might be an open restaurant, this being a national holiday. I ate my very last cookies the next morning, because my early flight required me to leave the hotel before its breakfast bar opened. When my airplane was finally airborne and the flight attendant served me a plastic tray with scrambled eggs and cold cuts, I blubbered like an old man who had just been reunited with his long lost twin.

When I was a boy, I once sat up all night in a pup tent with my cousin Alan, and over the course of twelve hours we each consumed a two-pound bag of red licorice. The next morning I deposited mine all over the backyard, and that was the last time the vile candy has ever passed between my lips. Better climbers than I have come home from the Himalayas missing fingers and toes. I returned from Mount Vesuvius having lost my taste for *speculaas*.

8 *Twin Peaks in Paradise*

When I received an invitation to lecture in Java, my first thought was to seize the opportunity and find a mountain to climb in that part of the world. After a bit of investigation I decided to add a side trip to a place ignored by most climbers—Bali. I had fantasized about the South Seas ever since reading *Mutiny on the Bounty* as a boy, but what sold me on Bali was the fact that it is home to a ten thousand-foot volcano, Gunung Agung. I could climb this prominent peak, and along the way I could sample the island's more traditional pleasures.

First, I had to accomplish my university business in Java, and it began with a stopover in the chaotic capital of Jakarta. The city was a disagreeable stew of shantytowns, crumbling colonial mansions, and sterile glass-and-steel towers. Although a few thoroughfares were impressively built, most streets had no business hosting automobiles, and yet every square inch of every road was occupied by smoking vehicles. The atmosphere was hot and sticky, brown with smog. The noise level was like an airport tarmac.

The taxi dropped me off at a no-surprises Hilton or Hyatt that could have been located anywhere, but after the din of my taxi ride, it was an oasis of calm. My eighteenth-floor room was on the back side of the building, and looking out, I saw a brown river.

On its banks, directly behind the hotel's high courtyard wall, were little shacks crowded together in a jumble that stretched to the horizon. Some women sat at river's edge, washing things in the water. Just upstream was a narrow wooden pier that jutted out fifteen feet into the river, and at its end was a small boxlike structure with no roof. People were lined up along the dock, and one at a time they would enter the box for a few minutes and then return to shore. I ordered something from room service, and when the valet arrived, I took him to the window and asked what was going on down there. Somewhat ruefully he explained that the cubicle on the pier was the neighborhood toilet.

The next morning I was driven to Yogyakarta, a smaller city that is home to Gadjah Mada University, Indonesia's oldest educational institution. Yogya is also the heart of Javanese culture. It is the center of *wayang kulit*, the elaborate shadow puppet theater, and the gamelan, a musical ensemble composed of xylophones, drums, gongs, and flutes. Local artisans also produce Indonesia's finest batik fabric. My university hosts made certain that I experienced the theater and music, and at dinner one evening they presented me with a lovely batik jacket of the sort that is worn on formal occasions. They seem to have overlooked the fact that they, the Javanese, are the smallest people in the world. The garment, which was labeled XXXL, would probably have been an XXS in the United States. It was highly entertaining as I tried to put the thing on. I was able to get my arms into it by thrusting them to the rear, but even expelling every ounce of air from my lungs, I couldn't bring them forward. Apparently, in Java it's the thought that counts, because my dinner companions merrily applauded my efforts.

One day, in lieu of meetings, I was taken to Borobudur, the massive and ornately carved Buddhist temple an hour's drive from Yogya. The largest Buddhist building in the world, it is Indonesia's premier tourist attraction. The complex is a series of platforms rising up to a main dome surrounded by seventy-two statues of the Buddha and capped with a spire. From bottom to top the structure stands 115 feet tall, and it displays a mind-boggling 26,000 square feet of detailed bas-reliefs that tell the story of Buddhism. The entire temple serves as a giant stupa, or holy mound. According to historian Daniel J. Boorstin, a typical stupa is a place of worship containing sacred relics such as the remains of a saint. It is also a stylized representation of the mythical Mount Meru—home of the deities, center of the universe, and the source of life-giving rivers. At a distance Borobudur indeed has the profile of a massive, symmetrical mountain with a sharp summit thrusting into the sky.

Like the Tower of Babel, Borobudur symbolizes humankind's efforts to reach the heavens and commune with the gods. A true pilgrim will circle and gradually ascend the monument to signify the achievement of enlightenment. The first stage, the base of the stupa, is Kamadhatu, the world of desires. Then comes Rupadhatu, represented by six square platforms. This is the world of focused meditations. Finally, the pilgrim climbs through three round platforms toward the central dome. This plane is Arupadhatu, the formless world of infinite consciousness. It is where earth and heaven meet and the mind can encounter the divine. The imagery of Borobudur is so complex that those of us who visit as Western tourists can scarcely appreciate its significance for a Buddhist. The best I could do was to feel the mountain imagery and ascend the temple as a climber moving toward a long-desired summit. The experience reminded me that I was on my way to climb a real mountain that was equally revered by the Hindu people of Bali.

Tropical breezes, fragrant flowers, exotic people—I was expecting Bali to be an unspoiled paradise. This is a place first seen by outsiders in 1597, when Dutch sailors landed, sampled the food and hospitality of the local women, and decided that they would never leave. Bob Hope and Bing Crosby filmed one of their "Road" pictures on the island—or at least in a studio decorated to look like it. I hoped that Bali would be as perfect as the

Hollywood version and that a Princess Lalah would be waiting for me.

My first letdown was Kuta. Located near the international airport, it has beautiful beaches, but the overwhelming impression was one of cocktail lounges filled with drunken Australians. There were souvenir stands, snack bars, and sunbathers. Blond-haired surfers rode the waves, and parasailors floated overhead. Kuta is a modern destination, and evidently many vacationers never leave its environs. The problem is that the beach resort has nothing to do with Balinese culture. It is Sydney transplanted, not Bali. I spent my first night there, and I felt trapped and betrayed.

The next morning I escaped. A taxi drove me along the south coast to Candidasa Beach, near the eastern tip of the island. This took several hours on a narrow, winding highway. As we left Kuta and passed through the nearby capital, Denpasar, the traffic was heavy, and the driver steadfastly kept his thumb on the car horn. Eventually, the congestion eased a bit, but the fellow kept honking. He beeped at every one of the thousand curves we negotiated along the way. It drove me crazy, so I finally asked whether it was really necessary.

"Oh yes, mister. Very good."

"But nobody is paying attention. Why bother?"

"Very good, mister. Very good."

"But it doesn't accomplish anything, does it?"

"Yes, mister. Very very good."

"Look, I'm going to sit back here and stab myself in the belly, and in a few minutes I'll be leaking abdominal fluid all over your back seat."

"Very good, mister. Very good."

Trying to concentrate on the scenery, I noticed that the countryside was lush with flowering trees and vegetation of the deepest green. Then, as the road veered from the coast and into the hills, I observed Bali's famed rice paddy terraces. These are marvels of engineering, rising hundreds of feet up the mountainsides. Farmers are able to turn three crops each year, and the terraces showed a range of color, depending on the stage of growth. Some had been recently flooded. Others showed the light green of new plantings. Then the dark green of maturity, followed by the ochre of drying plants. Finally, after the harvest, a terrace was burned black in preparation for the next cycle. The smoke from these fires could be seen here and there, and at times we passed through it. It was pungent but pleasant, reminiscent of any student party I had ever attended in the late 1960s.

My ears ringing from the car horn, I was dropped off at my hotel in southeast Bali. The Candidasa Bungalows was a humble establishment with plain rooms, but it sat on a pristine, south-facing beach, and in contrast to Kuta there wasn't a bar or nightclub in sight. It was a tranquil place, and it had a beachfront terrace that was everything you could ask for. I sat there, ordered lunch, and began to relax.

After my meal of rice and some exceptionally spiced mystery fish, I asked the owner to arrange for a car and driver the next day. I intended to travel to Besakih, a village on the lower slopes of Gunung Agung. There I would hire a local guide and stay the night at a guesthouse before getting an early start up the trail the next day. I expected the climb to take between eight and twelve hours, nothing more technical than a hike, but a strenuous one, with approximately 7,000 feet of elevation gain. I considered Mount Agung a worthy objective because of its physical prominence—at 10,308 feet it is an obvious ultra, and it dominates the eastern end of the island. Beyond its height, its periodic eruptions have engendered a good deal of respect and reverence among the Balinese. Even more significant, they believe that Agung is a fragment of the sacred Mount Meru, and the name *Agung* means "navel of the world." Bali's most important temple, Pura Besakih, sits on its flanks.

My travel arrangements confirmed, I considered how I might fill the afternoon. The hotel's owner suggested that I stroll down the beach a couple of miles to the Balina Diving Centre, where I could do some snorkeling. This sounded like an excellent way to relax before my climb. The tide was out, and I walked slowly past a few beachfront "losmen," Bali's version of a bed and breakfast. Most of them had the word *homestay* in their name and looked rather spartan. Then I left Candidasa behind, and in the distance I saw what I presumed was the Balina Beach Resort. The sand was soft, so I took off my sneakers and proceeded barefoot. I was lost in the lapping sound of the waves, the green of the coastal vegetation, and the serenity of the place.

Then I saw Her, the first woman I had ever seen whose personal pronoun deserved to be capitalized. She was walking toward me on the sand, also barefoot. Her shoulder-length hair, somewhere between brown and blonde, flowed in the breeze. She was wearing a string bikini, and it emphasized how her hips swayed as she walked. It also did little to hide her breasts, which stood out like perfectly formed twin peaks. As I write this, I am replaying the scene in my mind. I am walking toward her and she toward me, but we are moving in slow motion. It was like the episode in the movie 10 when Bo Derek walks up from the surf toward Dudley Moore and never seems to get any closer. I was in a trance. I kept moving with my eyes fixed on her. I knew that in another minute we would meet and the universe would change.

We were within twenty-five feet of each other when disaster struck. As I took a stride forward, still staring at her, I felt a piercing pain in my right foot. I looked down and saw that I had stubbed it on a rock; my little toe was sticking out at a ninety-degree angle. In a single motion I fell onto my back, pulled my right knee into my chest, and then grabbed my foot with both hands.

Squeezing hard, I pushed the toe into its proper position, parallel with its neighbors. It hurt like hell. Still grasping my foot, I rocked side to side on my back in a modified yoga pose, but I was no Happy Baby. Completely absorbed in my pain and moaning out loud, I momentarily forgot that I was not alone.

Then . . . I became aware that the woman was standing directly above me. I saw her face and realized that she was concerned, even a bit frightened.

"Are you okay?" the goddess asked in an accent that I took to be French.

"Yes, I'll be all right, *ça va*," I replied, trying to sound both manly and cosmopolitan.

"Can I help you?"

Well, for starters . . . I wanted to invite her to do any number of things, but I kept them to myself. "Thank you, I just broke my toe on that rock, but I think I can still walk."

She stepped back as I struggled to my feet. To prove I was in command of the situation, I took a few steps, then bent over and picked up my shoes. "I'm heading for Balina Beach," I said. "I'll just keep going. Thank you for stopping. That was very nice of you."

She touched my arm (the pain momentarily vanished) and cooed: "You are very bwave. *Bonne chance.*"

With that, she continued on her way toward Candidasa. I watched her and noticed how little of her derrière was actually covered by the fabric of her bikini. Twenty yards away she apparently felt my eyes burning laser holes into her cheeks, and she turned and waved.

I limped along barefoot, then stopped and sat to put on my shoes for better support, but I couldn't get the right one on over my throbbing toe. So, I continued without it and eventually arrived at the Balina Diving Centre. I thought a swim in the warm ocean might ease the pain, so I rented snorkeling equipment and walked into the water. There was a reef just offshore, and the fish were supposed to be spectacular.

Sitting in the shallow water to gear up, I discovered that I couldn't get the fin onto my right foot. It was just too painful. I tossed the fin onto the beach and put on the left one. After spitting into my mask (how many people before me had done that to this same rental mask?), I put it on, placed the snorkel into my mouth (similar question), and began to swim out toward the reef. Then two problems arose. The first was that I couldn't kick with my right foot—I had to just let it hang behind me as I fluttered my left fin. The second was that a one-footed swimmer doesn't swim in a straight line. There I was, barely into the bay, and all I could do was move slowly in a clockwise circle. When I realized this, I swore out loud into my snorkel and promptly ingested some seawater. Coughing and sputtering, I lifted my head, ripped off the mask, and stood up. I was in water only to my waist.

Back on the beach I bought a local Bintang beer and sat in a deck chair, looking out toward the bay. I was bemoaning my inability to swim when a larger thought entered my brain—I couldn't put on my shoe, nor could I walk without pain. That meant that I would not be able to climb Gunung Agung. In fact, I would be lucky to get back to my hotel for dinner. I had come all the way to Bali for nothing.

After limping back to my hotel, I went for dinner on the terrace. Nothing sounded good, so I ordered successive bottles of Bintang. After a while I began to feel Australian. I explained to the owner that I had broken my toe and wouldn't be able to climb Mount Agung. He was solicitous and offered to bring me a nice dinner of fish and rice. It sounded suspiciously like the lunch I had eaten, and it proved to be exactly the same, but on a platter of a different color. Okay, no problem; it was still tasty. Then I explained that I wouldn't be needing a driver the next day, because I didn't have to get to Besakih. Once again, the host was sympathetic, but he had a suggestion.

"You see," he said, "the driver is my nephew Wayan, and he speaks very good English. You can hire him for the whole day, and he can give you a nice tour to Ubud. Then he will take you back here to Candidasa. You won't have to walk much, and you will enjoy the day."

Two more Bintangs, and I agreed.

Wayan showed up the next morning in a small Nissan. He was twenty-two, and he did speak passable English, which he had learned taking care of guests at his uncle's hotel. Now he made his living as a tour guide and shuttling people to and from Kuta. Looking at the map, we agreed to take the direct route to Ubud, east along the coast and then inland into the hill country. I was in pain, and I was highly skeptical that the day would offer much. Nevertheless, I couldn't think of anything else to do.

Bali is nearly unique among the thousands of Indonesian islands in that its three million people are Hindu and not Muslim. Rather than mosques and the calls to prayer so ubiquitous on Java, Bali is a place of temples and ceremonies. A surprising fact is that despite all of the island's lovely beaches, the Balinese have traditionally avoided the sea, believing it to be the home of demons. They have also avoided the highest mountains, the home of their gods. The real life of Bali is in between, in the forested hills. Thus, Kuta is a modern development; Ubud is the keeper of authenticity.

On the road to Ubud we passed fruit stands and open-air markets, women carrying baskets on their heads, and countless statues and stone carvings tinged green with moss. Nearing the village, we saw more obvious indications of tourism, such as snack bars and displays of handicrafts. Wayan suggested we first visit Puri Ubud, a tiny palace in the center of the village where dances are often held. Sure enough, a crowd had gathered, and a Barong had already begun.

The Barong is Bali's most famous dance, featuring strange creatures, groups of frenzied humans, and energetic gamelan music. The core theme is the struggle of good versus evil. The good Barong, a dog-faced lion, battles the evil witch Rangda, a hag with gleaming fangs and an excessively long tongue. To accessorize, Rangda wears human intestines around her neck. Although Barong prevents her from doing her worst to the human characters in the play, the contest ends in something of a draw. The moral of the story is that good and evil will always coexist in this world, like day and night, yin and yang, bikini and beach rock.

The exotic dance lasted far too long for me, and I had the distinct feeling that it was being staged primarily for the hundreds of tourists who ringed the plaza. I told Wayan that I wanted to move on. He drove me to the famed Monkey Forest, where hundreds of supposedly sacred gray primates hover over a footpath screeching at the tourists and bombarding them with feces. Okay, it's not something you see in Seattle every day, but five minutes can give you a lifetime of satisfaction. Actually, I couldn't quite grasp the concept of monkey devotion. They are entertaining (let's all play Dodge the Droppings) and intriguingly humanlike (hey, there's cousin Wilbur) . . . but holy? My foot was throbbing, and I asked Wayan to take me back to Candidasa.

Shortly before we reached the hotel, Wayan (ever the tour guide) pointed out that his home village of Ngis was just up that road to the left, a few miles above the coastal highway. I had perked up a bit, and I responded that I would like to see it. He said that there was absolutely nothing there, but I told him I had enjoyed spending the day with him and it would be my pleasure to see his village. A little surprised and clearly flattered, he smiled and turned uphill.

Wayan was correct that there wasn't much to Ngis. The road we had taken into town was its only street, and it dead-ended into the hillside. The houses lining both sides of the street were modest to a fault, built of a random mixture of materials. The whole village wasn't more than three or four blocks long. What I appreciated, however, was that there was not a single tour bus or foreigner in the vicinity.

We sat in the car and surveyed the scene. I noticed that pairs of women were walking slowly up and down the street like Italians on a passeggiata. Young children scampered about, and a few older ones kicked a soccer ball.

"Where are all the men?" I asked.

"Behind building there."

"What are they doing?"

"Sunday today, they have cockfight."

I had heard that cockfighting still took place in Bali, but somehow I assumed it must be very hush-hush, as in the United States. "Is it legal?" I asked.

"Oh yes, no problem. It's okay."

"Are you going to the fight?"

"Yes, after I bring you to hotel."

"Would it be okay if I came with you?"

"You want to see cockfight?"

"Yes."

"It will be okay. You will be my guest."

We left the car and walked down a small alley between two houses, and then I heard the shouting. We emerged into a small plaza, a *banjar*—the community gathering place. Surrounded by houses, its perimeter was a tin-roofed portico fifteen feet deep. In the center there was a lower area, open to the sky, approximately twenty by twenty feet. The *banjar* was filled with men in a state of frenzy. The noise of their screaming hit me like a blast of air through the open window of a speeding automobile. It was one of those movie scenes in which everyone is trying to crowd onto the last plane before the volcano erupts.

I'm guessing there were 250 men jammed into that place—and all of them were focused on the sunken stage. Since it was a step or two down, from the back of the crowd we couldn't see the action. The shouting was sustained for a few minutes, and then all of a sudden there was a collective sigh and things calmed down a bit. Wayan took the occasion to shout that he had a visitor, an American with leprosy at a highly contagious stage. Everyone turned, and the crowd parted for us. We moved to the front, to the edge of the open area. I felt very self-conscious, not only because of whatever Wayan had said but also because I was a full head taller than everyone else. A lone Dutch American Goliath among a multitude of Balinese Davids.

I focused on the business at hand, and in the square several participants were setting up for the next bout. One man was holding a white rooster, while another held a brown. Each man was being assisted by an individual who was doing something to the bird's leg. On closer inspection I saw that the attendant was taping a wicked-looking stiletto blade just above the foot. This was a delicate operation because the blade looked razor-sharp, and neither cock was sitting still for the procedure. What seemed strange (as if the whole idea of taping a knife to a chicken's foot weren't odd enough) was the fact that the blade pointed to the rear, not to the front. How do you fight an enemy with your weapon aimed behind you? I do remember once sitting on the bleachers at a high school basketball game, thrusting my elbow back into the groin of my second cousin in the row behind me. He had been dropping popcorn down my neck. Never even turning my head, I launched that elbow into his soft parts, taking him completely by surprise. When he let out an agonizing "oomph," I turned and said, "Sorry, were those your nuts? Didn't see you back there." That—the element of surprise—might explain the stiletto placement. Or maybe it was to add a measure of whimsicality to the cockfight. Or perhaps PETA had convinced the elders of Ngis to adopt a policy aimed at reducing the psychological trauma that would arise if one chicken looked at the other and saw a blade extended in its direction. Be still, my giblets.

As the preparations continued, a fifth person, the master of ceremonies and eventual referee, moved back and forth between the two sides, inspecting their work. He pronounced the brown cock ready and then same for the white. At this the men holding the birds—who I assumed were the owner/trainer/handlers—started walking around the edge of the square holding them up for the crowd. The noise began to build, and suddenly each person in the crowd started waving money over his head. Several men appeared in the ring to collect the *rupiahs*.

"They are making bets," said Wayan. "Which one do you think will win?"

"The brown one, definitely the brown one," I responded, even though I obviously had no clue.

The noise continued until all bets had been placed. It became quieter for a moment, and then, on a signal from the referee, the two owners approached the center and started thrusting the birds toward each other, all the while gripping them tightly with one hand on the neck and the other on the leg just above the dagger. Like puppeteers, each one seemed to be mouthing derogatory comments for his rooster, like "You call that a wattle?" and "Who's that turkey I saw your hen with last night?" After exchanging a series of insults, the men placed their birds onto the center of the dirt floor. They did so gingerly, likely having seen a few handlers being hoist with their own petards in the past. Then they stepped back to the edge of the arena. I assumed the feathers would begin to fly.

At first the two cocks just stood there and looked at each other. They brought to mind an acquaintance who told me that he had been cut from the Harvard fencing team by his Hungarian coach, who explained, "You are too phlegmatic." The crowd started cheering the roosters on, but they were deep into data processing. After a few minutes the official directed the owners to prod them, which they did gently with some thin bamboo poles. The white bird reacted first, making a squawking fuss. This set off the brown one, and the two began to circle around just inches apart, staring at each other. A little more prodding, and they began to snarl and peck the air in each other's direction, like shadow boxers. The crowd got into it, pleading for brown or white to go for the kill. Responding to these urgings, the brown started flapping his wings, and the white responded in kind. They actually seemed to be making contact for a few moments, when suddenly the white one collapsed onto the ground. No feathers, no blood—it just lay down and died. I had been watching closely, but I had entirely missed the fatal thrust.

Now half the crowd cheered wildly, while the other half let out a collective "Oh shit!" The owner of the dead cock just stood there morosely, while the other carefully captured his bird and an assistant unwound the tape. With the winner disarmed, its owner then picked up the dead white cock, removed and returned the stiletto to the losing owner, and exited with the corpse.

"What happens now?" I asked Wayan.

"Winner takes dead bird home and cooks him for dinner."

"Does he get any prize money?"

"No, only dead bird and much respect in village." The betting masters now appeared and started moving through the crowd, handing out money to the successful bettors. When this was accomplished, two more handlers appeared with two more cocks, a white and a gray. Two men stepped from the crowd and started the taping process. Things were relatively quiet at the moment, and to my surprise Wayan stepped into the ring, pointed at me, and shouted something to the crowd. I assumed it had to do with another communicable disease, but in response many men from around the plaza started moving toward me. Okay, I thought, the *Lonely Planet Guide to Bali* never mentioned anything about cannibalism. I hope they don't want anything more than my wallet.

Actually, they started shouting at me and waving money in my face. That made me suspect that Wayan had declared me available for amorous activity, and with a bad foot I wouldn't be able to run away if things got a little rough. The bidding war for the tall, fair-haired stranger had begun. I involuntarily tightened up. Then I turned to Wayan and shouted, "What did you say to them?"

He chuckled, "I told that you said the brown cock will be the winner. Now they want to know who will win the next fight."

My haunches relaxed a bit, and I decided to play along. "Just tell them it will be the white bird this time."

Wayan reported this to the crowd, and they went wild. They sought out the nearest betting master and laid it all on white. Many of them continued to swirl around me, looking up in curiosity and anticipation. I was afraid someone would step on my foot, and I was still wary of being sold into white slavery.

The second bout started in the same fashion, but these roosters had no fight in them at all. When prodding failed, the official gestured, and someone brought in a large bell-shaped basket and placed it over the birds. This was now going to be the Balinese version of a professional wrestling Doomsday Cage Match. In such close quarters the cocks just couldn't ignore each other, but even then the expected flurry never happened. There was movement in the basket but no pecking, flapping, or squawking. Within two minutes the gray bird was down for the count, again with no gore. This time, however, I had seen the deathblow. It transpired that the white bird had turned away from the gray to gaze outside the basket, possibly looking for an ally in the crowd. In doing so, its stiletto was momentarily pointed back toward the gray. The gray had then moved toward the white, probably to inquire about what the white was looking at. In the process the hapless gray had inadvertently impaled itself on the white's blade. I decided then and there that cockfighting was inherently lame.

The crowd clearly disagreed with my assessment. Once again, they swarmed around me, waving their winnings in my face and shouting what sounded like "Have favor on us, O Steve, we dwell in your light!"

I grabbed Wayan's arm and yelled, "Okay, this is enough. I'm ready to leave."

"That is difficult. They want you to say next winner."

"Tell them I need to change the bandages on my bedsores, and it won't be a pretty sight."

He thought for a moment and then shouted something. The spectators looked very disappointed. Reluctantly, they cleared an opening, and Wayan and I moved toward the alley. As we departed, a few men came up to shake my hand and smile, but many of them just drifted away. When we got to the alley, I asked Wayan what he had told them.

"I say you did not really know who will win. It was only guessing."

Bali was not the paradise I had hoped for, and I was truly disappointed at losing the chance to climb Gunung Agung. Even so, there is no question that I will go back. I will keep my eyes open, my thoughts pure, and my shoes on.

9 *Expedition to Nowhere*

As I was making my plans for Bali, a grander idea was forming in my mind. I would be making two trips to Indonesia, and on the second one I wanted to climb Carstensz Pyramid. At 16,024 feet it is the highest peak in Australasia, the highest island summit in the world, and the highest point between the Andes and the Himalayas. It sits in Papua (formerly called Irian Jaya), one of the Indonesian provinces that occupy the western half of New Guinea. Now this was an interesting mountain.

Carstensz was originally named after Jan Carstenszoon, a Dutch sailor who in 1623 reported seeing a snow-covered mountain as he explored the south coast of New Guinea. Back in Europe his claims were met with derision, due to the fact that these were equatorial waters and snow was out of the question. Perhaps, it was surmised, the good captain had been nipping too enthusiastically on his flask of *jenever*. Subsequent observations—with or without the aid of Dutch gin—vindicated Carstenszoon, and the abbreviation of his surname was assigned to the mountain. The official Indonesian name is now Puncak Jaya (Peak Victory), but climbers still refer to it as "Carstensz." The peak is so remote that it was first explored by Europeans in the early twentieth century and not climbed until 1962. The first ascent was led by Austrian Heinrich Harrer, who had been a member of the first group to conquer the infamous north face of the Eiger in Switzerland, in 1938. Harrer's postwar book *Seven Years in Tibet* was an international best seller, and he lived long enough to see himself portrayed by Brad Pitt in the 1997 film of the same name. At the time I was invited to Indonesia, Carstensz had been recently talked about because of its arguable status as one of the Seven Summits. This is one of those debates that only the climbing community really cares about, and it goes like this: In 1985 a wealthy American businessman named Richard Bass became the first person to climb the highest peak on each of the world's seven continents. To do so, he had hired professional guides, spent lavishly, and essentially bought his way through the ultimate response to a midlife crisis. In a clever bit of marketing he coined the term *Seven Summits* and published a book by the same name.

The problem with Bass's feat was that one of these summits was Australia's 7,310-foot Mount Kosciuszko. It is indeed the highest peak on that continent, but Bass left Carstensz floating by itself somewhere on a large island in the Pacific Ocean. Enter Reinhold Messner, generally considered to be the greatest mountaineer of all time. He argued that Australia is simply part of greater Oceania or Australasia, and thus Carstensz should replace Kosciuszko on the Seven Summits list. That opened the door for Patrick Morrow, an accomplished Canadian mountaineer, who completed Messner's list with an ascent of Carstensz in 1986. Naturally, he wrote his own book—*Beyond Everest: Quest for the Seven Summits*—and the debate raged on. Both versions of the Seven Summits had their supporters and detractors, and as with Roger Maris's home run record, asterisks were liberally dispensed.

Having read Morrow's book, I was excited at the prospect of climbing Carstensz. But a problem immediately surfaced—lack of information. Those days were pre-Internet, so books were the only resources. The only volume I could find was Morrow's, which characterized the ascent as a one-day rock climb, nothing unusually difficult from a technical standpoint. The challenge for Morrow was getting to the mountain, and his book described in detail his two-year quest to obtain a climbing permit. The difficulty was that the most direct approach to the peak lay through private land owned by the Freeport Mine, an enormous gold and copper operation on the southern flanks of the Carstensz range. A rebel attack against the mine in 1977 had resulted in very tight security and the exclusion of visitors. An overland approach to Carstensz from the north would have involved weeks of bushwhacking through virtually unexplored country, so prospects of getting to the mountain were dim. Morrow ultimately involved the Canadian and Indonesian governments, which joined him in lobbying Freeport executives in New York. In his book Morrow speculated that a permit for a new climbing group would be a near impossibility.

I was obviously concerned about the logistics, so I tracked down Morrow's home in Canada and spoke on the phone with his wife, Baiba, who had climbed Carstensz with him. Although she was not encouraging, she did suggest that I get in touch with MAPALA, an outdoor activities organization affiliated with the University of Indonesia. The group had assisted Pat in selling his climb to the Indonesian government, and in fact two of the club's members had joined the team and summited the peak. This led to my correspondence and several telephone conversations with one of the MAPALA's officers, a young journalist named Adiseno. He was enthusiastic about helping me organize my own expedition, and the day after I arrived in Jakarta we met in my hotel.

Like many Indonesians, Adiseno used only one name. He was no taller than five foot four and was thin, bespectacled, and somewhat bookish. He did not look at all like a climber, but that is what he was. He was a key member of MAPALA's mountaineering section, and he was creating a career as Indonesia's first outdoor sports journalist. We discussed MAPALA for several minutes, and I got the distinct impression that many of its members came from Indonesia's elite families. All had attended the University of Indonesia, and they had the time and resources to engage in expeditions not only in their own country but around the world as well. One MAPALA team would be heading to Alaska the following spring for an attempt on Denali. Adiseno himself was organizing a voyage from Jakarta to Japan in a traditional Javanese outrigger sailboat.

Turning to Carstensz, Adiseno described his two ascents of the mountain. The first had been with a European group that had approached from the north. He did not wish to repeat what he described as a dangerous trek through country infested with armed rebels. For him the Morrow approach through Freeport land was the only sane alternative, and it was rather straightforward: From the coastal town of Timika, reached by air, Morrow's group had traveled by bus and then by aerial tramway with mine workers to the Ertsberg mine site at fourteen thousand feet. From there it had been a one-day, relatively level hike into the Meren Valley at the foot of Carstensz. The climb itself was two thousand feet of rock varying from forty to sixty degrees in angle. It was a technical ascent involving ropework, belays, and protection, and the exposure was great, but there were abundant hand and footholds, and the rock was sound. The crux move was rated at 5.8, a level of difficulty that experienced rock climbers can comfortably manage. The ascent was completed in twelve hours. An early start was necessary, because it rains on Carstensz virtually every afternoon.

After reflecting on Morrow's two-year permitting ordeal, Adiseno told me some surprisingly good news. Indonesia was planning a new campaign to promote tourism, including the new concept of adventure travel. The government, with urging from MAPALA and its supporters, had begun to realize that climbers, white-water rafters, and other hardy tourists would bring cash and favorable publicity. Thus, along with other outdoor activities, mountaineering in Irian Jaya would be possible for select groups of visitors. At the start only well-qualified climbers would be accepted. In addition, any climbing party would be required to pay the cost of having several MAPALA members accompany them from Jakarta. The last two points—climbing experience and travel expenses—led us to conclude that I would have to form a team rather than apply as an individual.

"Of course," I said. "That will be no problem. I'll be back next year with a group of first-rate climbers."

I returned to Seattle ready to form a party for Carstensz Pyramid. I had read books about the great Himalayan expeditions and had organized numerous weekend climbs in the Pacific Northwest. Professionally, I had structured complex international business deals and set up many foreign trips. I had never organized an overseas mountaineering venture of this sort, but I assumed I had the necessary skills to do so.

The easy part was my ongoing contacts with MAPALA. Adiseno and I exchanged letters about equipment, costs, and government requirements. We discussed the best time to carry out a climb. We debated about the number of climbers I should bring and who MAPALA would supply as our liaison officers. Overall, the Indonesian side of things seemed to be falling into place.

What I didn't anticipate is how hard it would be to find anyone with the slightest inclination to travel to New Guinea. Seven Summits or not, Carstensz proved to be of little interest to my climbing friends. Seattle probably has more mountaineering talent than any major U.S. city, boasting legends like Lou and Jim Whittaker, Ed Viesturs, and Jim Wickwire, but my acquaintances seemed content enough to stay within the cozy confines of the North Cascades.

After months of phone calls and lunch dates, a group of prospects finally emerged. Most of them were members of Seattle Mountain Rescue, which I had recently joined. All of them had known each other for years, and all were skilled mountaineers. They were relatively unassuming, typical of the Seattle outdoor crowd. The exception was a boisterous fellow named Andy. He was engaging but seismic, the brashest climber in the bunch. I hadn't had much contact with him, but I was impressed with his reputation.

Nine months before the expedition, our Carstensz group—six men and three women—met for the first time, at the home of a veteran climber named Jim. Sitting around the coffee table, we were drinking beer and nibbling on taco chips. I began the session with a description of my meeting with Adiseno in Jakarta, my continuing correspondence with MAPALA, and the climb itself. I had brought along Morrow's book, and we looked at his photos and maps. I had also prepared a rough budget and the start of a to-do list. Overall, everybody seemed enthusiastic in that laid-back, fleece-and-Birkenstock manner of the Pacific Northwest. Andy was especially keen to talk about the technical climb, itching to lead the 5.8 pitch. He was pumped up and ready to go!

We had just started dividing up the next set of tasks when Andy raised his hand and said, "There's one thing you should all know. I'm taking Toni with me."

In an instant there was a *whoosh* as the air was sucked from the room. It felt like the cabin of a depressurizing 747, and I expected oxygen masks to drop from the ceiling. I didn't know who Toni was or what was happening, but I had the feeling everybody else did. There ensued a long and decidedly awkward pause.

A throat was cleared, and someone said cautiously, "Are you sure, Andy? Do you really think she'll fit in?"

"Of course she will. She can climb, and I'll be responsible for her. She's definitely on the team."

A little bit of shuffling, and somebody said, "Hey, look at the time. I've got to get home. Great meeting, Steve. Thanks for putting this together. Let's all work on the plan and get back to you with more ideas." It turned out that everybody suddenly had urgent needs to attend to. That left only Andy, Jim, and me. I thanked Jim, gathered my materials, and slipped out.

An hour later I received the first call, and it went: "Steve, I'm not going to participate. I wouldn't travel to Tacoma, let alone halfway around the world, with Toni."

Then came the second call: "If Toni is in, I'm out."

Before the evening was over, everyone but Andy had quit the team. From the dropouts I was able to piece together that in the mountains Toni was legendary for insulting everyone around her. She was shrill, she was pushy, she was foulmouthed: "Somebody else carry this damned rope . . . hey you, get that anchor set . . . give me the goddamn chalk bag." To Andy, however, she was coquettish and flattering. "Oh, Andy, you're so strong! How did you *do* that!" And more: "Oooh, that seat harness makes you look so *hot!* Belay me, Big Boy."

It was reported that Toni looked great in spandex and that she had attracted a series of boyfriends in the climbing community. Behind her back she was known as the "Pony Express," because she had gone the distance with a succession of riders. As one team member described it, many a climber had had his piton tempered in the fires of her loins, and Toni had given new meaning to a standard mountain command—"Climb on!" Now it was Andy's turn, and he had let it be known that his primal needs were being met in spectacular fashion.

When I suggested that we simply disinvite Andy from the team, everyone said they didn't want to insult him. I argued that if he was getting such great stuff from Toni, he shouldn't really care that much about a climbing trip. But the others wanted to remain on good terms with him, and I suspected that a few of them were on Toni's Life List. No, it was easier for them just to tell Andy that the expedition would be too expensive, too inconvenient, too whatever. The mere mention of Toni had caused the team to vaporize. I had no choice but to throw in the towel.

A year later I heard that Toni had dumped Andy for a dentist.

There was a lot of speculation among the climbing community about whether anyone with a magnifier clipped to his eyeglasses could be capable of satisfying a woman who had been pleasured by so many mountaineers. Nobody ever found out. The Pony Express had disappeared, leaving behind a memory of the Wild West and an expedition to nowhere.

10 *The Mountaineer Unplugged*

Despite the Bali and Carstensz fiascoes, I still intended to climb something on my second trip to Indonesia. Expeditions were clearly overrated, so it had to be a mountain I could do without recruiting a team.

Further research brought my attention to Borneo, a place that many of us would associate with bubbling pots of missionary stew. It lies on the equator in the South China Sea, and at more than 288,000 square miles, it is the third largest island in the world and bigger than the state of Texas. Three-quarters of Borneo's land mass is composed of the Indonesian region of Kalimantan. The remainder, along its northwestern coast, is made up of Brunei and two states belonging to Malaysia. They are Sarawak and Sabah, home to isolated river tribes, riotously colored birds, and countless other subjects for the *National Geographic*. What might come as a surprise is that the island contains a very respectable mountain that is accessible and nontechnical.

The crown of Borneo, at 13,435 feet, is Mount Kinabalu, in the state of Sabah. I have seen it referred to in Malaysian travel brochures as the highest point in Southeast Asia, but that description somehow overlooks Carstensz Pyramid on New Guinea, which lies east of Borneo in what appears on the map to be the same chain of islands. What is clear is that Kinabalu and a few neighboring peaks in Borneo's Crocker Range are the only points that reach above the massive island's tree line. An exposed and dominating summit makes Kinabalu a highly desirable goal. In the language of the local Kadazan people, *Kinabalu* means "revered place of the dead." The Kadazan make annual sacrifices at the mountain's summit to appease the gods and honor the spirits of their ancestors. In a nice, practical touch, the chicken that they ritually slaughter is promptly cooked and eaten. Meanwhile, everybody else sees the mountain as a nature preserve and playground, and the area has been set aside as a national park since 1964. Non-Kadazan trekkers prefer to celebrate a successful climb with chocolate bars and energy drinks.

Kinabalu Park's natural attractions include exotic animals such as the orangutan, the bearded pig, the enigmatic barking deer, and the fabled waxing gibbous. The preserve is also home to the Kinabalu giant earthworm and the ever popular giant red leech. Orchids abound, as do rhododendrons, mosses, and something endearingly named "Miss Gibbs's Bamboo."

The superstar of Kinabalu is the *Nepenthes*, or pitcher plant. Primarily found in the park's cloud forest zone between six thousand and eighty-five hundred feet in elevation, these freaks of nature have adapted to the poor nutrients in the mountain soil by forming vertical cups or pitchers at the ends of their leaves. At the mouth of its pitcher, a plant secretes sweet nectar that entices insects to enter the orifice. Once inside, the unsuspecting prey finds itself sliding down the slick inner wall of the receptacle to a pool of enzyme-laden fluid. If the hapless bug manages to climb back up, it finds the exit blocked by downward pointing spines that ring the opening. Exhausted, it plunges pell-mell back down the slippery slope. The very last thing in life it notices are the carcasses of dozens of other insects floating in the liquid, slowly decomposing. The victims thus provide nourishment for the naughty plant.

Nepenthes are found throughout Australasia and as far away as India and Madagascar, but those found in Kinabalu Park are considered to be the best of the species. In the park they range in color from green and red to yellow and brown, with solids, stripes, and speckles. In size the pitchers may be as small as an inch or two deep, but the prize specimens may be five or six times that size. Among the larger varieties is the legendary *Nepenthes rajah*, whose deep purple pitcher sits close to the ground and stands well over a foot tall. Its mouth may be seven or eight inches in diameter.

The pitcher plant was first named in 1859 by a botanist who declared it to be "one of the most striking vegetable productions hitherto discovered." Three years later a Kinabalu explorer named Spenser St. John reported that he found one *rajah* that contained four quarts of fluid. Another, he noted, held a decomposing rat. More recent reports have confirmed this latter discovery, and the *Nepenthes rajah* stands as the only plant ever found to have eaten a mammal. Think of it. *Little Shop of Horrors* wasn't pure fiction after all.

Two further thoughts on these carnivores of Kinabalu: Early explorers picked them wantonly for transport back to the botanical gardens of Europe. This is now strictly forbidden because the plants are seriously endangered. Government regulations make it a federal offense to "pick, cut, or take pitcher plants" or even to "harm or disturb them in any way." The second point is that several varieties of *Nepenthes* grow alongside the Mount Kinabalu Trail. As if an airy summit were not enough, the Kinabalu climber has the opportunity to view in the wild one of nature's rarest and most unusual plant forms.

Before heading to Borneo, I visited Java to deliver my law lectures. On my final night in Jakarta I was invited by several university officials to a farewell dinner at a restaurant in an upscale hotel. The next day I was flying to Singapore for my connection to Sabah, and I was in a mood to celebrate. We ate an elaborate *rijst tafel*, the Dutch name for a table full of traditional Indonesian foods served over rice. There must have been twenty-five or thirty different dishes ranging from curries to seafood to goat meat, all served with a hot pepper sauce known as *sambal.* I had eaten this food many times in the Netherlands, but it was wonderful to sample it at the source.

At some point in the meal one of my hosts suggested that I should cap the occasion with a festive Indonesian coconut drink. I was anxious to show my gratitude, so I gladly accepted. The drink was served in a coconut shell with a protruding straw. It was sweet, delicious . . . and surprisingly cold. Trying to be discreet, I pried off the plug and looked inside. There I saw the milk and a handful of *ice cubes.*

At this point let me note how careful I had been on both of my visits to Indonesia. In Seattle I had visited the public health doctor, a ponytailed fellow wearing socks in his sandals. He had given me a rump full of shots against cholera, malaria, hepatitis C, typhus in D minor, very berry, and cherry garcia. He had also given me lists of dos and don'ts, such as Do Not Let Anyone into Your Pants, Wash Your Hands Often, and above all Do Not Drink Anything That Has Not Come from a Bottle Opened Six Inches in Front of Your Face. An adjunct to that final rule was Do Not Drink Anything with Ice in It, because of the established fact that all ice cubes produced anywhere between the Tropics of Cancer and Capricorn are made with water ladled directly from toilet bowls.

Until that coconut drink in Jakarta, I had had a perfect record. I had lived by the book, and I had never had the slightest case of gastric distress or anything beyond the occasional weird dream. Upon seeing those ice cubes, I experienced a wave of despair, all the while smiling at my hosts. But then my mind tried to reason that this restaurant was in a very expensive hotel; it must have its own water purification system. The management would never expose their executive clientele to germs, bacteria, viruses, or even social democracy, for God's sake. I convinced myself to relax, enjoy the rest of the meal, and be a gracious guest.

Gastric maladies are a regular feature of international travel, and they have impacted many an excursion into the mountains. Most adventure books and expedition accounts have chosen to ignore the subject, and I believe that as a public service it is time to correct that omission. Therefore, the remainder of this chapter is going to describe upset stomachs, eye-watering cramps, and related forms of distress, and a word of warning is in order: The subject may be just a tad bit indelicate. If, however, you have ever worked on a farm or in a hospital, there should be little ahead that is either new or disturbing. The same goes for anyone who has ever cared for an infant or walked a dog while wearing one of those plastic waste mitts.

If by some chance you do not fall into one of the foregoing categories, let me ask: Where the hell have you been? Are you some kind of germ freak? When you see a brown UPS truck do you swoon the way Tippi Hedren did whenever she saw the color red in *Marnie*? And while we're at it, what self-respecting corporation would have slogans like "The power of Brown" and "What can Brown do for you?" I digress. The point is that if you are squeamish, you are probably going to be better off not reading the next few sections. On a brighter note, if you are currently a thirteen-year-old boy or active mountaineer, what lies ahead may well be the most enjoyable material in the entire book.

Sometime in the middle of the night the hurricane struck. I had felt it coming when waves of nausea began pounding my shoreline. Like many people, I dread the thought of vomiting, and I will do anything to avoid it. Thus, I have a well-developed routine of getting out of bed, walking around, chewing Tums, breathing deeply through my mouth, and sipping cold water. I pace back and forth saying my mantra: "I'm okay. It's not going to happen. I'm okay . . . ." When this works, I am eternally grateful. When it does not, my stalling only provides more ferocity to the inevitable. That's how it was in my hotel room in Jakarta—an hour of shuffling and chanting ended in a mad dash to the toilet and a most energetic Heave-a-Thon. It was both colorful and prodigious. I have no idea how long I sat on my knees hugging the Porcelain Lady, but the clock hardly matters when you are engaged in this sort of activity. To the extent you have any lucid thoughts at all, you are certain that this has been going on for days and days.

The positive aspect of upchucking is that when you are finished, you do feel strangely glad that it has happened. You realize that you are still alive, and you take comfort from that fact that you have purged your body of all of its poisonous contents. You wonder why you fought it off, when you feel so much better now. In my hotel room I eventually found myself lying on my bed, exhausted and drenched with sweat, but certain that I had lived through the worst. As rational thought returned, I realized that it was still the middle of the night, and I recalled that my flight to Singapore was not until the next afternoon. I had time to fall asleep, which I did.

As I showered the next morning, grateful for another day of life, I started thinking ahead to a night in Singapore and the next day's flight to Sabah. I allowed myself a slight smile at the thought of having survived the worst that Jakarta could throw at me. I was a mountaineer and a tough old bird. I was heading to Mount Kinabalu. These sentiments lasted for several pleasant minutes, until the typhoon made landfall. Without warning my intestines tied themselves into figure eights, bowlines, and Prusik knots. I doubled over in pain, realizing that a gastric grenade was about to detonate. Bear in mind that I was still in the shower, and my options were limited. This was a fight-or-flight situation. Should I stand my ground or leap for the loo? In a panic I started flailing wildly and grappling with the shower curtain in Hitchcockian fashion. In the end it came out badly.

Once I emerged from the sewer that I had created in the bathroom, I did my best during intermittent periods of calm to attend to the necessary organizing and packing. As I dashed from the hotel lobby to a waiting taxi, I prayed that I could get to the airport between attacks. In this regard I was mostly successful. Somewhere en route I was hit with cramps, but I fought like a tiger. There is a yoga pose in which you lie supine and alternately tighten your muscles and then relax them. Let it be said that in the back seat of that taxi I tensed every fiber of my body to retain control. I must have looked like one of those weight lifters in the Iron Man competitions. I knew if that I relaxed even the slightest amount, it would literally be all over. In this state of rigor mortis I held on gamely until the cramps eased off.

In the days before security screening, airports were well designed for sufferers of desperrhea, and I was able to pace myself through the ticket line and down the concourse by hopping from one restroom to the next. Once on the airplane I settled into my seat and hung on until we were airborne. When I was free to move about the cabin, I dashed to the comfort station and occupied it during the entire trip. I have read about holiday charter flights returning from Mexico to the States on which half the passengers have contracted Montezuma's revenge and there is a protracted struggle over the water closets. People have been known to stand in the aisle pounding on toilet room doors, wailing and begging to be let inside. Flight attendants have threatened to break down the doors and man-haul the selfish occupants to make room for others. I suffered no such competition, and I traversed the South China Sea in self-centered bliss.

Airplane toilets do leave much to be desired. During a flight they quickly become smelly and unsanitary, so the key is to be first in line, to use the facilities before takeoff or immediately afterward. As the trip progresses, the cabinettes become truly intolerable because Absolutely Nobody heeds the admonition to wipe the sink after using it. Also, after the first few users, the soap dispensers either dispense nothing or send it out in a horizontal stream that lands on your shirt. The paper towels are released either in small shreds or clumps of ten, which explains the clutter on the floor. The air is invariably foul, and the ineffectual ventilator makes a constant whistling noise. Despite all of this, I became rather fond of my chamber on that flight to Singapore. Not only was physical relief available on demand; the psychological pressure was gone. I could actually relax. Then I discovered that from my sitting position I could reach the sink and wash my hands from time to time. On top of this there was an airline safety card for my reading pleasure and occasional announcements from the flight crew. All in all a five-star experience. If I had felt like eating, I'd have had my meals delivered.

My night in Singapore was busy and unpleasant, but I did learn a valuable lesson there: If you drape two bed pillows across your knees, it is possible to put your head down and sleep while sitting on the Throne. Please add this to your list of handy travel tips.

The following morning I flew to the capital of Sabah. Kota Kinabalu at that time was a city of a quarter-million people, a surprisingly modern place that had been completely rebuilt after being razed during World War II. I checked into the multistory Hyatt, a business hotel for the nonadventurous, and promptly flung myself onto the bed. Cramps were hitting me with less frequency, but I was exhausted. I had not eaten since Jakarta, nearly two days earlier. I desperately needed to rest for the following day's two-hour ride to Kinabalu Park.

In the late afternoon I got up to survey my surroundings. The hotel was right on the harbor, and my room offered a commanding view of the South China Sea. Feeling a bit better, I decided to take a short walk, and after a few blocks I stumbled into the Central Market. I had seen it on the map and had anticipated an open-air venue, but this was a massive warehouse. It was dimly lit and smelled like wet straw that had already been used for cleanup purposes. I wasn't sure I had the stomach for it, but I was curious enough to go inside. The market was a well-organized place with rows of stalls where farmers were selling exotic fruits and vegetables. Except for bananas, I didn't recognize a thing. At one stand I saw some spiky melons and asked the seller, "Durian?"

He nodded enthusiastically and held one up, hoping I would buy it. All I wanted to do was sniff it. It was my first encounter with the fabled fruit.

The durian is native to Borneo and a few other parts of Southeast Asia. The size of a cantaloupe, it contains pods whose inner pulp is edible. The flavor of this pulp is said to resemble almonds, raspberries, or custard pudding. Although the fruit's taste is generally described as heavenly, its notoriety arises from its odor. Some have likened it to a dead animal, stale vomit, or used surgical swabs. Celebrity chef Anthony Bourdain has said that after eating it, your breath will smell as if you have been French-kissing your dead grandmother. Food author Richard Sterling has written that the durian's odor "is best described as pig-shit, turpentine and onions, garnished with a gym sock." The smell of a ripe durian can be so strong that many hotels in Malaysia have signs prohibiting patrons from bringing one onto the premises.

Standing in the Central Market with my nose against the fruit, it was just as if I had opened the door of an Iowa slaughterhouse in mid-August. The smell was offal. I recoiled, and in that instant I had urgent business to attend to. Another intestinal attack was mounting, and I was several blocks from my hotel. I scrambled for the exit, leaving the befuddled farmer with his stinking fruit.

That evening I started to feel feverish again, so I just lay in bed, occasionally sipping some water from a bottle I had taken from the minibar. My mind began playing tricks on me. I found myself back in my first day of freshman English class at Iowa State University in the fall of 1966. I was staring at my instructor, James McGurny, and he was doing everything possible to look and act eccentric. Probably no older than thirty, he had his hair slicked back like a gangster, but he also wore narrow women's glasses, skintight black pants, and little pointy-toed boots. He had a small gold stud in his left ear. Sitting cross-legged on the desk at the front of the room, he gazed upward as he drew deeply on some sort of perfumed cigarette. To a group of aw-shucks Iowa farm kids in 1966, he looked like an extraterrestrial, and we squirmed in discomfort.

After a few drags and exaggerated exhales, he looked down at us and said scornfully, "I'm supposed to teach you how to write. Let's be clear that I don't expect any results. Most of you are here for the agriculture or engineering schools, so it doesn't really matter."

Mr. McGurny went on to say that he would start with the assumption that we were functionally illiterate and that initially we would be shown how to put subjects and verbs together. After that, perhaps some complete sentences and simple paragraphs. The grand finale at the end of the term, for those of us who did not drop out, would be essays composed of three or four paragraphs. Should any of us actually demonstrate an iota of writing skill, he would consider accepting us into his limited-admission creative composition seminar in the spring term. In the seminar he would have us expand our creative vocabulary by writing synonyms for "*urinate, vomit,* and *defecate.*"

When Mr. McGurny said those three words out loud, I believe he was trying to intimidate us even more. We had been raised not to say those things in public. Nevertheless, I relaxed a bit and smiled, thinking, "This isn't going to be so tough after all." Heck, from the age of nine my friends and I had been listing variations of the McGurny Big Three. It's what you do during the endless summers in Iowa and during those long winters too. I was well ahead of the game. After I had proven myself in the creative composition class, I might just declare a double major in literature and scatology. Undoubtedly, I had the tools to be a great writer.

Possibly because of Mr. McGurny's English class, I have always been something of a language buff. I carry a phrase book with me at all times when I travel, and I always try to say something to someone in the local tongue. It makes me feel more connected to the place I am visiting and the people who live there. In this regard I have long been fascinated by the fact that French for Travelers, German on the Go, and every other travel book ever published contains the phrase "I have diarrhea." I can understand the necessity of "Good morning" or "Two beers please," because you actually hope to use them. But how many of you (mountaineers excepted) really want to run around in a foreign country announcing that you have a case of the skitters?

Lying in my room at the Hyatt Kinabalu, old phrase books appeared before me like the dancing brooms in *The Sorcerer's Apprentice.*

French: *J'ai de la diarrhea.*

Dutch: *Ik heb diarree.*

Czech: *Jsem průjem.*

German: *Guten Tag meine Damen und Herren. Ich habe ein großes Shitstorm.*

Beyond these basics it has always been curious to me that the word *diarrhea* is so similar to the word *diary.* Is there a connection here? Did the inventor of the diary see fit to record the details of his rioting rectum, or did someone with a serious case of the trots decide it was time to start writing down his daily experiences? In other words, was the first diarist a diarrhist?

In my hotel bed I was depressed and confused. What had begun as a Jakarta jive had morphed into a Singapore tsunami and was now a full-blown case of the Kinabalu kraps. I was riding the gravy train, and it was careening down the tracks. Was I going to die here in Borneo? Did I have consumption, or was that something else? If cowgirls get the blues, do climbers get the browns? Should I just fly home? After canceling Gunung Agung and Carstensz Pyramid, why not make it a trifecta and scratch Mount Kinabalu as well? I hadn't eaten for two days, so how could I possibly have the strength to climb a mountain? If I did set out on the Kinabalu trail in my weakened condition, would I be attacked by a barking deer or a bearded pig? Would I have my blood sucked out by a giant red leech? Would the Cubs ever win the World Series? I drifted off, dreaming of Grey Poupon.

A private car had been arranged by the hotel, and the driver was a Chinese Malay named Peter. He spoke perfect English, and he explained that he ran his own tour business. When he picked me up, there were three people in the back seat. They introduced themselves as Charlie and Martha, a retired couple from Los Angeles, and Dieter, a middle-aged single man from Germany. The three had booked an excursion to Sabah's renowned orangutan sanctuary at Sepilok, on Borneo's northeastern coast. It was a seven-hour drive from Kota, and the only highway to Sepilok passed near the southern end of Kinabalu Park, where I would spend the night.

While I sat quietly in the front, the three in the rear talked on and on about their previous travels. Charlie and Martha: Puerto Montt. Dieter: Perth. C&M: Marrakesh. D: Kathmandu. Capetown, Halifax, Reykjavik, San Juan. It was Centre Court at Wimbledon, and the volleys were fast and furious. The set appeared to be heading for a tiebreak.

The point was driven home to me (and since then confirmed on many other occasions) that there is nothing more boring than listening to other people talk about their past vacations. Now, if you are part of the discussion, things are invariably more interesting, not necessarily because your companions' tales are better, but simply because you are in the game. Actually—if we can be brutally honest here—even when you are participating in a travel conversation, it is satisfying primarily when you are the one doing the talking. You don't really want the other folks to say much more than "Oooh, that's *so* fascinating. What happened next?"

In any event, passively overhearing someone else's travel stories is nearly unbearable. At several points during the drive I wanted to turn around and beg them to cease and desist: "Please, I'll do anything if you just shut up. Take my money, take my wristwatch, my camera. Just say it, and I'll do whatever you want. I'll renounce my U.S. citizenship. I'll convert to your religion. I'll even move to Omaha, Nebraska. Anything. Please just stop."

The road from Kota runs north through the coastal lowlands for fifteen miles before turning inland to the east, where it climbs into the Crocker Range. In approximately twenty miles it crosses a divide and begins to drop into the forested highlands of northern Borneo. The road is paved for its entire length, although its twists and turns inhibit any speed. It was a scenic trip, actually enjoyable when I could forget about my innards and tune out the latest installment of *Passport to Adventure* in the back seat.

What I had not expected in the Crocker mountains was the extent to which the forests had been cut down. I had read that logging was under way, but it was shocking to view it with my own eyes. Clear-cuts are commercially practical, but they look awful. Climbers in the Pacific Northwest have gotten used to seeing them all over the Cascade Range, but the scourge has spread. I remember my disappointment when, taking a vacation cruise north from Vancouver, I found that all along the Inside Passage there were loggers at work. The entire coast of British Columbia was checkerboarded with clear-cuts.

Borneo was once covered with dense rainforests, but for decades they have been leveled to supply the world with necessities such as garden benches and boat decks as well as paper pulp and chopsticks. For many years the logging industry was Sabah's main source of revenue. I could see evidence of impending devastation, and by the early years of this century Sabah had been all but denuded, having lost an estimated 80 percent of its forests. The effects are likely irreversible—take your pick: erosion, flooding, extinction of plant life, destruction of animal habitat, forced relocation of indigenous peoples, global warming, loss of patio furniture. Although smaller in scale than the ruination of the Amazon rain forest, the deforestation of Borneo is a tragedy.

One of the strangest things I discovered in Borneo was that I never had to stray very far from civilization. I didn't really expect headhunters, but I certainly anticipated infested swamps, poisonous snakes, and killer insects. I had assumed that my base camp at Mount Kinabalu would be no more than a tent, erected over a wooden platform if I was lucky. In addition to all of those tropical disease shots I had received, I carried in my knapsack some industrial-strength bug repellant, a snakebite kit, yards of mosquito netting, and a hundred feet of nylon cord with various hooks, clips, and fasteners to erect a safe barrier at nighttime. Imagine my surprise when Peter deposited me at the portico (yes, portico) of the Hotel Perkasa. It was a completely modern seven-story building. After several minutes of emotional farewells with Charlie, Martha, and Dieter, I entered the marble lobby.

When I presented myself to the front desk, the clerk on duty asked whether I would need to borrow any tennis equipment or make a reservation at the nearby golf course. You could have knocked me over with a feather or even a soft breath. I asked him how on God's green earth there was demand for a modern hotel out here in the middle of absolutely fucking nowhere. Actually, I was more diplomatic than that, but I couldn't fathom what this facility was doing here. The clerk's explanation was simple: A Japanese corporation owned an enormous copper mine just down the road, and there was a steady stream of visiting managers and executives. Hence the golf course and other amenities.

On the heels of my arrival and check-in, the surprises continued in my room, where I found two beds, a private bathroom, and a television set. I dropped my knapsack onto one of the beds, sat on the other, and cradled my head in my hands. It was so different from what I had expected. What was going on here? Had I accidentally strayed into another business trip? But then, on reflection, I was grateful that in my current state of health I could sleep between clean sheets and use a flushing toilet. Surely the following night in the mountain hut would be more primitive. Later, for amusement, I covered the extra bed with my mosquito net.

The clerk had told me that the Malaysian cuisine in the hotel restaurant was "superb," but I didn't feel like eating. Instead, I sat in the bar, the only patron at that time, and ordered a bottle of soda water. The bubbles felt good in my stomach. When I was finished, I retreated to my room and turned on the TV. Not surprising, the only live channel was in Malay, but the hotel also had an on-demand movie selection. After passing over Bruce Lee and some Japanese monster films, I chose a romantic comedy with Cary Grant and Doris Day. There I was, in the middle of Borneo with my survival gear spread out on the bed next to me, watching *That Touch of Mink*.

The next morning I desperately needed some food. It had been three full days since my farewell meal in Jakarta, three days with no more than some water and a bit of toast. Fortunately, my intestines had quieted down, and I had survived the night with a few minor tremors but no major seismic events. So, I staggered to the breakfast room and gave it another shot. This time I had a small bowl of white rice and a few sips of clear soup. It tasted good, but I was very nervous about how my system would handle it.

A hotel car drove me several miles to the Kinabalu Park headquarters, elevation five thousand feet. It was a modern building with display rooms, canteen, and souvenir shop. At the front desk I signed in, paid a modest entrance fee, a mandatory guide fee, and a bit more for a van to take me to the trailhead. I could have paid extra for a porter, but I was just carrying my knapsack. At this point breakfast was settling in nicely, and I assumed I had finally seen the last of my galloping grunts.

For most climbers Mount Kinabalu is a two-day outing. You leave the park headquarters during the morning of the first day, take a van to the trailhead, and hike approximately five miles to get to the overnight hut. On Day 2 you leave before dawn for the final twenty-four hundred feet to the summit. Then you try to get all the way down before the inevitable midday rain shower.

The total climb involves seventy-four hundred feet of elevation gain—a good workout but primarily a hike.

My guide's name was Lasius. He was a local Kadazan, no more than twenty-five years old and somewhat shy. In contrast to my mountain togs, hiking boots, and knapsack, he wore street clothing and sneakers, and he carried a plastic sack containing what appeared to be a windbreaker and a small water bottle. We silently sized each other up for a few moments, and then I decided to break the ice. I extended my hand and said, "My name is Steve. I'm a mountaineer." He smiled and accepted the handshake. Then it occurred to me that it was only fair to advise him of my condition.

"I want you to know that I have diarrhea," I said.

He rocked on his heels, glanced down at his hand, and delicately took a half-step back. The corners of his mouth twitched slightly. I wasn't sure if he had understood me. In fact, at that moment I didn't know if he spoke any English at all. I fished in my pocket for my Malay phrase book, turned to the medical page that is always near the back, and said, "*Saya diare*—I have diarrhea." He tilted back again but then caught himself and shrugged as if to say, "So what?"

Not knowing if he had gotten the message, I put my hands on my abdomen and said "*Diare*—diarrhea." To illustrate, I doubled over a bit, made a grimace, and simulated a cramp. "I want you to know in case I have to head into the woods in a hurry." He shrugged again, as if to say, "Look, Mr. Steve the Mountaineer, my people have been here for a hundred thousand years. You are here for two days to bag another peak. I'm happy to walk you up the mountain for a month's wages, but let's not clutter this fleeting relationship with intimate details of what is happening south of your Mason-Dixon Line. Do what you have to do but don't paint me a picture."

He offered a third shrug, and then he said out loud, "You

want see pitcher plant?" I said yes, and he responded, "We go now, get in van."

The van left at around 8:30 a.m., snaking up the Kamborongoh Road to the trailhead at six thousand feet. On foot Lasius and I passed through the Timpohon Gate, a stylish pagoda-shaped hut where we had to show our permits and receipts to enter the trail. The trek began with a few hundred yards of descent to cross a gully, and then the path headed upward.

The temperature was cool and the skies clear. We were in a montane oak forest, said to be one of the most diverse in the world, with over forty oak species identified. The path was generally rocky, and it was occasionally muddy where streamlets flowed. One thing I quickly discovered was that park officials had placed trail markers every hundred meters, a European custom that I find distracting and annoying. On the other hand, there was an open shelter (*pondok*) placed every kilometer along the path, and these struck me as reasonable amenities, nice places to take a short break.

We soon came to a cascade named Carson Falls. The trail brochure suggested it was a good place to fill water bottles (not for me, thanks) and look at the variety of mosses and other plants growing in the wet environment. As we proceeded, the trail became a series of steps formed by tree roots. It was dry at that point, but I imagined that coming down on this section in the rain would be treacherous. We soon arrived at the first shelter, Pondok Kandis, at sixty-five hundred feet, where we paused to look back. In the distance we could see the highway snaking back toward Kota Kinabalu. That dark blue on the horizon must have been the South China Sea.

Resuming our walk, Lasius said, "Now we find some *Nepenthes.*" He suggested I step off the trail and look around. I saw nothing, and I said so. We walked a bit farther, and he told me to look again. I did, and again I reported that pitcher plants must be the figment of someone's imagination. The third time this happened he seemed truly puzzled and walked back with me to where I had been searching.

"See," I said with a note of frustration, "no pitcher plants."

He then started pointing: "Here and here and here—look." Sure enough, there were indeed many pitcher plants growing at eye level on vines, but they were much smaller than I had anticipated. I had been looking near the ground for the big dogs like the *Nepenthes rajah*. I had not thought to look higher for little ones. They were, in fact, the small mountain pitcher plant, *Nepenthes tentaculata*.

The trail steepened, and we climbed a series of staircases made of horizontal logs anchored across the path. At the second shelter we stopped briefly for a drink, and just above that point we entered the rain forest, locally called the "Cloud Forest Zone." This was a place of twisted trees, hanging mosses, abundant ferns, and exotic flowers—exactly what I was hoping to see in Kinabalu Park. The canopy overhead was dense, so there was no direct sunlight, and the air was dank. Lasius mentioned that larger pitcher plants could be found here, but I had little enthusiasm for the pursuit. I said I wanted to keep moving.

Before long I began to feel light-headed and fatigued. Whatever the breakfast rice had done for me, I needed something more, some quick-acting nourishment. In my pack I found a granola bar that I had carried from Seattle, and I wolfed it down. After a brief rest I was ready to resume, hoping for an energy spurt.

Fifteen minutes later I was hit with a fierce abdominal cramp that caused me to double over. My eyes crossed, and my vision blurred. The thought flashed into my head that what I had eaten was, after all, a *high fiber* energy bar. These bars are quite useful for climbers, who tend to get constipated from dehydration. It wasn't exactly what I needed under the circumstances.

Calling to Lasius, who was ten yards ahead on the trail, I shouted, "I'll be right back!" and began crashing through the trees, wanting to get out of sight. The moment was upon me, and my abdomen was welling up like a helium balloon. Fireworks flashed before my eyes as I tore open my clothing, grabbed the nearest tree, and doubled over.

What ensued was impressive. A lion roared, the earth trembled, and the trees began to shake. There were scurrying noises as little forest creatures scattered in all directions. Birds took flight, screeching in fear.

When it was over, the woods were dead silent. Then, as I started to pull myself upright, a shaft of sunlight pierced the canopy above and lit the ground just behind me. Centered in the ray was a long, pale arm with a bony hand and an extended index finger pointing toward the forest floor. I heard a sonorous voice proclaim, "Behold what thou hast done."

Obediently, I turned and beheld. There in that pool of light was a large pitcher plant attached to its vine just above the ground. I was looking down the maw of an exquisite and endangered *Nepenthes rajah.* It was what I had been hoping to see, but certainly not this way. To my everlasting mortification I had filled the *rajah* with my personal business. What was once a wonder of nature now hung there cheerlessly, a foul caricature of a Starbucks grande no-whip mocha.

I staggered back to the trail to find Lasius sitting on a log, waiting for me. When I emerged from the trees, he looked up and asked, "You find pitcher plant?"

I responded, "Uhhh, no. Not my day."

As we proceeded up the path, my abdomen felt better, but my enthusiasm was at its nadir. I no longer gave a damn whether I succeeded in ascending this ridiculous mountain. I would simply slog to the overnight hut and head back in the morning. This was the dumbest thing I had ever done—travel halfway around the world, get violently ill, and then set out to climb a thirteen thousand–foot peak. I swore that as soon as I got home, I would sell all my climbing equipment.

Then it started raining.

The effect was rather curious. First, it turned the trail into a slimy, slippery obstacle course. Then, despite my waterproof clothing, it soaked me to the skin. But for some reason I started laughing. My response might have begun as hysterics, but the rain actually seemed to wash away my self-pity. I realized that there was nothing special or unusual about my circumstances. There were fifty other climbers on the mountain that day, some heading up and some coming down. All of us were wet and tired, God knows how many of us had the runs, and there was little we could do about any of it. Nobody had forced us to come here. This was our choice, our form of recreation, and that was that. I would get through it.

Soon we encountered the first of perhaps thirty climbers who were returning from the summit. They were drenched, and their misery was exacerbated by the difficulties they faced in walking down the wet trail.

A couple of drowned rats, Lasius and I eventually stumbled into the Laban Rata Resthouse, the overnight hostel situated on a rocky outcropping at eleven thousand feet. It was two o'clock, about five hours after we had left the trailhead. Normally, I would have felt silly taking that much time to travel only five miles, even with the five thousand feet of elevation gain. Yet factoring in my lack of inner fuel and the time it had taken to assault the *Nepenthes rajah*, I was satisfied enough at my performance. Even more, I was pleased that I hadn't died along the way.

Like my hotel outside the park, Kinabalu's Laban Rata was a surprise. I had expected some sort of primitive shelter, but this was a large two-story building. In the Pacific Northwest an overnight climb means carrying tent, sleeping bag, stove, and food. Laban Rata was positively European—a hostel with beds, showers, toilets, and a restaurant. It had been built a few years earlier by British troops as a gesture of goodwill to the people of Sabah—thanks very much, Tommy. The building had a dozen or more bunk rooms itself, and with a few smaller buildings nearby, there were beds for approximately one hundred guests. Websites and other sources today indicate that reservations at Laban Rata must be made six months in advance. On my visit there weren't more than fifteen other guests, so it was quiet. Especially pleasing was the fact that I was assigned a four-bed room by myself. It had an electric heater, and soon my clothes were hanging on the bunks and drying out.

For a Seattle climber a hot shower on a mountain is pure fantasy. At Laban Rata it was real, and after my encounter with the pitcher plant I needed it desperately. No waiting lines, no soapy mess from previous users—pure bliss. I did some necessary hand laundry as well, and I felt like a new man. I resolved that I would go for the summit the next day. Taking a table in the restaurant area, I sat down to relax awhile before retiring early. I wasn't sure if I would eat anything, but for starters some hot tea would be just what the doctor ordered.

All of the other guests were Asian, and they were clustered in small groups at other tables. One man saw me sitting alone and came over to introduce himself. He was David Choi, and he invited me to move to his table, where he presented his teenage daughter, a girlfriend of hers, and David's cousin, Bill Choi. All four were from Kota Kinabalu, and all were ethnic Chinese. David said that he was an administrator at the Sabah Foundation, a government agency that was created in the 1960s to manage Sabah's timber wealth. Bill owned several small businesses. David said he was climbing Kinabalu for the tenth time; the others hadn't tried before. Over tea my new friends and I spent several hours comparing life in Kota and Seattle. We talked about schools, houses, and shopping centers, and yes, we shared travel stories. This was the first companionship I had had since Jakarta, and it was as welcome as the hot shower.

Eventually, the girls said that they *needed* to have some dinner. The restaurant—actually more of a canteen—had a variety of foods, heavy on the rice and noodles. David explained that the food was pricey because it was carried up the trail by porters. There was a helipad nearby, but it was used only for emergencies, not for transporting supplies.

Sparing the details, I told my new friends of my recent digestive problems, and David strongly suggested I try again and eat some rice and broth. With some trepidation I did, and the initial results were pleasing—the carbs and David's encouragement made me feel much better. At seven o'clock I turned in for the night.

After a light breakfast of rice and hot tea, Lasius and I left the hostel at 3:30 a.m., somewhat later than the other parties. I had heard that the final climb would take two to four hours, and I was betting we would be at the top before sunrise at six o'clock.

Just above Laban Rata is a series of roughly made staircases snaking their way up through scrub bushes. Here and there the steps were steep enough to count more as ladders than stairs. Fortunately, it had dried out during the night, and footing was relatively secure. The night sky was moonless and heavy, and we proceeded in near total darkness. Lasius carried a small flashlight, but I was grateful to have my headlamp. Nighttime is cold at 11,000 feet, even on the equator, and both of us started out wearing jackets and caps. Fifteen minutes into the hike I was warmed up and able to stuff the outerwear into my pack. After forty-five minutes we passed the mountain's highest huts at 12,500 feet, a station called Sayat Sayat. The views both up and down from there are spectacular but not, of course, in the middle of the night. At that point the brush disappeared entirely, and we stood at the base of the summit plateau.

The upper thousand feet of the mountain is a pluton, a mound of granite formed from a ball of molten rock that was forced up through the Crocker Range. Ten thousand years ago a retreating glacier carved the granite into undulating, striated slabs. To a mountaineer, slab walking is heaven—as long as the rock is dry. If wet, it is treacherous. We stepped onto the slabs, took a few careful steps to gauge the texture of the rock, and then started moving upward. At this point several thoughts came into my head. First, I was grateful that Lasius was doing the route finding in the dark. Second, my digestive system was behaving to the point that I actually felt good. Most of all, I was glad to be there, doing some real climbing.

As we began negotiating the slabs, I saw lights bobbing just above us, indicating the other climbing groups. According to the manager at Laban Rata, some of them had left as early as two. I said to Lasius, "Look, I'm feeling great. Let's go faster and get around the other groups." We soon caught up with the first pair, who were climbing very slowly. In the steeper sections there were thick white ropes strung as extra handholds, and these climbers were hanging on nervously, hauling themselves up with great effort. Then we overtook a team of three, also panting and struggling. Then David and his party, who were moving cautiously. We exchanged greetings in the dark, and David said, "Glad you're feeling better. See you on top."

In short order Lasius and I had passed everyone. Up and up we scrambled for nearly an hour. Then the angle of the slope eased off, and in the distance I could make out the jumble of boulders that is the summit of Kinabalu. It was five fifteen, and the sky was turning from black to gray.

Once we stopped climbing, the predawn cold hit me. I quickly put on all the clothing I had in my pack and found a place just below the summit to sit against a rock. Lasius did the same. We drank some water and shared some crackers I had taken from Laban Rata. This was time to rest and simply wait for the sunrise. Mercifully, the air was calm.

After half an hour of crouching at the summit, we had company as the other groups began to arrive. The Choi party joined us at six, just as the horizon was bursting with streaks of red, yellow, and orange. We congratulated each other, and they sat down to rest. At six fifteen we all stood together to witness a spectacular sunrise, one of the mountaineer's hard-earned rewards. With a laugh I recalled a family vacation to Maui, where my wife and I had roused our three young teens at 3:30 a.m. for a long drive to see the sunrise atop ten thousand–foot Mount Haleakala. Tourist brochures had proclaimed the mountain dawn to be a "breathtaking sight that will bring tears of joy to the onlooker." All we got was a bone-chilling, swirling gray mist. The kids were mortified and grumpy for the rest of the day. In contrast, Kinabalu delivered its best, to the appreciative oohs and aahs of the successful climbers. Looking north, we could see the upper reaches of Low's Gully, a mile-deep chasm that splits the mountain in two. Beyond it stood Victoria Peak, the slightly lower twin of our summit, Low's Peak. Even farther off was the Sulu Sea (of *Star Trek* fame) and a cluster of offshore islands. As daylight began to warm us, we took pictures of each other, ate some snacks, and prepared to leave.

At six thirty Lasius and I headed down, but I told him I wanted to climb St. John's Peak, a prominent spire a quarter mile from Low's Peak. Together we scrambled down Low's and up a series of smooth slabs to St. John's airy summit. As we came down, a few other climbers noted our success and decided to give it a try. To the consternation of my guide, I then said I wanted to climb South Peak, a Matterhorn-shaped fang of rock a half mile away, at the southern edge of the summit plateau. Lasius said he wasn't interested but would wait for me at the saddle between South Peak and St. John's. Alone, I scrambled up the 12,900-foot pinnacle. Its final pitch was sharp indeed, and a summit monument provided a convenient final handhold. I stayed there only a few moments and then hustled back to join the impatient Lasius. By seven fifteen we were heading down the mountain.

One of the pleasant aspects of ascending in the dark is that on the descent everything is new. The summit plateau displayed itself as an impressive jumble of needles and outcroppings with colorful names like Lion's Head, Donkey's Ears, Ugly Sister, and, appropriately, Phallus. Also before us were the rain forest, the distant Sabah coast, and the shimmering South China Sea. I had to constantly remind myself either to stop and gaze or to ignore the scenery and concentrate on my footing. Looking down the climbing route, the exposure was occasionally impressive, a fact entirely missed in the dark. As I descended, I freely used the ropes to speed my progress.

By nine o'clock Lasius and I were back at Laban Rata, eating a warm breakfast of tea and noodles. Then I packed my overnight things, filled my water bottle, and checked out. As we left, we saw that the summit had clouded over, but mercifully it never rained on us. The mountain gods gave us a break that day, and all those stairs and rocky sections of trail offered firm footing. By noon we were back at the Timpohon Gate, where I signed out and was given a certificate memorializing my successful ascent.

This had been a great excursion. In addition to making the summit of Mount Kinabalu, I had seen a marvelous sunrise and made new friends. To me, however, my most significant accomplishment was that during my overnight in the hostel, nine hours of climbing, twenty-four hundred feet of elevation gain, and a descent of seventy-four hundred feet, I had eaten four times and had not taken a single dump.

Several months later, after I had regaled my friends in Seattle with tales of my impressive ascent of Mount Kinabalu, David Choi sent me a clipping from the *Sabah Daily Express*. The article reported on the second annual Kinabalu International Climbathon, a running race from the Timpohon Gate to the summit and back. It had taken place a few days after our ascent. The winner was a park ranger named Salikun Nasun, who completed the round-trip in two hours, fifty-five minutes, and thirty seconds. He apparently had not stopped along the way to look at the pitcher plants.

"Minister Pooh-Poohs Stories of Man-Eating Plant,"
Singapore Straits Times, July 27, 2004:

KOTA KINABALU, SABAH. The Minister of Natural Resources for the Malaysian state of Sabah today dismissed persistent rumours that an immense pitcher plant (nepenthes), capable of devouring a human being, has been observed on the slopes of Mount Kinabalu, Borneo's highest peak.

"These plants occasionally exceed their normal size," he stated, "but we do not believe that such extraordinary growth is possible."

Scientists at the Southeast Asia Institute for Botanical Research confirm that floral gigantism is known to occur in nature, but is extremely rare. They note that there are no naturally occurring nutrients in the meager alpine soil of Mount Kinabalu that would support plant growth of the sort that is being suggested.

Despite these disclaimers, authorities at Kinabalu Park have warned hikers to be especially careful and to stay on designated trails at all times.

Northern Exposure

On my first trip to Norway I was calling on fishing industry clients in the west coast town of Aalesund, and I was invited to dinner at the home of a banker named Harald and his wife, Gudrun. Over cocktails we chatted about vacations, and my hosts enthusiastically handed me a photo album from their recent trip to the Canary Islands. It was typical stuff, with snapshots of people lying on blankets, standing in shallow water, and sitting on beach chairs with colorful drinks. What I wasn't prepared for was the fact that in most of the pictures Gudrun was topless. She was a strikingly attractive woman, and let's just say that she had outstanding features. Now if there is a social convention for how to react when you are shown photos like that in what is otherwise a polite situation, it escaped me. I found myself sucking in my breath and repeating, "My oh my." At one point Harald pointed to an artistic shot he had taken of a bronzed and exposed Gudrun stretching out her arm to feed a hovering seagull. When he asked me what I thought, I responded "They're amazing . . . I mean . . . the picture . . . this picture that you took . . . it's amazing." I'm not sure how I made it through dinner, because every time I looked at Gudrun across the table, well. . . .

A year later I paid a return visit, and this time I took along one of my law firm partners, a short-statured and bookish man named Monty. As we checked into the Parken Hotel, where I had previously stayed, we looked at a photo display in the lobby. There were pictures of the hotel's conference rooms, restaurant, and fitness center. One photo showed two stunning blonde women enjoying the hot tub. I suggested that we had enough time to relax in the spa, and Monty jokingly asked whether the two women would be there. I assured him that they would.

Imagine my shock when we entered the spa and found the hot tub occupied by the very women from the lobby photo. With a slight swagger I said to Monty, "Just stick with me." He and I were wearing swimsuits, but I quickly noted that the ladies were not, and their towels were hanging on the wall six feet behind them. As Monty and I climbed into the tub, one of the women hastily reached for a button that started the bubbles. Okay, fair enough, I thought, but let's take this to the next level.

"Hello, I'm Steve, and this is Monty. We're from Canada."

Helga and Ingrid, or whatever their names were, did not respond or even make eye contact with us. Instead, they began to talk to each other in low tones, in Norwegian of course.

Helga: "Look at these losers. They're wearing swimsuits."

Ingrid: "The tall one has nice legs."

"They're both wearing glasses, probably to see our body parts more clearly." In fact, we were wearing glasses, and they were steaming up. We found it necessary to remove them frequently and wipe them.

Ingrid: "Let's get out."

Helga: "The towels are over on the wall."

"Great, they want to watch us climb out, the little twerps."

"You go get the towels."

"No, you do it."

"We can wait them out, while their little sausages cook down to bite size."

There was a pause in the conversation. We waited patiently.

Helga: "I'm getting hot, and it has nothing to do with them."

Ingrid: "I'm turning into a prune."

"Well, go and get me my towel."

"You do it."

"Shit, let's get out together, very slowly, and give these Canucks a good show."

Monty never forgot his first trip to Norway.

Norway is wonderful, and my fondness for the country goes well beyond a photo album and hot tub. Let me put that into perspective. My family's roots are in the Netherlands. I have worked and studied there, and my son was born in Amsterdam. I love the Dutch people and feel that I am one of them. And then there is Greece. After six or seven visits I am under its spell. Even more so with Italy, whose language and food are pure music. I have a soft spot in my heart for Slovakia, where I taught for one year. Switzerland is in my dreams, and I could happily disappear into France, Portugal, Spain, or England. Nevertheless, if I could reincarnate in any country on earth, it would be Norway.

For me the most beautiful sight in the world is a snowcapped peak hovering over a body of water. With so many mountains and so many fjords, Norway has an endless supply of picture-postcard vistas. So does western Washington, and it is no surprise that a substantial number of Norwegian emigrants gravitated to Seattle in the nineteenth century. On the other hand, it is a complete mystery why even more of them opted for Minnesota, Wisconsin, and North Dakota. Okay, cheap farmland was a draw (only 3 percent of Norway is arable), but didn't they miss the scenery?

By nearly any human measure—health, education, social welfare—Norway offers the highest standard of living in the world. It is also the cleanest place you will ever visit. With vast reserves of offshore oil, the country is ridiculously rich, so much so that in two separate public referenda its people have opted to stay out of the European Union on the ground that EU membership would offer them absolutely nothing.

I suspect that an additional reason the Norwegians decided

against joining the EU was that Denmark and Sweden were in the process of doing so. Norway has a long-standing love-hate relationship with its neighbors because of their shared history. Fully independent only since 1905, Norway had spent the nineteenth century in an imposed union with Sweden and the four hundred years prior to that under Danish control. In modern times the three countries share close commercial and cultural ties, but Norwegians have an ingrained resistance to outside domination.

Norwegian identity can reveal itself when the people comment on their Nordic cousins. Here's what a friend once shared over a beer: What does Norway do with its high school dropouts? Answer: Send them to Sweden as teachers. Or try this one: A Norwegian shrimp fisherman sails into port with his holding tanks full. A man on the dock asks him how much he has caught. "Well," says the fisherman, "I've got five million Norwegian shrimp and one Danish shrimp." The other man asks, "How do you know that one of them is Danish?" "Because he's standing on top of the pile waving his little arms and shouting 'I'm a lobster. I'm a lobster.'"

The Norwegian lifestyle is immensely appealing to anyone who enjoys outdoor activity. Like Seattle and Denver, Norway is a place where many people measure themselves not so much by their possessions or careers, but by their weekends in the countryside. Nearly every Norwegian family owns a mountain hut for winter ski touring, and in their short summers everyone is hiking, fishing, and sailing. They are a hardy lot who relish fresh air and physical challenge. It's in their blood.

The Norwegians' Viking forebears sailed to Iceland, Greenland, and Canada across the storm-tossed and frigid North Atlantic—in open boats. In 1888 a young Norwegian biologist named Fridtjof Nansen led a team in the first crossing of Greenland. They did it on foot, pulling heavy sleds, and much of the time they were chewing on rawhide because their stoves had failed. Then came Roald Amundsen, who in 1912 was first to reach the South Pole. He and his men were so well prepared that they came home from Antarctica fit as a fiddle and ready to pose for that year's Men of the Pole bare-all calendar. Meanwhile, Robert Falcon Scott and several companions reached the Pole a month after the Norwegians, but on their return the entire English team perished of starvation and poor oral hygiene. In late 1992 a Norwegian lawyer named Erling Kagge made the 840-mile journey to the South Pole on skis, and he did it alone. He made up for lack of companionship by consuming six thousand calories a day. Americans toast their baseball stars, while people in most other countries cheer their football champions. In Norway they celebrate their explorers.

The inherent Norwegian toughness is on display indoors as well. I have never seen such a hard-partying crowd. I remember a few all-nighters in college, but my friends and I quickly outgrew the practice. Not so in Norway, where birthdays, anniversaries, weddings, and graduations are cause for a celebration that begins with dinner and ends with breakfast. Let me offer an example.

When our friends Dagny and Hans-Christian got married in Oslo, my wife and I flew over for the occasion. The ceremony started in the courtyard of a rented mansion. In response to a single question by the magistrate, the bride and groom each responded with one word—*Ja*—and the formalities were concluded. Then it was upstairs to the party room, where sixty people were crammed in at long tables. The sit-down dinner started at six, and during the course of the evening every single person in the room gave a speech that was followed by a stand-up toast to restore circulation in our legs. My wife and I didn't understand a word, but we consumed a lot. Around midnight the dancing began. By three o'clock we couldn't take any more, and we begged someone to call a cab. As it turned out, the taxi drivers had retired for the night, and we found ourselves walking several miles through the streets of Oslo back to our hotel, in the rain. I later learned that the Norwegians had held on until eight in the morning.

The wedding was typical for a formal event in Norway. If it had been a smaller group at someone's home, there is a pretty good chance that at some point the hosts and guests would have started taking off their clothes and heading for the sauna. If it had been winter, they might have dashed outside in the altogether to roll in the snow. And here I want to offer a note of clarification: Do not get the impression that Norway is one big nudist colony with a seat at the United Nations. Far from it. When working, shopping, and going to a movie, the Norwegians are always fully clothed. The only indoor places they like to strip down are hot tubs and saunas, while outdoors they will expose themselves only at beaches, swimming pools, parks, gardens, terraces, and balconies.

As I am writing this, I have been to Norway forty or fifty times, and I am in a position to say that its people are enthusiastic about life, filled with good humor, and liberal in their thinking. They are essentially secular, setting foot in a church only for baptisms and funerals. Most significantly, they are unfailingly warm and generous. Thus, in all respects they are the polar opposite of the dour immigrants in Garrison Keillor's Minnesota. Lake Wobegon has everything to do with the American Midwest and nothing whatsoever with modern Norway.

Some preachers believe that every exhortation must end with a note of caution, and here is mine: Do not travel to Norway for the food or the weather. Norwegian cuisine consists of overcooked meat and boiled potatoes accompanied by twenty-seven varieties of pickled herring, and that's just breakfast. The weather is either cold and wet (June through August) or cold and snowy (the other nine months). Survival tip: Get outside for some vigorous exercise and then quickly return indoors to that bottle of aquavit.

The first time I sampled Norway's mountains on foot was near the city of Stavanger on the country's southwestern coast. I had arrived on a Friday morning after a sleepless overnight flight from Seattle. My clients picked me up at the airport, and after I had a quick shower, we went into a series of meetings. By the end of the afternoon I was a zombie, and I was looking forward to my bed. My clients had other plans, beginning with cocktails, then dinner. After dessert and coffee I started to thank them for a nice evening, when they informed me that there was more. Stavanger, home to Norway's offshore oil industry and thousands of expatriates, is known as a swinging town, and my clients wanted to prove it. The city's liveliest and loudest nightclub happened to be in the basement of my hotel.

I do not like discos, and I hate noise, so the next four hours were pure hell. For a long time I just couldn't bring myself to bail out, so I gamely stayed with my hosts, standing cheek to jowl with Texans, Brits, and misbehaving Arabs. Finally, around two in the morning I shouted, "I think I am going to die." My clients had a good laugh and said I should go up to my room for some sleep. Then they added that two of them would pick me up at seven to go hiking.

If I was a sorry sight in the lobby five hours later, Paul and Jøstein were even worse. They looked as if they had been run over by a truck. They had stayed at the club until six and had gone home just to change clothes. Paul's girlfriend, Thorhild, was driving, and she was not amused with her tough-guy companions. During our short ride to a ferry the three of us fell asleep in the car, and during the voyage each of us found a bench to lie on. Thorhild bought three cups of coffee and forced them on us.

Our destination was Preikestolen, which translates as the "Pulpit" (literally, the preaching chair). It is the most dramatic feature in any Norwegian fjord.

When a continental glacier retreats, as at the end of an ice age, it scours the earth's surface as it moves. Where the underlying rock is soft enough, the receding ice gouges out a channel. At the same time, when the remaining, more resistant bedrock is freed of its heavy glacial blanket, it may float upward in what is referred to as a "rebound." The combination of carving and thrusting can result in a deep gorge bordered by high mountains. If this activity takes place near the sea, water may seep in and partially fill the new valley, thus creating a fjord. Our English word, not surprisingly, comes directly from Norwegian. Interestingly, the original Norse term *fjǫrðr* referred to the act of traveling over water, because coastal inlets were convenient for transportation. The related English verb *ford* also refers to movement over water, as in crossing a shallow river or stream.

In a narrow fjord the exposed walls may be sheer, nearly vertical. From the tops of those precipitous faces, however, the land will usually slope gently away. As a result, a mountain flanking a fjord will have a distinct shape and will offer two dramatically different options to the climber. Its water side will present a daunting, technical ascent, while its back side may be a walkup. On Preikestolen we took the easy route.

The tourist track begins at a parking lot at 886 feet above sea level, and from there it is a straightforward hike of two and a half miles, with 1,100 feet of elevation gain. We started in forest and gradually climbed into an alpine zone with little more than bushes and scrub. In mid- to late summer the path is bare and easily negotiated, but we were hiking in early May, and much of the time we were walking on snow. That is not normally a problem for me, but I didn't have hiking boots, and my basketball shoes did a lot of slipping and sliding. On top of that, I was exhausted, my stomach was queasy, and my ears were still ringing from the nightclub—in those respects I was a typical Norwegian on a typical Saturday morning.

Nobody spoke much for the ninety minutes of our walk—that is, until we arrived at the top. Reaching the crest of the mountain mass, we could see in the distance a narrow finger of water. "That's the Lysefjord," Paul said. "We're going right up to the edge for a better look."

The Pulpit is a square column of stone that juts out from the high plateau. It has a flat top roughly eighty feet on each side.

One edge of the pillar is attached to the mountain, while three drop straight down. The outermost side falls two thousand feet directly to the water below. Walking out onto the lid of the Pulpit is not difficult, and standing in its center is comfortable enough. It's only when you start working your way to the edges that it gets hairy. You can hear the wind rushing up the sides, and eerie voices seem to be rasping, "Jump, jump."

In a typical summer more than 100,000 people will hike to the Pulpit, and on a good day hundreds may be crowded together on the top to enjoy the breathtaking views up and down the Lysefjord. The four of us had no other company on that gray and windy day. We took turns photographing each other, but none of us got very close to the edge. When Jøstein pointed out a metal spike fixed at the very lip, I was persuaded to crawl to it on my belly, grasp it with both hands, and extend my head into space. There I learned for the first time that under the right circumstances I can be stricken with intense vertigo. I nearly passed out from a combination of exhilaration, abject terror, and nausea, and I hung on for dear life. I am surprised I didn't get sick, but if I had, the fierce updraft would have driven everything into the sky, and I would have gone down in history as the first person to literally throw *up*. I have seen pictures of people standing at the very edge and even sitting there with their legs dangling into the void. My only thought on that is: No Fucking Way.

Years later I was on a cruise that sailed into the Lysefjord for a sea-level view of the Pulpit, and the captain invited me to the bridge to give a narration over the ship's public address system. I hadn't talked about the hike for a long time, but as I described it to my fellow passengers, the feeling of vertigo returned. I found myself drawn to the edge of the rock, ready to answer the Siren's call and leap into the void. I started sweating and clutching a rail to maintain my balance. Fearing that my lecture would lapse into amplified heavy breathing, and hoping to avoid getting sick all over the ship's navigation charts, I did a quick wrap-up—"In closing, folks, just remember that moving ice is called a glacier. Thank you for your attention"—and headed straight to the Oceanview Bar for a Bombay Sapphire martini, extra dry and straight up.

After visiting Aalesund and Stavanger, I began to make regular stops in Bergen and Oslo as well, but I was merely city hopping to visit clients, and on the map of Norway I was just nibbling at the edges. When a trip came up in late June one year, I decided it was time to tack on a few days and head inland to the mountains.

In most states and countries there is no doubt about the highest spot above sea level, but I am aware of two places where the question has been muddled. One is my home state of Iowa, which for a hundred years identified as its high point the Ocheyeden Mound outside the town of Ocheyeden (pop. 545) in the northwestern part of the state. The hill is a random deposit from the receding Wisconsin ice sheet, and it rises slightly above the surrounding cornfields to a height of 1,655 feet above sea level. It is the crown jewel of Osceola County, whose other attractions include a border with Minnesota, two tiny lakes, and a nine-hole golf course. When I was a boy, we once drove the forty-five miles from Sioux Center just to see the Mound and marvel at this wonder of God's creation. This was before we took our vacation to the Rockies.

In 1973 Ocheyeden's world was turned upside down. A surveying crew creating a topographic map of the region discovered that ten miles northwest of the Mound lay a farm lot whose barely perceptible "summit" measured in at 1,670 feet, and at that precise spot stood a receptacle for feeding hogs. A nice couple named Sterler woke one morning to learn that their swine were feasting at the high point of both Osceola County and the entire state. They named the place "Hawkeye Point," and Iowa proudly stepped forward as the only jurisdiction whose upper extremity was a slop trough nestled in pig shit. Actually, this was metaphorically apt because, as writer Paul Engle has noted, the state of Iowa is shaped much like a hog facing to the east.

Its snout is that great curve of the Mississippi River jutting into Illinois, while its tail is my own northwestern corner along the Big Sioux. Just below the tail Sioux City occupies an unenviable position, but it could be worse—whatever Sioux City produces is certain to trickle down and land squarely on Council Bluffs. *Sic simper swinum*, or, as we learned in Latin class, *pigo — pigare — squeali — gruntum.*

Norway has also had difficulty determining its high point, and in defiance of all odds the Norwegian narrative also involves a pig. The country is famously shaped like a spoon, with most of its population living along the coastal perimeter. The bowl of the spoon consists entirely of mountains, and at its center stand the highest peaks of all—the region called Jotunheimen, "home of the giants." Few people live there, but its valleys and ridges are peppered with alpine hostels joined by well-developed walking paths. When I decided go for a hike, my first question was "What is the highest mountain in Norway?" I was not expecting people to respond, "Well, that depends."

In the heart of Jotunheimen lies Visdalen, a valley named after the rushing Visa River, whose most prominent feature is the MasterCard Falls. Towering above are the nation's two highest peaks, and of them, Galdhøpiggen is the more easily defined. Its rocky summit rises to 8,100 feet, and its name refers simply to the peak (the Norwegian word is *pigg*) in the Galdhø area—Galdhø-piggen. Across the valley soars a sister peak, Glittertind, which is named after the Glitra (glittering) River. Glitra's peak (*tind*) also glitters, because its summit is a pointed crest of hard-packed and windblown snow. And that is precisely the problem. From year to year the elevation of Glittertind's white mantle varies, depending on winter snowfall, summer temperatures, and hours of direct sunshine. The rock beneath Glittertind's snowcap reaches a height of 8,045 feet—well below the summit of Galdhøpiggen—but at times the top of the snow may reach to a level *above* its neighbor. Thus, the highest point in Norway depends on the vagaries of that season's snowpack.

The year I traveled to Jotunheimen my maps showed Gald-høpiggen at 2,469 meters, its permanent height, but Glittertind was identified at 2,470 meters (8,103 feet). I had decided to tackle Glittertind, but shortly before my climb I was told that after the maps had been printed, Glittertind had shrunk by more than a meter. I adjusted my plans accordingly.

Most climbs of Galdhøpiggen begin at Spiterstulen, a modern hostel at road's end, high in the Visdalen valley. At an elevation of thirty-six hundred feet, the main lodge and a dozen outbuildings stand just above the Visa River. I arrived in the evening after a grinding all-day drive from Aalesund through the most spectacular terrain in the world. In fact I was suffering from Scenic Overload, a potentially fatal condition that can be alleviated only by hearty food and strong drink. As I registered at Spiterstulen and requested the Cure, I also told the desk clerk of my plans to climb Galdhøpiggen. He said that conditions were excellent, and he added, "To climb to the top of Norway on Midsummer's Eve is a special experience."

I hadn't given much thought to the calendar, but the next day was June 23. The Christian church observes June 24 as the feast day of John the Baptist, and thus the twenty-third is Saint John's Eve. The Norwegian words are *Sankt Hans Aften*, but under questionable German influence they run it together as *Sankthansaften*. Despite its name, however, the twenty-third has no religious significance in contemporary Norway. It is, as the hotel clerk described it, Midsummer's Eve, the day to celebrate the summer solstice.

With the technology available today, many of us live without regard to the rhythms of nature. At night we turn on the lights, in winter the furnace, and in summer the air conditioner. Seasons come and go with little effect on most of our activities. To be sure, we complain about the weather, but we can avoid its influence, and most of us completely ignore markers such as the equinoxes and solstices. Nevertheless, without even realizing it, our lives may reflect how our more nature-bound ancestors responded to the cycles of Mother Nature.

Take Christmas, for instance. Many of us forget that there is only a 1 in 365 chance that Jesus was born on December 25. Nobody is sure of the exact date, but December 25 is what the early church fathers selected. At that time it was the winter solstice, and our forebears may have been drawn to the symbolism of light coming into the darkness. On the other hand, they may have wanted their feast day to co-opt or coincide with the pagan midwinter celebrations then prevalent in Europe.

Like the birthday itself, the Twelve Days of Christmas (December 25 to January 6) carry astronomical significance. The word *solstice* comes from the Latin *sol* (sun) and *sistere* (to stand still), and in our northern latitudes the sun reaches its nadir and appears to hold its position for twelve days before reversing direction. Technically, the solstice occurs at a particular moment on December 21 or 22, but without sophisticated instruments the perception is that of a series of equally short days and long nights. The church seized on this phenomenon to create an extended Christmas season that begins with the Nativity and ends with the Epiphany.

Before we take a closer look at today's midwinter celebrations and their midsummer counterparts, I want to give a brief description of several Norse gods who are relevant to the festivities. The mighty Thor, son of Odin, created thunder with his hammer. His lightning would often strike a towering oak tree, the natural connection between heaven and earth. Thor's second cousin Freyr was more laid-back. He was the god of agricultural bounty and was often depicted straddling a boar, presumably for transportation. Most significant for our purposes were Frigga and her son Baldur. One of Odin's wives, Frigga was the patroness of marriage and fertility. She gave birth to Baldur at midwinter, but years later he was stabbed to death at midsummer with a sharply pointed branch of mistletoe. He was cremated and then brought back to life by Frigga's tears, which fell as mistletoe berries. In hindsight wouldn't the resurrection have been easier to pull off if it had been done before the cremation? In any event Baldur and Frigga became identified with the beginning of the sun's return at midwinter, the solar zenith at midsummer, the cleansing fire, and the overall cycle of life, death, and rebirth—a very nice package.

At midwinter the ancient Nordic people would build large outdoor fires to ward off the darkness and call for the sun to come back. Or, they might drag an oak log into the fireplace, douse it with lighter fluid, and let it burn for twelve days. Another option was to incinerate an entire tree, preferably outside, or bring one indoors and decorate it with dripless candles. Whatever its form, the fire would summon Baldur or Thor while incidentally providing light and warmth for cavorting. People would join hands in a circle and dance around the flames, and a boar would be roasted in Freyr's honor. Some folks added spice to the occasion by hanging mistletoe, and under the sacred plant they would honor Frigga through acts associated with fertility. Throw in some mead, and it was a friggin' party.

Traditional midsummer celebrations made use of the midwinter elements but with a few twists. Bonfires were lit to celebrate the longest day of the year and to beg the sun not to begin its retreat. People danced around the fire, and anyone who successfully leaped over the flames was ensured good luck in the ensuing year. Those who didn't leap quite high enough or far enough were delivered their bad luck instantaneously. No risk, no reward. A counterpart to the midwinter tree was a midsummer pole wrapped in greens and flowers, somewhat akin to the maypole in Britain. In Sweden the vertical post had a cross-arm with two large rings attached, and the whole thing screamed "phallus and testicles." There was circle dancing around the pole, and the men would try to maintain self-control by thinking about baseball.

Although Frigga was present at midwinter, she was queen of

the midsummer celebrations. Maidens would honor her by wearing flowers in their hair and engaging in ritual baths. Children carried out mock weddings, and the countryside was believed to be crawling with nymphs and fairies—you will recall that Shakespeare employed these elements in *A Midsummer Night's Dream*. Taken together, the midsummer rituals encouraged the fertility of crops and procreation of the human race—all thanks to Frigga.

Carrying the symbols forward, many of today's Christmas customs reflect the ancient midwinter practices. Norwegians still dance around the Christmas tree and build bonfires, and on New Year's Eve they light sparklers and fireworks. The English eat roast boar or its less intimidating cousin, ham. They also hang mistletoe, although beneath it they limit themselves to a sanitary, dry-mouthed peck on the cheek (no tongue, please, we're British). In several countries the Yule log is retained, and the English word *yule* derives from the Norse *hjul* (wheel), reflecting the cycle of the seasons. Around the world people decorate their homes and cities with lights, and they prepare special dinners. At the end of the festivities, perhaps on Twelfth Night, many celebrants burn the Christmas tree—one last tribute to Baldur.

Now maybe it's because I have lived through too many American Christmases and may be suffering from overexposure, but it seems to me that my fellow countrymen have done more than any other nationality to purge the meaningful elements from our year-end celebrations. We pay no mind to the sun cycle and little regard to the Nativity, instead filling our lives with office parties, Santa-themed Ice Capades, and sappy made-for-TV movies on the Lifetime network. Any traditional symbolism that we have retained has been crassly placed into the service of pedal-to-the-metal, take-no-prisoners, 24/7 Power Shopping and other extravagances—think of professionally decorated Christmas trees, Lexus sedans wrapped in giant bows, anything from Nieman Marcus, and chocolate Yule logs (damn those French, they're really onto something with that Bûche de Noël). Humbug on us all.

While reminders of the midwinter traditions live on, albeit obscenely, I cannot think of a single American custom that celebrates Midsummer's Eve as an astronomical or religious event. We have summer rituals like picnics and Fourth of July fireworks, but nothing we do is intentionally related to the solstice or John the Baptist. Nevertheless, midsummer is alive and well in other countries, and here is where we work our way back toward Galdhøpiggen.

Modern Scandinavians think that midsummer is a very big deal. In Sweden they still erect—if that is the correct word—their suggestive midsummer poles and dance around them. Throughout the northern latitudes people celebrate the solstice by gathering flowers, mushrooms, and herbs, and in Latvia midsummer is called "Herb Day." One herb that is said to bloom precisely on that date is St. John's wort, which is used to treat depression, and I'm not sure if the two are connected, but late June is also a favorite time for marriage ceremonies in northern Europe. Yes, I know that June is also the wedding month in the United States, but I'd bet that not one in a thousand American couples would even think of the solstice in setting their date. One of the most enduring Scandinavian traditions is the building of bonfires on Midsummer's Eve. Anywhere you travel in the Nordic countries, in fields or along the fjords, people celebrate the longest day with Baldur's fire.

Simply enjoying the sun is the key to midsummer for many Scandinavians, probably because for half the year they suffer through so much darkness. Even after the vernal equinox, as daylight lengthens, the weather may be cool and cloudy, so it is no wonder that a bit of sun makes the Nordic people so giddy. In the 1960s there was a series of films—*Mondo Cane, Mondo Pazzo,* and *Taboos of the World*—that purported to show bizarre slices of real life in different countries. My high school friends and I went wild over the finger amputations, mouth castration (don't ask), and other gross behaviors, but oddly, one scene that that I haven't forgotten was rather tame. It showed Swedish office workers bursting forth from their buildings when the summer sun came out. The narrator mentioned that direct sunshine was so rare that normal activity came to a halt and everyone went outside to catch a few rays. How lucky for me that my Midsummer's Eve in Norway was a blue-sky day.

From Spiterstulen, at timberline, to the top of Galdhøpiggen is an ascent of forty-five hundred feet. For most people it is a hike of three to four hours, and there is no technical difficulty whatsoever. In fact, two-thirds of the elevation gain takes place on a well-worn path that zigzags steeply up through low-lying tundra grass. For me that part of the trek was tedious and boring. At the crest of the slope, however, the scenery opened up, and the remainder of the climb was an exhilarating stroll up a broad and gently sloping ridge, most of which was covered with well-consolidated snow. The upper section was pure delight under clear skies and a warm midsummer sun.

During the trail slog I paused now and then for a drink or a bit of food, and each time I noticed another hiker below me. Whenever I stopped, he did too, but at first I didn't think much of it. When I reached the snow, the views were so spectacular that I began to take more frequent breaks to look around and shoot photos. As I did so, I realized that the man following me stopped each time and watched me, and when I started moving again, so did he. At one point I decided to sit on a rock and eat a snack, figuring the fellow would catch up, but he didn't. He again stopped climbing and waited for me to continue. Eventually, his behavior rattled me because I couldn't figure out what the man was up to.

I have read about Himalayan climbers suffering from hypoxia, and some have reported delusions such as the feeling that someone was hiking beside them. That just couldn't be the case here, because there was plenty of oxygen on Galdhøpiggen, and that man following me was no figment of my imagination. He was the one behaving strangely, not me.

As I moved along the ridge, I paused half a dozen times, and so did my shadow, always about fifty yards back. Finally, in exasperation, I turned and started walking down to him. He looked startled, but he stayed where he was as I approached.

"Hello," I said as I came to him. "Is everything all right?"

He was a thirtyish, slender man with a mop of dark hair. He looked shy but quite normal. In response to my greeting, he said, "Yes, I'm fine. Why do you ask?" He accent was British.

I wanted to respond, You're creeping me out, dipstick. What are you, some kind of sociopath? But instead, I said, "Well, I couldn't help but notice that you've been staying the same distance behind me, and every time I stopped, you stopped. I was curious why you didn't just catch up."

"I didn't want to bother you," he replied. "I thought you might want your space."

It might have been appropriate for me to point out the obvious—that it was far more peculiar for him to stay behind me as he had been doing, than to come up to me or pass me. However, he seemed harmless, so I simply introduced myself and suggested that we sit down and take a break together.

His name was Martin, and he was indeed from England. He was an atmospheric scientist spending the summer on leave from his research job at the Amundsen-Scott South Pole Station. He had been down there for six years, including several polar winters. As he described his life, I began to understand his behavior.

According to Martin, working in Antarctica gives a person an unusual combination of intense feelings. On the one hand, you are isolated from the rest of the world, cut off from your friends and family, and if you winter over, you have no way to leave in an emergency. On the other hand, you are living in very close quarters with other people, much as you might on a submarine. Personal privacy is lacking, and the mannerisms of your colleagues can drive you crazy. So, it is not unusual for a person in Martin's situation to crave companionship while dreading it at the same time. Putting two and two together, I concluded that he had wanted to hike with me but had been afraid to make the first move. Then again, it was all a bit too much. All I wanted to do was climb the mountain. I didn't care if I was alone or not, and I really wasn't interested in anyone else's psychological complexities.

"Well," I said. "Let's just head up together."

As Martin and I neared the summit, a group of climbers was approaching on the slope off to our right. There were eight of them, six men and two women. All were dressed in nothing but gym shorts. Actually, the women also wore bikini tops. Everyone was walking with ski poles.

We converged at the summit hut, which was closed, and after Martin awkwardly excused himself, I sat to talk with the group. They were members of a ski club from the nearby town of Høyanger, and they had come up from the northeastern side of the mountain, where there was a small ski resort. From the top of the chairlift they had hiked up carrying their skis and had stashed them just below the point where I first saw the group. They were going to have lunch on top, walk back to their skis, and leave the mountain with a long, graceful run on spring snow.

In contrast to sad-sack Martin, the skiers were a gregarious lot, and we enjoyed our visit together. They were delighted to meet an American on Galdhøpiggen, and they were very interested in the Seattle climbing scene. When I felt comfortable enough, I mentioned that it seemed a bit strange for all of them to be sitting around essentially in their underwear while I was fully dressed in my climbing clothes. They had a good laugh at this, and one of them said, "Stephen, today is midsummer. This is how we enjoy the sun in Jotunheimen."

When the skiers left, I decided to explore the summit area. I found a tripod marking the high point, and I walked along the rim taking pictures. Galdhøpiggen has the classic shape of a Norwegian mountain, with a relatively gentle slope coming up from Spiterstulen and a back side that drops straight down. However, the valley below the sheer wall was not a fjord—we were much too high above sea level for that. Rather, it was a glacier, the Storgjuvbreen, which was flanked by impressive peaks with what to a Norwegian must be divine-sounding names: Storgjuvtinden, Storgrovtinden, and Skardstinden.

Normally, I would have started down after seeing the sights, but the skier's comment about midsummer had impressed me. I was in no hurry whatsoever—I could get back to Spiterstulen in less than two hours, it would be light until 11:00 p.m., and I was staying another night. Better to kill time on the mountaintop than in a spartan hotel room. I decided to find a comfortable place to stretch out and drink in the sun.

I found my spot on a slab of rock facing the glacier. I cushioned my hips with spare clothing, lay my head on my knapsack, and drifted off to sleep.

When I awoke, I was greeted by a remarkable sight. Not ten feet away, stretched out on an adjacent rock with her eyes closed, was a naked woman. Let me correct that—she was wearing hiking boots. She was buxom, had long blonde hair, and was either a true blonde or had gone to a lot of trouble to look like one. Breathless, I lifted myself onto one elbow and stared. Was I awake or dreaming? It was Midsummer's Eve, after all—had fairies come to Galdhøpiggen to mess with my mind, as Puck had done in Shakespeare's play? I felt my face to be sure I hadn't been turned into an ass. No, it was still me, but this phenomenon had to be supernatural. Perhaps Frigga had returned to earth to warm herself beside me in Baldur's sunshine.

When my elbow started to hurt, I realized that I was very much awake and that the goddess was human. That only made things worse because I didn't know what to do next. Should I say hello? Should I ask for directions—"Pardon me, but do you know the way to Oslo?" Maybe I should offer her some sunscreen. I once read about a man who claimed the first nude ascent of Mount Rainier, and his biggest concern was having his privates exposed to ultraviolet rays. I could be noble and save this woman from a painful burn. I could offer to administer the lotion myself. Maybe she . . .

"Snap out of it, Weenie Boy," said a voice in my head. "This is as close as you get. It's midsummer in Norway, and this is nothing more than a typical Norwegian enjoying a rare bit of sun at the summit of Galdhøpiggen. Don't insult the entire Nordic culture by gawking. If you can't go with the flow, then gather up your gear and leave quietly."

I couldn't, and so I did.

So the Last Shall Be First

It is odd to describe a mountain in the past tense. You talk that way about your climbing experiences, such as "I led that pitch" or "We skirted the crevasse," but stepping back to say something about a peak itself usually calls for present tense—"Snowdon is the highest point in Wales" or "The Matterhorn dominates the skyline above Zermatt." Not so with Mount St. Helens.

St. Helens was the jewel of the Pacific Northwest. Not as dominating as Washington's Mount Rainier or Oregon's Mount Hood, the 9,677-foot neighbor was nonetheless lovelier and more sublime. Often referred to as "America's Mount Fuji," its elegant cone defined what a volcano should be, and its symmetry beckoned countless artists and photographers. To the native Klickitat the peak was a maiden. To climbers she was an easy but prized conquest simply because she was so damned beautiful.

By the fall of 1979 adventurers had been climbing St. Helens for well over a century. The first known trek to the top was reported by Thomas J. Dyer, founder of Portland's now venerable *Oregonian* newspaper. On August 27, 1853, Dyer and three other men reached the summit from the mountain's south side. Fred

Beckey describes the feat as "the first climb of a major snow peak on the Pacific Coast."

I needed a glacier ascent to complete the requirements of the Mountaineers basic climbing course, and the season was nearly over. The club roster listed St. Helens as the final snow outing of the year, but when I tried to sign up, I learned that the climb was fully subscribed. I called the leader, a lawyer named Jon, to plead my case. "Look," I explained, "I need this climb to graduate, and I'm moving to Europe at the end of the year, so it's now or never." Jon agreed to add me to his team, and that is how, on September 23, 1979, I became one of the last people to climb Mount St. Helens.

A few days before the weekend, Jon called to coordinate ride sharing. Most of the party wanted to drive down on Saturday afternoon and spend a few hours relaxing at Spirit Lake on the mountain's north side. They would enjoy stunning views across the water to the mountain, and they would stop at the iconic Mount St. Helens Lodge to pay their respects to its proprietor, a former bootlegger and full-time curmudgeon named Harry Truman. I had never been to St. Helens, and I wanted to see its attractions, but I told Jon that I didn't have any spare time. I would have to do those things on my next visit. Jon was also juggling several commitments, so he and I agreed to travel together during the evening.

After sleeping next to our cars at the Timberline Campground, Jon and I met the rest of the party early Sunday morning, and we set out in the chilly fall weather carrying only our day packs. Late in the season the lower two-thirds of St. Helens was clear of snow, revealing a series of parallel ridges running up and down the mountain's north slope. Between these rock ribs lay narrow gullies filled with fist-sized pieces of brown and black pumice as light as popcorn balls. We found it impossible to climb the loose material—the pumice was even less stable than the climber's usual bane, scree and talus. With each step we slid back to where we had started, like walking on a treadmill. As a result, we moved onto the spines of solid rock and enjoyed a pleasant scramble up to a prominent buttress known as the Dog's Head.

Just above us lay the Nelson Glacier. At the snow's edge we strapped on our crampons, roped up, and continued in teams of three. Had it not been an official Mountaineers outing, we might well have dispensed with the ropes. The glacier was so melted out that its crevasses were glaringly obvious. It would have taken a deliberate act to fall in, and we simply walked around the cracks as we threaded our way upward. Here and there we were dwarfed by ice towers known as seracs.

Near the mountain's crown we traversed to the upper reaches of the Forsyth Glacier, where a gap in the skyline offered an entrance to the broad, shallow summit crater. The top point of the mountain, at one end of the crater, was a snow-covered hump. Near it there were outcroppings of exposed lava rock, where we sat to savor the view—Mount Hood to the south, Adams to the east, and Rainier just north. Even in autumn the icy mantles of these giants glistened in the midday sun. In all, perhaps twenty-five climbers shared the summit that day. Nobody in my group was in a hurry, and ours was the last party to leave.

On the descent we paused at the snowline, unroped, and carefully packed away our glacier gear. We stuffed ropes and harnesses into our knapsacks and strapped ice axes and crampons on the outside. Looking at the lower part of the mountain, we decided against working our way down the ridges. Rather, we calculated that we could move much more quickly by entering the gullies and negotiating the loose pumice with exaggerated downward strides on our heels. On snow this type of controlled sliding is called "plunge-stepping."

To avoid getting in each other's way, we separated, and I found myself in my own private ravine. After cautiously trying a few steps to get a feel for the pumice, I discovered the proper technique and with a whoop of joy started sashaying downward. In a series of rhythmic whooshes, I moved rapidly and began to pick up speed. I would be at the bottom in a matter of minutes.

Suddenly, just ahead of me, I spotted a piece of solid rock protruding from the rubble. It was directly in my path, and I was moving too fast to avoid it. Without really thinking, I decided to land on it with both feet and bounce over it. My plan worked, but with one unexpected add-on. When my feet hit the boulder, my downward momentum and the spring in my legs caused me to launch up and out, like a diver from a diving board.

I flew into the air and inexplicably turned a forward somersault. By the time I rejoined the slope, I was feet-down again, still in tuck position, and I landed with a jolting crunch. My heavy knapsack drove my torso forward, and I heard (and felt) a distinct crack as my lower ribs impacted against my thighs. I was amazed that I hadn't damaged anything except my ribcage, but my sense of relief did not make the last section of down-climbing any less painful. By the time I gingerly exited the gully, my teammates were wondering what had taken me so long.

Shortly after our day on St. Helens, the winter storms moved in, and the autumn climbing season came to an end. I have often wondered . . . were we the final humans to stand on its summit? We very well might have been. Of course, it is possible that a handful of mountaineers ascended the peak during the ensuing months, but at that time winter climbing in the Pacific Northwest did not have many practitioners. Even today, with the increasing popularity of backcountry skiing, few climbers are willing to endure the hallmarks of winter climbing: long approaches in deep snow, short days, foul weather, and the constant threat of an avalanche. So, if anyone was masochistic enough to climb St. Helens after we did, I will give them credit for having made the mountain's Last Ascent.

Alpine activity for the sane resumes in March and April, as days lengthen, snow consolidates, and the sun makes more frequent appearances. Just as the spring of 1980 was arriving, however, and just as the climbing community was waking up to another year of weekends in the high country, Mount St. Helens was put off-limits.

The trouble began on March 20, when seismologists recorded an earthquake near the peak. Then another and another, and on March 25 Forest Service officials issued an emergency edict: No Trespassing. And well that they did, because two days later a cloud of ash and steam shot into the sky from the mountaintop, and a black 250-foot hole suddenly appeared in the summit crater. Further eruptions enlarged the opening to 1,700 feet across and 850 feet deep. At the same time an enormous bulge began to appear on the north slope of the mountain. The Klickitat maiden was suffering from a serious case of gastric distress.

On the morning of May 18 all hell broke loose. First, a series of violent earthquakes caused the north face of the mountain to slide down. Then a lateral blast blew out what was left of the north side, and the summit was launched heavenward. Every tree within seventeen miles to the north of St. Helens was leveled, and a black plume shot eighty thousand feet into the atmosphere. The high ash cloud was carried by the jet stream, its dust fell across the United States, and remnants circled the globe. Poisonous gasses moving three hundred miles per hour killed every living thing near the mountain, including fifty-seven people. One victim was Harry Truman, whose refusal to evacuate his home had made him something of a media darling during the previous weeks. The old man, his sixteen cats, pink 1956 Cadillac, and the lodge itself disappeared under mudflows that obliterated Spirit Lake and caused extensive flooding in nearby rivers. In all, it was the most cataclysmic eruption ever recorded in United States history.

Everybody in the Northwest remembers exactly what they were doing on that Sunday morning when they learned of the event. The woman who is now my wife recalls shopping for plants at a nursery near Seattle and looking up to see an ominous black cloud billowing to the south. A friend was sitting in church when the minister announced the disaster in apocalyptic tones. Meanwhile, a lawyer I know was wrapping up an overnight date by rocking his sailboat in Puget Sound. At their moment of fulfillment he and his passenger were engulfed in the thunderous rumbling of St. Helens, and as he reports it, his companion ran her fingers through his hair and sighed, "That was wonderful."

As luck would have it, I missed the show entirely. Some months earlier I had taken a job in Amsterdam, and I first heard of the eruption when I showed up for work on Monday morning. As I walked into the office, several of my coworkers jumped up and started waving Dutch newspapers in my face. I was stunned, but they were even more incredulous when I told them I had climbed that same mountain just before I left Seattle. Later, when the stratospheric ash cloud blocked enough sunlight to cause a noticeably cooler summer in northern Europe, my colleagues speculated that somehow I might have been responsible.

As for St. Helens itself, Princess Leia had morphed into Jabba the Hutt. When viewed from east, west, or south, the mountain's symmetrical cone was reduced to a squat and unattractive mass. Its north side was completely gone, and it emerged from the black cloud as a horseshoe-shaped, hollowed-out peak with a crater 2,000 feet deep and more than a mile wide. The 8,363-foot high point of the jagged crater rim—the new summit—was 1,314 feet lower than the plateau on which I had eaten my lunch eight months earlier. Except for its location on the map, it was literally a different mountain.

The ultimate measure of St. Helens's reduced state was the fact that the Mountaineers summarily removed it from their roster of significant peaks in Washington. Many years earlier the club had designated it as one of Six Majors, along with Rainier, Adams, Baker, Olympus, and Glacier Peak. The list was created to recognize the accomplishments of a serious climber, and completion of all six ascents was celebrated with the awarding of a Six Majors pin to wear on your Tyrolean hat. After the eruption the Mountaineers dropped St. Helens like a hot cinder—they now bestow a Five Majors award. The same thing happened recently to Pluto, which has been downgraded from planet to space lump. If you were lucky enough to climb St. Helens before the spring of 1980, you are part of a vanishing breed. You can claim your Six Majors pin, but be aware that the icy winds of old age are beginning to penetrate your GORE-TEX.

*

St. Helens lay in mountaineering limbo for seven years. Volcanic activity continued as a new lava dome began to build up on the crater floor, and the Forest Service considered the mountain too dangerous for public access. Furthermore, a spate of lawsuits had followed the eruption, with the federal government and the state of Washington as defendant stand-ins for God Almighty and Mother Nature. Litigation-shy officials did not want to open the mountain to recreation only to have additional people swept away, leaving behind family members with legal claims.

Mountaineers are inherently antiauthoritarian, and they didn't like being told that St. Helens was too dangerous to climb. They complained and lobbied and complained some more, but the Forest Service turned a deaf ear. When a few journalists were given access and wrote tantalizing stories about the views from the new crater rim, the climbing community became even more restless. A number of scofflaws were rumored to have made "pirate ascents" at night or in white camouflage clothing, and there were occasional reports of people being arrested and fined for such misbehavior. Finally, in late 1986 the Forest Service announced that the mountain had stabilized sufficiently and that it would be opened on December 1 of that year. For bureaucratic reasons the date was pushed back several times, until "any day now" materialized as May 4, 1987.

Although I had moved back to Seattle in 1982 and had been climbing actively, I didn't think too seriously about an Opening Day ascent of St. Helens until a television reporter called. Jack Hamann of Seattle's KING-TV Channel 5 had received my name from a producer at the station, and he was looking for someone to lead him and a camera crew to the summit on May 4. In addition to shooting footage for a later feature, he hoped to broadcast a live report for the evening news. Would I be interested? That was an easy yes. I thought it would be great fun, and I was curious to see firsthand what the new mountain looked like.

Jack and I met to arrange logistics. After I described the climbing details, he proceeded to educate me on the gear that would be required to broadcast from a remote location. Bear in mind that in 1987 the words *digital* and *micro* didn't exist in their current sense, and portable satellite transmitters were only a gleam in some engineer's eye. As a result, we were faced with an equipment list that was daunting, and Jack insisted on at least two of most items to ensure a fail-safe operation. My notes (and God only knows why I still have this piece of paper) reflect the following:

- 2 shoulder cameras—8 lbs. each
- 2 tape decks—8 lbs. each
- 6 batteries—30 lbs. total
- 8 videotapes—1 lb. each
- 2 microphones—2 lbs. each
- 1 scanner—2 lbs.
- 3 two-way radios—2 lbs. each

So, eighty-two pounds of TV equipment plus their carrying cases and all of our climbing gear. I asked Jack how big his crew was, and he said it would be him plus two camera operators. When I suggested that we might want another climber or two to help with the load hauling, he readily agreed.

I contacted Al Errington, a six-foot-five-inch character who bore an uncanny resemblance to Clint Eastwood. He was a prominent member of Seattle Mountain Rescue, an occasional climbing partner of mine, and a longtime friend. Most important, he was a Minnesota Norwegian, and because of our common roots in the Midwest, we had shared many a story about prairie life. Big Al was a certified expert on the nocturnal habits of North Country farm boys and their complex relationships with livestock, and as such, he was an entertaining companion on any weekend outing. Happy to join us, he promised to dust off his collection of tall tales and flat-out fabrications. He also agreed to bring his wife as an additional load carrier.

Climbing is normally a quiet sport, a chance to escape the bustling city and share the wilderness with a few friends. The first day on St. Helens II was something entirely different. It began on the warm, clear evening of May 3, with at least a hundred cars crammed into the trailhead parking lot and along the approach road. The mood was festive as die-hard climbers, reporters, and assorted hangers-on wandered about swapping stories and drinking beer as they would at a football tailgate party. Our KING-TV group joined the scene in a company van, and after sorting our loads for the following morning, we sat together on some rocks to get acquainted and throw back a few brews of our own. Al was in fine form as he regaled us with graphic stories of rescue missions and colorful descriptions of the lowlife characters he had climbed with. I didn't believe much of it, but the TV crew seemed to be impressed.

At one point Jack pulled me aside and said, "Thanks for bringing Al. He's great. I'm going to interview him during my live report at the summit tomorrow, but don't tell him. I want to keep it spontaneous."

The most straightforward route up the new St. Helens was its south side, through the woods to timberline and then up a feature called Monitor Ridge. Because it was early May, the entire

climb was on snow, and we carried both snowshoes and crampons. Neither proved to be necessary—the snow was perfectly
consolidated and not icy.

We had more than four thousand feet to climb, but it was
straightforward. Actually, the route had little variation, and it
was tedious. We set an easy pace because of our heavy loads and
because we literally had all day to get to the summit. The first
broadcast would be at five that evening.

As we climbed, long-legged Al couldn't seem to hold himself
back. With each stride he separated himself from us, soon disap-
pearing from sight. Eventually, we would find him sitting in the
snow, relaxing and waiting for us. Then, as we arrived at his resting
place, he would hop to his feet, move out, and vanish again. The
rest of us stuck together, and soon Jack started grumbling that
Al wasn't much of a team player. The higher we got, the more
Jack vented his frustration, and when we decided at one point
to redistribute some of the weight, he was, in his own words,
"highly pissed off" that Al wasn't available to carry more. I tried
to explain that Big Al was the strongest, fastest climber I had
ever known and that he really couldn't help himself, but Jack
was not buying it. He told me that he would not be interviewing
the Minnesota Stud on his broadcast.

The party atmosphere of the previous evening continued at
the top of the mountain as one group after another arrived and
engaged in backslapping and photo taking. The descent would
be easy, so people lounged in the warm sunshine, alternately
napping and chatting. Now and then they would stand up and
walk to see the star of the show, the crater rim.

No amount of climbing experience can prepare you for the
top of Mount St. Helens version 2.0. A typical mountain summit may be a mound of snow, a pile of rocks, or even, rarely, a
pointed pinnacle. New St. Helens is entirely different. From the
center of its crater rim, the two sides of its horseshoe extend out
left and right, like arms poised for an embrace. Behind you is
Heaven, the gentle white slope that you ascended. Before you is

Hell, a brown chasm emanating sulfuric fumes. In the distance, beyond the extended arms, looms Mount Rainier.

Everyone on that Opening Day reacted with shouts of surprise and wonder, marveling at the view and standing in awe of the power that had so dramatically changed this mountain. Seven years of waiting were forgotten. We were part of history, the first people to climb this peak legally. We were jubilant, and yet we felt so small.

Our party had work to do. First, Al and I set snow anchors and attached climbing ropes, and then all of us in the party took turns tying in and walking to the crater rim. We discussed the best locations for establishing shots and other video footage. Al and I began working with the two camera operators, belaying them to various points for filming. After an hour or two the preliminary work was done, and Jack started preparing for his live report. There is a direct line of sight from the summit of St. Helens to Portland, Oregon, and the TV crew could shoot a signal directly to KING's network affiliate in that city. The feed was instantaneously bounced to Seattle. Once the initial connection was established, Jack was able to have a videoconference with his studio producers.

Meanwhile, several helicopters came and went, depositing other television crews onto the slopes just below us. Jack was particularly disdainful of these freeloaders, as he called them, saying that he had wanted to earn his summit broadcast by doing the full climb. He did note that the KING helicopter was positioned with extra gear in the nearby town of Castle Rock, but it would be used only in case of equipment failure. Jack truly hoped that he could do his report with what we had carried up the mountain on our backs.

With everything set up, we had more than two hours to kill before the first broadcast. We made ourselves comfortable in the snow, looking south toward Mount Hood, Mount Jefferson, and other peaks in Oregon. As we stretched out, I casually mentioned to Jack that if his gear hadn't been so ridiculously heavy, we might have carried some beer to the top. He chuckled and agreed, and a moment later he stood up and walked a few paces away, engaged in an animated conversation on his radio. I assumed that he had thought of some additional details to discuss with the station in Seattle. When he had finished, he rejoined us for further idleness.

Thirty minutes later another helicopter approached from below. I expected Jack to make some scathing remarks, but as the machine turned and hovered a hundred feet below us, I noticed a prominent 5 on its side. It was from KING-TV. One of the camera operators scampered down the slope and crawled to the cockpit door, opened it, and extracted two brown bags. Spare batteries, I thought. The cameraman knelt with his packages as the helicopter lifted up and floated away. Returning to us, he reached into the first sack and produced two six-packs of Rainier beer. From the second he removed hamburgers and French fries. It was the best summit food I have ever eaten.

Jack's first live report opened the five o'clock news hour. He repeated the segment at six, and afterward he told me that there would be a third feed at six thirty. Then he told me that he wanted to interview me. He was still angry at Al, and I was apparently his only alternative. In our segment together Jack identified me as a Seattle lawyer and mountaineer who had climbed St. Helens shortly before its eruption. He asked for my impressions of the new climb and the crater rim, and he asked me to open my jacket and display the dress shirt and necktie I had worn for the occasion. Nothing I said on camera was memorable, but I garnered my fifteen minutes of fame. During the next few weeks a number of people stopped me on the street and asked if I was the lawyer who had been interviewed on Channel 5. Months later, sitting on the summit of Vesper Peak, I overhead someone in another party say to his group, "Did you see that guy on St. Helens wearing the tie?"

By seven o'clock we were finished, and the camera operators began packing their equipment. I did not want to get back to the cars after dark, and I was urging the two men to hurry when Jack stepped over. "I've just spoken to our pilot," he said. "He's willing to give us a ride, and he's on the way up. With six of us and all the gear, it will take three trips."

I wasn't going to argue, and two by two we were plucked from the mountain. Al and I were the last pair, and as I started moving toward the noisy helicopter, he grabbed me and shouted, "Be sure to approach from the front, where the pilot can see you. That little rotor in the rear will turn you into sausage." I hadn't given any thought about how to board a helicopter, because I had never done it before. Al had been on many rescue missions, and he knew exactly what he was doing. After nearly crapping in my pants, I shouted my thanks. The big guy had more than redeemed himself, and I vowed that in the future I would believe anything he said.

Matthew 20:16 says, "So the last shall be first." I have no idea what that means, but as we lifted off from the rim of St. Helens into the yellowing sky, I was on the verge of giddiness. I had been one of the last to climb the old mountain and one of the first to ascend the new. This achievement was highly unusual and apparently biblical; I felt a special connection to this peak. I had been interviewed on television for the first time, and it happened on top of a mountain. Just this once, I was publicly recognized as a climber. I hadn't been turned into sausage, and I was leaving my mountain in style.

If someone was sitting behind me whispering, "Glory fades," I didn't notice. At that moment, in my own mind I was exceptional, a man set apart like J. LeRoy Harrington-Pumphrey of the Matterhorn. I put my hands to my cheeks and felt my sideburns flaring out. My face was glowing, and my clothing seemed to evaporate from my body. Well, I thought, when I get home, I just might call a photographer.

Epilogue

THE SIRENS' CALL

Writing these accounts has forced me to address a fairly obvious question: Why didn't I just take up golf? The worst that can happen in a golf game is that the battery of your electric cart will go dead and you will have to walk. Even then, it's only a couple of 3-irons to the clubhouse, where the bartender will be waiting with your usual Scotch on the rocks.

The fact is, I can't explain what would cause me to invest valuable time and good money trying to find and get to the top of a mountain somewhere. I know that as a boy I had a romantic notion of becoming a climber. I also believed that I could woo Dale Arden away from Flash Gordon and then be elected president of the United States. Eventually, I grew up, but only partially. What happened there?

Why would anybody—not just me, but lots of other folks as well—engage in an activity that may offer great satisfaction but can just as easily leave you feeling like dog dirt and wondering whether you will ever see your loved ones again? I don't much buy into the idea that mountaineering is the perfect metaphor for human endeavor. To be sure, climbing contains elements common to most people's experience (endangered tropical plants, talkative gigolos, sunbathing nudes, for example), but to say that mountaineering is life itself seems overblown.

Maybe it's a vestige of my childhood Calvinism coming back to haunt me. Activities like golf are too comfortable, too slothful, when what you need now and then is a good dose of misery to keep things in proper perspective. Hair shirts are so Last Millennium. A weekend of climbing can teach you what a pathetic little pissant you really are. Therefore, it is good for you. Hey, I think I'm onto something. Lutherans, Catholics, Jews—feel free to jump on board here.

All right, all right. In the end, the best I can figure is that I climb mountains because I am mysteriously drawn to them. I can't stop thinking about them, so I keep going back. Stand on a summit, and you're on top of the world. And there's always the bright side when things go wrong: The best stories come from the unexpected.